HINDU
TRIBES AND CASTES

HINDU
TRIBES AND CASTES;

TOGETHER WITH

THREE DISSERTATIONS:
ON THE NATURAL HISTORY OF HINDU CASTE; THE UNITY OF THE HINDU RACE; AND THE PROSPECTS OF INDIAN CASTE;

AND INCLUDING A

GENERAL INDEX OF THE THREE VOLUMES.

BY THE

Rev. M. A. SHERRING, M.A., LL,B., Lond.;

FELLOW OF THE CALCUTTA UNIVERSITY;
CORRESPONDING MEMBER OF THE BENGAI. ASIATIC SOCIETY;
AUTHOR OF "THE SACRED CITY OF THE HINDUS," "THE HISTORY OF PROTESTANT MISSIONS IN INDIA," ETC.

"Homo sum; humani nihil a me alienum puto,"

VOL. III

ISBN: 978-93-5128-480-2(HB)

ISBN: 978-93-5128-477-2(Set)

First Published in 1881
Indian Reprint in 2017

Published by

Kalpaz Publications
C-30, Satyawati Nagar,
Delhi – 110052
E-mail: kalpaz@hotmail.com
Website: kalpazpublications.com
Ph.: +91-9212142040

PREFACE.

THIS volume was left by the late Mr. Sherring in a complete state, and was placed in our hands shortly after his death. It has not had the benefit of the Author's revision in passing through the Press; but the want of it is the less to be deplored, as it was Mr. Sherring's habitual practice to make his manuscript quite perfect before entrusting it to Printers; and we therefore feel confident that no material errors can have crept in.

The Index to the first and second volumes was made by Mr. Sherring; the Index to the third volume has been incorporated on the same plan.

Mr. Sherring contemplated a Map showing the location of the various castes, which would have added greatly to the value of the work; but we regret it was impossible, without his participation, to prepare one.

THE PUBLISHERS.

List of Books, Reports, Records, and other Documents, quoted or referred to in the third volume of "Hindu Tribes and Castes."

Extract from the General Memoir of the Survey of Travancore. By Lieutenant P. E. Conner, Madras Journal of Literature and Science, for October, 1833, and January, 1834.

Geographical and Statistical Memoir of a Survey of the Neilgherry Mountains, under the superintendence of Captain J. Ochterlony, 1847. Madras Journal of Literature, Vol. XV.

Descriptive Sketch of the various Tribes and Castes of Mysore. By Mr. S. B. Kristnasawmy Iyengar.

The Land of Charity—A Descriptive Account of Travancore and its People. By the Rev. Samuel Mateer, F. L. S.

Tribes of South India. By the Rev. J. F. Kearns, Missionary of the Society for the Propagation of the Gospel, Tinnevelly.

Description of the Administrative System of Travancore. By V. Kristno Row, late Dewan of Travancore. Edited by Major Drury, at the request of F. N. Maltby, Esq., Resident at the Courts of Travancore and Cochin.

The Aboriginal Tribes of the Neilgherry Hills. By Lieut.-Colonel W. Ross King.

The Native States of India. By Colonel Malleson.

Report on the Census of the Madras Presidency for 1871. By Surgeon-Major W. R. Cornish, Sanitary Commissioner for Madras.

The Tribes inhabiting the Neilgherry Hills. By the Rev. F. Metz, Missionary of the Basle Missionary Society.

A Phrenologist among the Todas. By Lieut.-Colonel W. E. Marshall, Bengal Staff Corps.

Manual of Vizagapatam. By Mr. D. F. Carmichael, Magistrate, and Agent of the Governor of Fort St. George.

The Madura Country. A Manual compiled by order of the Madras Government, by J. H. Nelson, Esq., M.A., Madras Civil Service.

Transactions of the Ethnological Society, New Series, Vol. III, Article on some rude Tribes of Southern India. By Dr. Shortt.

Manual of the Nellore District in the Presidency of Madras. By John A. C. Boswell, Esq., M. C. S., Collector and Magistrate of the Kistna District.

Gazetteer of Ajmere-Merwara. By Mr. J. D. Latouche, B. C. S.

Gazetteer of the Bikaneer State. By Captain Powlett, Political Agent, Ulwar.

Gazetteer of the Karauli State. By Captain Powlett.

Gazetteer of Marwar. By Major C. K. M. Walter, Political Agent, Marwar.

Gazetteer of Mattani. By Major Walter.

Gazetteer of Jeysalmere. By Major Walter.

Gazetteer of Rajputana, 1st and 2nd Volumes.

History of Mewar. By Captain J. C. Brookes.

Gazetteer of Southern India. By Messrs. Pharoah & Co., Madras.

Essay on the Creed, Customs, and Literature of the Jangams. By Charles P. Brown, Esq., Madras Civil Service.

Grammar of the Dravidian Languages. By the Rev. Dr. Caldwell. Second Edition.

Manual of the District of Cuddapah. By J. D. B. Gribble, Esq., M. C. S., Sub-Collector of the Cuddapah District.

Hindu Tribes and Castes, Vols. I and II. By the Rev. M. A. Sherring.

The Tinnevelly Shanars. By Bishop Caldwell.

Mysore and Coorg. A Gazetteer compiled by the Government of India, by Mr. Lewis Rice, Director of Public Instruction, Mysore and Coorg. Vols. I and II.

The Indian Antiquary, Vol. V, p. 354. Extract from the work of Von Philipp Van Mokern, entitled 'Ostindien seine Geshichte, Cultur, und seine Bewohner.'

Indian Caste. By the late Rev. Dr. Wilson, F. R. S., Missionary of the Free Church of Scotland, Bombay. 2 Vols.

Manual of the South Arcot District. By J. H. Garstin, M. C. S., Collector of South Arcot.

The Chiefs of Central India. By G. R. Aberigh-Mackay. Vol. I.

CONTENTS.

PART I.—THE TRIBES AND CASTES OF RAJPUTANA.

CHAPTER I.

The Tribes and Castes of Rajputana.

CHAPTER II.

The Brahmanical Tribes.

CHAPTER III.

The Rajpoot Tribes.

CONTENTS.

CHAPTER IV.

The Rajpoot Tribes—(*Continued.*)

CHAPTER V.

Castes.

CHAPTER VI.

The Mair, or Mar Tribes.

CHAPTER VII.

CHAPTER VIII.

The Mahomedan Tribes.

PART II.—THE TRIBES AND CASTES OF THE MADRAS PRESIDENCY.

CHAPTER I.

CHAPTER II.

CHAPTER III.

CHAPTER IV.

Aboriginal and Low-caste Tribes.

CHAPTER V.

Aboriginal and Low-caste Tribes.—*(Continued.)*

CHAPTER VI.

Tribes and Castes of Mysore.

CHAPTER VII.

Tribes of the Neilgherry Hills.

CHAPTER VIII.

Tribes and Castes of Travancore and Tinnevelly.

SECTION I.—TRIBES OF TRAVANCORE.

SECTION II.—TRIBES OF TINNEVELLY.

CHAPTER IX.

CHAPTER X.

PART III.—DISSERTATIONS ON

PART I.

THE TRIBES AND CASTES

OF

RAJPUTANA.

CHAPTER I.

THE TRIBES AND CASTES OF RAJPUTANA.

DISTRIBUTION OF THE RULING RAJPOOT TRIBES AMONG THE RAJPOOT STATES. NATURE OF THE GOVERNMENT OF A RAJPOOT CHIEF. THE AGRICULTURAL CLASSES. BHUMIA TENURES. THE CUSTOM OF GAVELKIND. THE WORSHIP OF THE SNAKE. SACRED AND CELEBRATED PLACES IN RAJPUTANA:—THE PUSHKAR LAKE; THE DARGAH AT AJMERE; THE GREAT MOSQUE AT AJMERE; THE TEMPLE AND MONASTERY OF DADU PANTH AT BARAHNA, NEAR THE SAMBHAR LAKE; THE OLD ROYAL PALACE AT AMBER, IN JEYPORE; THE GUTTA; THE OBSERVATORY AT JEYPORE; THE SILLA DEVI TEMPLE; THE AMBER-KISWAS SHRINE; THE MONASTERY AND SHRINES OF THE DADU PANTHIS AT NARAINA; THE TRIPOLIA; JAIN TEMPLES AT SANGARER; THE CHARAN-PADH; THE SHRINES AT BAIRAT; THE JAIN TEMPLE AT LADORVA; THE ANCIENT JAIN TEMPLES OF JESALMERE; THE MAHA SUTTEE AT BUNDEE. MARRIAGE CUSTOMS IN RAJPUTANA.

THE country of Rajputana possesses an area of about hundred and thirty thousand square miles, separated into the following nineteen States, namely:—Banswara, Bhurtpore, Bikaneer, Bundee, Dholpore, Dungarpore, Jeypore, Jesalmere, Jhalawar, Karauli, Kishengarh, Kotah, Marwar, Meywar, Pertabgarh, Sirdhee, Tonk, Ulwar, and Ajmere-Merwara. With the exception of Ajmere, which is a British province, all the remaining States are independent and have their own ruling chiefs, who are, however, more or less controlled by the British Government through its Political Agents. Tonk is governed by a Mahomedan prince, Bhurtpore and Dholpore by Jâts, and the remaining fifteen States by Rajpoot chiefs. There is also a sixteenth Rajpoot State, that of Shahpore, which is of small extent, and has no treaty with the empire.

At what date Rajpoots first entered Rajputana is unknown. There is reason to believe that, at one time, the great Râthor kingdom of Kanouj once included a portion of this tract; and it is quite certain that, at the period of the commencement of the Mahomedan rule in India, the Chauhâns were in Ajmere, the Râthors were in Kanouj, the Solankhis were in Gujerat, the Gâhlots were in Meywar, the Râthors and Sodas were in the barren deserts of the north-west, and the Kachwahas were in Jeypore. When the Mahomedans entered India, Rajpoot kings were ruling over extensive tracts, extending from the Punjab to Ajudhiya, the ancient term for Oudh. Had these monarchs and their tribes united together firmly, and placed themselves under one or two sagacious commanders, they would have stemmed the tide of Mahomedan invaders, and driven them back again beyond the Himalaya mountains. Unfortunately, they were at constant feud with one another, and hence, gradually, fell a prey to the sword of the conqueror. In the latter half of the twelfth century a fierce war broke out between the Solankhis of Anhalwara and the Chauhâns of Ajmere, and between the Chauhâns and the Râthors of Kanouj. Weakened by tribal strife, and before they had recovered themselves, these tribes were attacked by the Mahomedan invaders; and Shahabuddin, aided by his great lieutenant Kutbuddin, gained possession of Delhi, Ajmere, Kanouj, and Anhalwara.

The tribal wars of the great Rajpoot houses, and their eventual subjugation by a foreign foe, produced the separation and dispersion of the Rajpoot tribes, and led to their occupying, for the most part, new territories. The Bhâtis, after many vicissitudes, settled in Jesalmere, the Râthors in Marwar, the Sisodiyas in Meywar, and the Jâdons in the vicinity of the Chambal. These and other tribes have experienced various fortunes down to the present time, which would be better discussed in a history of Rajputana than in a work restricted to an account of the individual tribes and castes. One important event, however, in regard to these tribes must not be passed over. This is the growth of the Oodipore State in the sixteenth century and its predominance in Central India under its great chief, Rana Sanga, and the complete overthrow of this Prince, and of all the Rajpoot tribes attached to him, at the hands of Babar, in the famous battle of Futtehpore-Sikri, in the year 1527. In consequence of this serious defeat the Sisodiyas lost their supremacy, which passed over to the Râthors. But the Rajpoot tribes lost their independence. Moreover, some of the chiefs entered the service of the Mahomedan emperor, and some permitted their daughters to marry Mahomedan princes. Up to the time of Akbar, the Rajpoot chiefs, more or less, preserved their independence; but in a short time they lost this position and became simply feudatories of the emperor.

When Nadir Shah entered India, a compact was made between the three great tribes of the Sisodiyas, Râthors, and Kachwahas, which would have had an important result politically, had it not been for the haughty stipulation of the Sisodiyas that the sons of Râthor and Kachwaha chiefs by Sisodiya wives should take precedence of sons borne by wives of other tribes. The consequence was, that a feud arose, which broke up the compact. At the end of the last century

Rajputana fell almost completely under the sway of the Mahrattas, who 'exacted tribute, ransomed cities, annexed territory, and extorted subsidies.' Its oppressors were, for the most part, Sindia and Holkar. These potentates succumbed to the British army after severe fighting and various changes; but it was not until the years 1817 and 1818 that the Rajputana chiefs were finally taken under British protection, and firmly established in their territories again. The State of Bhurtpore was not settled till afterwards, and not indeed till a British force had stormed the city, which event took place in the month of January, 1825.

Eighteen of the Rajpoot States are of the first rank, and are under treaty with the British Government. Sixteen States, including Shahpore, are governed by Rajpoot chiefs of six tribes, namely, Râthor, Sisodiya, Chauhân, Jâdon, Kachwaha, and Jhâla, which are distributed as follows :—

Distribution of Rajpoot States among Rajpoot Tribes.

State.	Ruling Tribe.
Jodhpore (Marwar)	Râthor.
Bikaneer	Ditto.
Kishengarh	Ditto.
Meywar (Oodipore)	Sisodiya.
Banswara	Ditto.
Dungarpore	Ditto.
Pertabgarh	Ditto.
Shahpore	Ditto.
Bundee	Chauhân, of the Hâra branch.
Kotah	Ditto ditto.
Sirohee	Ditto, of the Deoria branch.
Karauli	Jâdon, of the Bhâti branch.
Jesalmere	Ditto ditto.
Jeypore	Kachwaha.
Ulwar	Ditto, of the Naruka branch.
Jhalawar	Jhâla (*a*).

In addition there are various chiefships not reckoned as States. One of these is Khetri, in the Shekhawatee District, which is held on a tenure similar to that of Shahpore. Beyond Bundee and Kotah, on the eastern side of Rajputana, are seven small tracts, called the seven Kotris, possessed by seven families

(*a*) The Rajputana Gazetteer, Vol. I, pp. 54-5.

of the Chauhân Hâra Rajpoots, under special compact with the British Government. Their chiefs are responsible to the head of the Hâra tribe. There are also the chiefs of Sikar in Jeypore, Nimrana in Ulwar, Fathgarh in Kishengarh, and Kusalgarh in Banswara, Then, too, there are the Bheel chiefs of the Meywar hill regions, and the Thakur of Lawa. Besides these minor chieftains there are others of a still lower rank, such as the Rao of Salumbar, in Meywar, a ruler of much influence in the Chappan.

Three Rajputana States are not governed by Rajpoot princes. One of these is Tonk, consisting of six separate districts, three of which only lie within the boundaries of Rajputana. They are ruled by a nawab, according to the convention made with Ameer Khan in 1817. The remaining,—namely, Bhurtpore and Dholpore,—are held by Jât chiefs. These States were not included within the treaties of 1817 and 1818, which were of so much importance to the consolidation of the other Rajputana States (*a*).

A Rajpoot chief rules as the head of a tribe divided into numerous clans, at the head of which are petty chiefs, generally members of his own family, all of whom acknowledge his sovereignty and pay him tribute, while his own authority is only absolute over those tracts which are not in their hands or under their control. The tenure differs in different States, but this is the general type which it assumes. The domestic and clannish character is seen more prominently in the western than in the eastern States of Rajputana. It will be obvious that this mode of tenure contributes greatly to the maintenance of an extensive Rajpoot aristocracy, and to the self-reliance, pride, and love of display, for which it is famous. Although the smaller chiefs are obliged to pay tribute and homage, and also to perform certain services to their paramount lord, nevertheless, their right to their estates and to lordship over them is indefeasible, and in some cases is as ancient as the right of the ruling prince to the State which he governs. The Thakurs, or great landholders, similarly claim from their dependants customary dues or services. The clannishness of the eastern States, as just remarked, is weaker than in the western. This arises from the fact that those provinces were much more accessible to Mahomedan and Mahratta invaders, and hence were brought much more under their influence than those further west. Moreover, the former contains a much small Rajpoot population than the latter. Zalim Singh well nigh ruined the clans of Kotah. The head of the Bundee State rules almost absolutely, for although in that province there are several persons, relatives of the Bundee Rajah, holding large estates, yet they have no separate jurisdiction.

(*a*) The Rajputana Gazetteer, Vol. I, p. 56.

In Bhurtpore and Dholpore, the power of the chief is supreme, as it is also for the most part in Tonk. The rule, however, is not without an exception, for Karauli, in the east, exhibits the clannish system to perfection.

The Rajpoot population, while considerable in some States, in no State outnumbers all the other classes put together. The Rajpoots, however, are everywhere first in rank and influence, and next to them come the Brahmans. The Chârans and Bhâts are genealogists and bards. The Jâts and Gûjars are agriculturists. The Meenas, Mers, and Meos were, probably, in closer alliance than they are now, and may have proceeded from the same original stock. Their traditions state that they have partly sprung from old Rajpoot tribes. Moreover, they are, to some extent, in intimate association with the Bheels. The Meos were formerly Hindus, but are now Mahomedans. Some of the Bheel tribes, those of purer blood, inhabit wild and desolate tracts, and are semi-independent. Other Bheels, a rude people, have intermingled with Hindus in their villages away from the civilization of the cities.

Respecting the geographical distribution of the principal Rajpoot tribes in Rajputana, the Râthors are most numerous in Marwar, Bikaneer, Jesalmere, Kishengarh, and the central tracts of Ajmere. Jesalmere is under the government of the Bhâtis. The Kachwahas predominate in Ulwar and Jeypore, while the territory in the north of Jeypore belongs to the Shekhawatis. The Chauhâns, especially the Hâra tribes, are strong in the eastern States. The Deorias, also Chauhâns, hold Sirohee. Nimrana is likewise in the hands of the Chauhâns, and so is Kusalgarh. The Sisodiyas are paramount in Meywar and the north-west States below the Arvalis, the head of the tribe being the Maharana of Oodipore. The Parihars, Pramaras, and Solankhis, once powerful tribes, are found in some of the States, but they are few in number, and without much influence (*a*).

These Rajpoots of Rajputana are not so rigidly attached to caste as their brethren in other parts, and are not very respectful to Brahmans. They eat animal food, especially the flesh of goats and wild pigs, drink the strongest spirits, consume opium inordinately, and are exceedingly superstitious, the poorer classes being profoundly ignorant. With the exception of the States of Mallani and Shekhawatee, the law of primogeniture prevails in all the States.

In some States the authority of the principal chief is of a very limited character. For example, the Thakurs, or great landholders, of Banswara, of all ranks, are said to possess full and entire jurisdiction within their several estates, and will neither allow their subjects (as they are termed) to be summoned to the

(*a*) The Rajputana Gazetteer, Vol. I, pp. 66, 67.

capital of the State, nor to be interfered with, or any way punished, by orders of the sovereign prince.

Mr. Aberigh-Mackay, in his interesting book on the Chiefs of Central India, makes a significant and important statement respecting many of the great Rajpoot families at the present time. I shall quote his observations on this point: "The saddest thing in all Rajwarra at the present day," he remarks, "is the condition of the royal caste. The children of the sun and moon, the children of the fire-fountain, seem to have forgotten the inspiriting traditions of their race, and have sunk into a state of slothful ignorance and debauchery that mournfully contrast with the chivalrous heroism, the judicious and active patriotism, the refined culture, and the generous virtue of their ancestors. The memory of a hundred noble deeds that adorn their annals, is still fresh in the minds of all men; and the names of many Rajpoot princes, of comparatively recent times, will never die while a history of India remains. Rana Sanga of Mewar, enemy of the Moghul; Jai Singh Sewai, of Jeypore, scholar statesman, and soldier; Sur Singh, Gaj Singh, Jeswant Singh, the glorious paladins of Marwar,—these are surely names to conjure with—yet they would now seem to excite but little emulation in the breasts of many of those in whose veins their blood flows, and who still bear their undying names. Hardly able to read or write his own language—ignorant of all pertaining to his country, pertaining to his race, pertaining to his State, pertaining to his sacred office as a ruler of men—the petty Rajpoot of the present day often saunters away his miserable existence in the society of abominable creatures that cast discredit on the name of servant. Besotted with spirits and opium, dull, morose, and wretched, he knows nothing of his affairs; and leaves everything to plundering 'managers' and 'deputy managers.' He is generally hopelessly in debt. He seldom cares for anything but the merest shadow of his dignity, the ceremony with which he is treated. Of this he is insanely jealous. That all the honours due to royalty and Rajpoot blood should be paid him; that he should be saluted with guns, and received at the edge of carpets, and followed by escorts of cavalry; that his daughters should be married at an early age to princes of higher clans than his own; that his Thakurs should attend him at the Dassehra, and perform the precise ritual of allegiance—all this is what he craves. It never occurs to him to consider whether he wears his princely honours worthily, and whether those who show him the outward observances of respect, love or honour him in their hearts. But there is reason to believe that a new generation of Rajpoot princes is springing up, who will add to the courtly manners of which the most degenerate Rajpoot is never destitute, a knowledge of affairs, a desire to govern well, and an enthusiasm for manly sports, the battles of peaceful days. They, however, will have much to do to restore the drooping prestige of the royal caste" (*a*).

The agricultural classes in Rajputana occupy a higher social status than they commonly do in the provinces of British India. They are a manly, independent race exhibiting a good deal of self-respect, and are treated with consideration by native chiefs. They will only perform agricultural duties, and regard themselves as much superior to day-labourers and menial servants, who, unlike the similar class under British rule, are a down-trodden, mean-spirited people.

Bhûmia Tenures.

There is a peculiar tenure prevalent among Rajpoots, known as Bhûm, which properly means the soil, by virtue of which the Bhûmia, or holder of land under this tenure, has a proprietorship very different from that of feudal chiefs and tenants of crown-lands. Originally, they seem to have belonged to the aristocratic class, but gradually sank from that position to that which they now occupy, which is, however, one of respectability and of considerable independence. They still pay a small quit-rent to their chief for their lands, but are otherwise left uncontrolled. This old form of the Bhûm tenure has assumed various phases, arising from changes in grants of land in addition to the original kind of tenure; yet they were alike in this, that an "hereditary, non-resumable, and inalienable property in the soil was inseparably bound up with a revenue-free title. Bhûm was given as compensation for bloodshed, in order to quell a feud—for distinguished services in the field—for protection of a border—or for watch and ward of a village" (*b*). In all cases the tenure is the same, and is very highly esteemed by Rajpoots of all classes, so that some chiefs of superior rank think it no dishonour to be styled Bhûmias. "The Maharaja of Kishengarh," says Mr. J. D. La Touche, "the Thakur of Fathgarh, the Thakur of Junia, the Thakur of Bandunwara, and the Thakur of Tantoti, are among the Bhûmias of Ajmere" (*c*). In this province there are no less than one hundred and nine tenures of this nature. It is somewhat singular that the old Rajpoot families, which formerly held rule in Ajmere as kings, should be so little represented in these Bhûmias. A few are in the hands of the Gaur Rajpoots, but the Chauhâns and Pramars seem to be entirely without any in their possession, while most of them, in fact nearly all, are held by Râthors.

(*a*) The Chiefs of Central India, by G. R. Aberigh-Mackay, Esq., Vol. I. pp. xxx, xxxi.

(*b*) The Rajputana Gazetteer, Vol. II, p. 30.

(*c*) *Ibid.*

Certain public duties were required of the Bhûmias, namely, to defend their own villages from robbers, to afford protection to travellers, and to compensate those who had through their misadvertence been plundered. This last condition is still carried out through the instrumentality of the International Court of Advocates. Thus, if a robbery has happened within the jurisdiction of any village, its head or chief is bound to make good the loss (*a*).

The Bhûmia chiefs of Ogna, Panurwa, Jowra, and Jowas, in the Meywar State, are partly of Bheel and partly of Rajpoot origin. They pay tribute to the Maharana. One or two of them, it is said, can muster a considerable body of men armed with bow and arrow.

The Custom of Gavelkind.

This custom, which has the force of law, prevails in Mallani, where it seems to have been productive of much disorder and strife. On the death of a father his property is equally divided among his sons. The land, therefore, has been divided and subdivided from generation to generation among a great number of claimants, so that it is split up into a multitude of proprietorships. Endless feuds arose in former times among families and clans from these minute divisions of estates, and, on account of the bloodshed which often occurred, the Jodhpore chiefs at length interfered, and eventually asserted a right of sovereignty over the whole province (*b*).

The Worship of the Snake.

Every village in the State of Mallani has a sacred slab with the figure of a serpent sculptured upon it, which is an object of devout veneration by all the inhabitants. The slab is placed in a prominent position under a tree, generally the *khejra*, and is especially resorted to by anyone who has been stung by a snake (*c*).

SACRED AND CELEBRATED PLACES IN RAJPUTANA.

The Pushkar Lake.

This is a spot of great sanctity in the estimation of Hindus for two reasons,—the first of which is, that Brahmâ is supposed to have performed a great religious ceremony; and the second, that the formerly famous and now extinct River Sâras-

(*a*) The Rajputana Gazetteer, Vol. II, p. 30.
(*b*) *Ibid*, p. 266.
(*c*) *Ibid*, p. 282.

wati is believed to reappear in this lake, not in one stream, but in five,—namely, the Suprabha, flowing into Jyesht Pushkar; the Sudha, which enters the Madhya Pushkar; the Kanka, falling into Kamsht Pushkar; and the Nanda, flowing past Nand; and the Prâchi, flowing by Hakran. No other lake bears so sacred a character as the Pushkar Lake, with the single exception of the Manusarowar Lake in Thibet. An account of the legends connected with it is found in the Pushkar Mahâtam of the Padma Purâna. So many Hindus are said to have bathed in the lake after Brahmâ had performed the ceremony, and to have gone to heaven in consequence, that it became inconveniently crowded; and therefore Brahmâ, to remedy the difficulty and to stay the influx of saints into heaven, abolished the sanctity of the Pushkar Lake, except during the days intervening between the eleventh day of the month of Kartik and the full-moon next succeeding. From this, or from other reasons, the sacred virtues of the lake were lost sight of, until they were re-discovered by Rajah Nahar Rao Parihâr, who was cured of a skin disease by bathing in its waters. He, in gratitude, built several ghâts on the banks of the lake, and had it newly excavated and thereby cleansed. There are five important temples in Pushkar, of comparatively modern date, erected to Brahmâ, Savitri, Badri Narayana, Vârâha, and Shiva Atmateswara. The ancient temples formerly here were destroyed by the Moghal emperors, especially Aurungzebe, who raised a mosque on the site of a temple dedicated to Keshu Rae. The mosque is still standing. It is worthy of remark that the temple to Brahmâ is the only one in all India consecrated to the worship of that deity, who, although regarded by Hindus as the creator, is nevertheless one of the most unpopular of Hindu divinities. The reason of his unpopularity is well-known, and arises from gross licentiousness, of which, according to tradition, Brahmâ was once guilty.

The fish of the lake, and the wild fowl floating upon its surface, together with all animals within certain limits of the lake, are protected by ancient charters. As animal life is sacred to the religious Hindu, it is a crime to take the life of any creature either within the lake or in its neighbourhood. Not long since the entire population around the lake was greatly excited at hearing that an English officer had fired at an alligator. Petitions in great numbers were sent to the Government on the subject, and the people, especially the Brahmans, were with difficulty appeased (*a*). A fair is held at Pushkar in the autumn of every year, when as many as one hundred thousand pilgrims are present, and bathe in the sacred lake.

(*a*) The Rajputana Gazetteer, Vol. II, pp. 67—70.

The Dargah at Ajmere.

This is a tomb in which was buried the pîr or saint Khwaja Micaiyin-ud-din Chisti, in the year 1235, shortly before India was invaded by the Emperor Shahâb-ud-din. It is so sacred that pilgrimages are made to it. Akbar himself is said to have performed a pilgrimage on foot to the sacred spot. He erected a large mosque close by. Shah Jehan also built a mosque, the materials of which were of white marble. The edifice is still as fresh as it was on the day it was built, some two hundred and fifty years ago. On the left of this mosque is the tomb of the saint, a square-domed building with two sandal-wood doors, the spoils of Chitore, and a silver arch, the gift of Siwai Jai Singh of Jeypore.

The Arhai-din-kâ-jhompra, or Great Mosque of Ajmere.

This mosque, says General Cunningham, is "one of the earliest and finest monuments of the Mahomedan power in India. Like the great Kutb Masjid at Delhi, the Ajmere mosque was built of the spoils of many Hindu temples, which were thrown down by the bigotry of the conquerors. Its very name, the 'shed of two days and-a-half,' which is the only appellation by which it is now known, would seem to point directly to the astonishing rapidity of its erection, and as this could only have been effected by the free use of the ready dressed materials of prostrated Hindu temples, I accept the popular name as confirmatory proof of the actual origin of the masjid, which is amply attested by an inspection of the edifice itself. The Great Mosque of Ajmere consists of a quadrangle cloistered on all four sides, with a lofty screen wall of seven pointed arches forming a magnificent front to the western side. The side cloisters are mostly ruined; but the whole of the seven noble arches of the screen wall, as well as the grand pillared cloisters behind them, are still standing. Altogether it is the finest and largest specimen of the early Mahomedan mosque that now exists. It is of the same age as the Kutb Mosque at Delhi, but is considerably larger, and in very much better preservation. Externally, it is a square of 259 feet each side, with four peculiar star-shaped towers at the corners. The interior consists of a quadrangle 200 feet by 175, surrounded on all four sides by cloisters of Hindu pillars. The great screen is no less than 11½ feet thick and 56 feet high. I am inclined to believe that the two mosques must have been designed by the same architect, and that even the same masons may have been employed in the decoration of each." "In the Ajmere mosque we have the earliest example of a pair of *muazzin* towers in two small *minars*, which are placed on the top of the screen wall over the great centre arch. This arrangement was impracticable in the

Delhi mosque, as the screen wall is only eight feet thick" (*a*). On one of these minars is an inscription, from which the information is obtained, that the mosque was completed in the reign of the Emperor Altamish, or between A. D. 1211 and 1236. The mosque is a vast pillared hall with five rows of columns, numbered altogether three hundred and forty-four. Each pillar, it is conjectured, is made up of at least two original pillars; no less than seven hundred columns are represented by those now standing, an enormous number, equivalent, in General Cunningham's judgment, to the spoils of from twenty to thirty Hindu temples. It is his opinion that the two great mosques of Delhi and Ajmere belong to a higher and nobler style of art than the Saracenic architects ever reached. "In gorgeous prodigality of ornament, in beautiful richness of tracery, and endless variety of detail, in delicate sharpness of finish, and laborious accuracy of workmanship, all of which are due to the Hindu masons, I think that these two grand Indian mosques may justly vie with the noblest buildings which the world has yet produced. In attributing the design to the Musalman architect, and all the constructive details to the Hindu, I am chiefly influenced by the fact that the arch has never formed part of Hindu structural architecture, although it is found in many specimens of their rock-hewn temples" (*b*).

The Temple and Monastery of Dâdu Panth at Barahana, near the Sambhar Lake.

Dâdu was the founder of a Hindu sect in the sixteenth century. His followers are found in many parts of the country. Dâdu died in the neighbourhood of the lake, and these edifices have been erected to his memory, and to perpetuate his creed. His precepts have been recorded in a book which is held in great veneration by his disciples. These persons eschew idolatry, shave their heads, teach morality, and wander about in all directions preaching the doctrines of Dâdu. The head-quarters of the sect are said to be in the Jeypore State. The armed Nagas are attached to the sect.

The old Royal Palace at Amber, in Jeypore.

For nearly seven centuries Amber was the capital of the Jeypore kingdom, that is, from A.D. 1037 to 1728. The old palace of the great chiefs of this principality is still standing, and commands a grand and picturesque view of the surrounding country. This ancient city, however, is almost abandoned, and its former splendid buildings are falling into ruins.

(*a*) Archæological Survey of India, General Cunningham's Report, Vol. II, pp. 258—261.
(*b*) *Ibid*, p. 263.

The Gutta.

A very sacred shrine dedicated to the sun, on the summit of the hills, about one mile and-a-half to the east of Jeypore. A spring issues from the rocks below the shrine, and falls seventy feet. Its water is regarded as exceedingly sacred, and a tradition prevails among the people fostered by the priest of the temple. that the water is as holy and efficacious as that of the Ganges at Benares or Hurdwar.

The Observatory at Jeypore.

This was erected by Maharajah Siwai Jai Singh II. The instruments are of enormous size, but are in decay, and have probably not been used since the Maharajah's death in 1743.

The Silla Devi Temple.

This temple, reputed to be of great antiquity, is situated within the palace at Amber, the former capital of Jeypore. A goat is daily sacrificed to the goddess, in the place, it is said, of a human victim formerly offered.

The Amberkiswas Shrine.

This is a very old shrine, dedicated to Shiva, and still standing in Amber. It is commonly believed that the city took its name from the sacred shrine.

The Monastery and Shrines of the Dâdu Panthis at Naraina.

The monastery is built of the finest Makrâna marble, and has a very striking appearance. The great enclosure inside is decorated with pillars rising from a platform. In the inner part are deposited various sacred objects, among which are the Dâdu Panth's writings and the bed on which Dâdu lay. The impressions of his feet are also shown.

On the shores of the lake at Naraina is a mosque of considerable beauty, a composite of Mahomedan and Hindu styles. Its five rows of richly carved pillars, differing very greatly in their characteristics, are of Hindu art, having been taken from shrines and temples, and put together by Mahomedan architects according to their own designs. These pillars resemble those at the Kutb near Delhi, and are considered to date from A.D. 961, the era of the temple of the 'Lord of Joy,' in Shekhawatee (*a*).

(*a*) The Rajputana Gazetteer, Vol. II, p. 161.

The Tripolia.

This singular building was erected in A.D. 1603, and is situated at Naraina. It is largely composed of materials taken from older edifices. It has four angles of a ceiling, 'exactly similar to that of the portico of the temple of Baroli, dedicated to Shiva, near the Makundara Pass on the Chambal' (*a*).

Jain Temples at Sangarer.

This ancient spot is seven miles from Jeypore. It contains many old Hindu and Jain buildings, the most remarkable of which is a temple reputed to be more than a thousand years old, constructed of marble and sandstone. Its style resembles that of the celebrated Dilwâra Jain temple on Mount Abu. Foreigners are not admitted into its most sacred parts.

The Charan-padh.

Two miles from Jeypore are, as is supposed, the impressions of the feet of Ram Chandra, over which a shrine was raised in former times, and is, with the Charan-padh, an object of great veneration to Hindus.

The Shrines at Bairât.

Bairât was the ancient capital of Matsya, the name by which the territory of Jeypore was formerly known. It was famous in Hindu writings for being the residence of the five Pându brothers during their twelve years' exile from Indraprastha; and is referred to in the seventh century of our era as being an important city, and having within its circuit several Buddhist monasteries (*b*).

The Jain Temple at Ladorva.

Ladorva was the capital of the Bhâti rulers before they built Jesalmere. It is now in ruins; but an ancient temple of the Jains is still standing.

The ancient Jain Temples of Jesalmere.

These are situated inside the fort, and are famous for their exquisite sculptures. The oldest dates from the year 1371 (*c*).

The Maha Suttee at Bundee.

This spot is famous for the cremation of the bodies of former chiefs of Bundee, and the burning of many of their wives. Very handsome monuments have been

(*a*) The Rajputana Gazetteer, Vol. II, p. 161.
(*b*) *Ibid*, p. 162.
(*c*) *Ibid*, p. 182.

erected to commemorate these events, on which are recorded not merely the names of the chiefs, but also the number of the unfortunate ladies who at their death performed the terrible rite of suttee. According to these inscriptions, as many as two hundred and thirty-seven women thus voluntarily surrendered their lives on the death of nine chiefs, as follows :—

At the death of	Rao Raja Sattra Sal,	ninety-five women were burnt as suttees.		
Do.	Rao Raja Bhao Singh,	thirty-five	do.	do.
Do.	Maharaja Jodh Singh,	three	do.	do.
Do.	Rao Raja Ajit Singh,	two	do.	do.
Do.	Rao Bhojh Singh,	two	do.	do.
Do.	Rao Ratan Singh,	one	do.	do.
Do.	Maharaj Bhurt Singh,	twelve	do.	do.
Do.	Rao Kishen Singh,	eighty-four	do.	do.
Do.	Rao Budh Singh,	three	do.	do. (a).

Marriage Customs in Rajputana.

According to Hindu law, no money is allowed to be given by a Hindu on the marriage of a daughter, a law which, among some castes and in some places, is more frequently honoured in the breach than in the observance. The reason of the law is mainfest, and approves itself both to humanity and civilization. It is simply that the Hindu law abhors anything having the appearance of the sale of a girl to her husband. Yet not a few Hindu tribes in their marriage ceremonies are notoriously guilty at the least of such appearance. Rajpoots especially in all parts of the country are accustomed to give large sums of money on the marriage of their daughters, which circumstance has been a fruitful cause of female infanticide, parents preferring to slaughter girls in their infancy to bearing the ruinous burden of procuring costly husbands for them on their attaining a marriageable age. In Rajputana this evil custom of giving a considerable amount of money on the marriage of a young woman is said to prevail among three-fourths of the Rajpoot population, and also among most other Hindu castes. It is important to state, however, that an opposite custom, namely, of giving money on the marriage of young men, is also observed among some tribes. In inferior castes, the bride's mother expects a large present of money from the bridegroom in return for her daughter.

The ceremonies of betrothal and marriage are very curious among Rajputana tribes, and differ greatly in different tribes. The following customs prevail in Jodhpore : Among Rajpoots and Chârans, the bride and bridegroom eat opium

(a) The Rajputana Gazetteer, Vol. I, p. 237.

together in the presence of their caste. With Tailang Brahmans, the bridegroom's father sends a handkerchief to be put on the bride's head. With Sâraswat Brahmans, the bride's father places a ring on the bridegroom's finger. Among all other Brahmans the custom is for the girl's father to make presents of fruit, sugar, cocoanuts, and so forth, to the bridegroom's friends, or to receive them. The Oswâl bankers, at the time of marriage, send a garland of flowers and a ring from the bridegroom's family to the bride. Among other Vaisyas the betrothal is confirmed by simply giving to the other party sugar and cocoanuts. The Jatia Kumhârs bind a thread round the bride's wrist. The general custom among the great majority of the castes as a token of the binding of the contract between the parties, is the exchange of sugar and cocoanuts. At the time of the celebration of the marriage, the bridegroom takes hold of the bride's hand, and together they go round a fire in the centre of the room three times, and then a fourth time, the bride on this occasion walking before the bridegroom. The Srimâli Brahmans wait till the morning after the marriage before encircling the fire, when the bridegroom takes the bride up in his arms, and carries her four times round the fire. The Maheshwari and Panchoti Vaisyas observe a singular custom. The bride's maternal uncle, on the bridegroom entering the house of the bride, catches her up in his arms, and takes her round the bridegroom seven times (*a*).

As every Rajpoot takes a wife from a tribe other than his own, the abduction of the bride, real or professed, is the universal practice. This custom arose in times when a tribe, being dependant for wives on the good-will of neighbouring tribes, found itself thwarted in its matrimonial inclinations through their enmity and hostility, and hence the frequent feuds which arose between them. Although such tribal strifes have largely ceased, yet the manner of forcible abduction continues. "The ceremony may be witnessed in great perfection at any marriage in high life, when the bridegroom arrives with his wedding band of armed kinsmen, who clash their arms and rush in with a shout upon the bride's party" (*b*).

(*a*) The Rajputana Gazetteer, Vol. II, p. 251.
(*b*) *Ibid*, Vol. I, p. 69.

CHAPTER II.

THE BRAHMANICAL TRIBES.

The Brahmans of Ajmere hold no social intercourse with those of Merwara, the chief reason being, perhaps, that the latter eat animal food. They hold lands in nearly all the villages in these States with the important privilege of paying no revenue for the same. They seldom cultivate the soil themselves (*a*).

The hills in the vicinity of Kalinjar, Laroth, and Bhadan were, according to tradition, first occupied by Brahmanical tribes.

Section I.—Brahmans of Pushkar.

The Brahmans of Pushkar are divided into two branches, the Barâ Bâs and the Chhotâ Bâs, between whom a great feud has always existed. The former are regarded as having preceded the latter in the town; but they have both been there for many generations. A charter of the Emperor Jehangir is extant, referring to the division of offerings by these two tribes, and endeavouring to heal the animosity between them by ordering two-thirds to be given to the older tribe, and one-third to the younger, which rule still exists.

The entire population of Pushkar numbers nearly four thousand persons, of whom the greater part are Brahmans of the two sects just referred to. There seems good reason to believe that the Barâ Bâs are older than the Chhotâ Bâs (*b*).

(*a*) Gazetteer of Ajmere-Merwara, by Mr. J. D. LaTouche, p. 32.

(*b*) The Rajputana Gazetteer, Vol. II, p. 70.

1. *The Barâ Bâs Brahmans of Pushkar.*

The tradition of these Brahmans is, that they are descended from Parâsar, father of Veda Vyâsa, through Bhopat, who, in common belief, was a Mair. The *sewaks*, or priests of the Jain temples, intermarry with the Barâ Bâs Brahmans, which is a very remarkable circumstance, seeing that the Jains are not Brahmans, but Vaisyas. It is needless to add, therefore, that other Brahmans decline to hold intercourse with the Pushkar sect.

2. *The Chhotâ Bâs Brahmans of Pushkar.*

These Brahmans are divided into the following four clans :—

1. Gaur.	3. Gujrâti.
2. Sanâdh.	4. Raj Purohit.

The Chhotâ Bâs Brahmans are *purohits*, or family priests, to the Rajas of Jeypore, Bikaneer, Bhurtpore, and Dholpore (*a*). They have no writing or tradition stating when they first came to Pushkar.

Section II.—Brahmans of Bikaneer.

The Brahmans of Bikaneer are chiefly of two classes, namely :—

1. Pokarna. These are ten times more numerous than any other Brahmanical tribe in the State. They are traders and agriculturists, and are an energetic, hard-working people. Astrologers are of this clan.

2. Paliwâl. Enterprising trading agriculturists, inhabiting twelve villages west of Bikaneer. Many of this tribe emigrated into British territory a few years ago.

The priests of the Darbar, or Court, as of Râthor Rajpoots generally, are Kanoujiya Brahmans of the Sanâdhiya branch. The teachers of the Shâstras are Gour Brahmans.

Section III.—Brahmans of Karauli.

The Brahmanical tribes of Karauli are the most numerous of all the tribes in the State. They are mostly small traders, and convey their goods from place to place on pack-cattle. They bear various designations, such as :—

1. Borârs or Ladeniâs (carriers of merchandize). In addition to trading they are often "the village money-lenders, or cultivators, especially of hemp, which they prepare in large quantities, and work up into *tât*, the coarse cloth of which their packing bags are made. They carry salt from Lâmbar, sugar from

(*a*) Gazetteer of Ajmere-Merwara, by Mr. J. D. LaTouche, p. 58.

Agra, cotton, ghi (clarified butter), and piece-goods, to the marts, where they are wanted" (*a*). The Borârs are mostly Kanoujiya Brahmans of the Sanâdhiya sub-tribe. They are nearly all able to read and write.

2. Brinjârâs. Although bearing this name, these Brahmans are very unlike the wandering Brinjârâ tribes of the Dekhan.

3. Haiwâsis. These have been carriers of merchandize for many generations, and some of them journey over a wide extent of country. Not a few feed their cattle on the waste lands of Shopur, Badowra, Duma in Gondwana, and other parts of Central India, while still keeping up intercourse with their brethren in Karauli. The Haiwâsis of this State are settled at Laknipur, in Mâchilpur. There are members of the tribe in Bâri, Ulwar, Gwalior, and on the banks of the Nerbuddha. The Haiwâsis mostly worship Raghunâth. Some of the tribe in Marwar have become converts to Mahomedanism.

4. Gujrâtî Brahmans. Of these, there are about sixty families in Karauli. They are worshippers of Vishnu.

5. Gor or Gaur Brahmans. A few families.

6. Gor Beas. A few families.

7. Nandwânî. These are Brahmans from Marwar, and are found in the city of Karauli and in all the large villages. They are active traders. They have a higher social position than the Borars (*b*).

Section IV.—Brahmans of Marwar.

These are said, by Major Walter, to be subdivided as follows :—

1. Tailang.	8. Srimâli.	15. Gujar-gor.
2. Parik.	9. Sâraswat.	16. Sanâwar.
3. Sankhwâl.	10. Khandelwâl.	17. Nadwâni.
4. Gor or Gaur.	11. Sarwaria.	18. Lâchora.
5. Kanoujya.	12. Gujrâtî.	19. Palliwâl (*c*).
6. Pushkarna.	13. Parohit.	20. Asopa.
7. Sâwug.	14. Daima.	

This is, however, a very confused and unsatisfactory list of subdivisions. The Parohits are simply village priests, and may belong to any of the Brahmanical tribes. The Sarwarias form one of the great branches of the Kanoujya Brahmans; as also do the Sanâwars or Sanâdhs.

(*a*) Gazetteer of the Karauli State, by Capt. P. W. Powlett, p. 17.

(*b*) *Ibid*, p. 18.

(*c*) Gazetteer of Marwar, by Major C. K. M. Walter, Political Agent, Marwar, p. 24.

Asopa Brahmans have held important posts in the Marwar Darbar. Pushkarna Brahmans held the offices of Dewan and Bukhshi in the reign of Moharaja Takht Singh. Among the Tailang Brahmans the custom prevails of the father sending a handkerchief for the decoration of the head of the girl who is about to espouse his son. A Sâraswat Brahman father places a ring on the finger of the youth who is about to be his son-in-law. A Srimâli Brahman bridegroom carries his bride four times round a fire lit in the centre of the room, on the morning after the first marriage ceremony. The Srimâlis are not cultivators in Mallâni, but traders on a small scale.

Section V.—Brahmans of Mallâni.

In Mallâni, Joshis, or astrologers, are very numerous. Instead of following the uncertain pursuit of astrology, however, they are, for the most part, engaged in trade and agriculture. They enjoy special privileges, paying neither export nor import dues, and only a fourth part of their produce as revenue. The Paliwâl Brahmans came originally to Mallâni with the Râthors. The Sârsat or Sâraswat Brahmans have only recently entered the State from Bikaneer. They are the priests of the Jâts, and are cultivators and beggars. The Râjgur Brahmans are family priests of the Thakurs of Mallâni. One of their duties is, on the death of the head of a family, to take his ashes to the Ganges and to throw them into the stream. Their lands are rent-free.

The Lohânas are trading Brahmans in Mallâni, paying less duty on goods than other castes. They are low in social rank, and eat meat and drink spirits. They are not treated with such consideration as the Joshis.

The Bhojaks are beggars, and cooks in the families of Oswâls. They are worshippers of Shiva, but are lax in principle, and readily pay their devotions in the Jain temples. The Bhojaks are inferior Brahmans.

The Kârtakias are low Brahmans who receive the clothes thrown over dead persons when burnt; and eat the food given in charity during twelve days after the death of any one (*a*).

The Srimâli Brahmans are strict in the observance of their caste rules. They will not work in the fields, but engage in trade in a small way, and of course, like most Brahmans, rigidly adhering to caste, are incorrigible beggars.

Section VI.—Brahmans of Sanchore.

This district is almost exclusively populated by Brahmans, who bear the designation of Sanchora Brahmans.

(*a*) Gazetteer of Mallâni, by Major C. K. M. Walter, p. 66.

Section VII.—Brahmans of Jesalmere.

These belong to two classes, the Paliwâls and Pokarnas or Pushkarnas, who are the principal sects of Brahmans in the State of Bikaneer. In numbers the Paliwâls equal the Rajpoot tribes, while they far surpass them in wealth. Tod considers that they are the descendants of the ancient Pali or pastoral tribes of this region. They never marry out of their tribe. They worship the bridle of a horse (*a*).

The Pokarnas are numerous in Marwar, Bikaneer, and Jesalmere. As to their origin, there is a tradition that they were formerly Beldars, and as such excavated the Lake Pushkar or Pokar, for which service they were raised into the rank of Brahmans, and permitted to bear the designation of Pokarnas. They worship the khodala, or pickaxe (*b*).

In this State, besides the above Brahmans, there are others of the following tribes, namely:—Srimâli, Joshi, Râjgur or Kesuria, and Gujar-gor.

Section VIII.—Brahmans of the Rajputana Desert.

The most numerous Brahmans of this region are Vaishnavis, who are agriculturists, cowherds, and to some extent traders. They are found in greatest numbers in Dhât. Their dead are buried near the thresholds of their houses. The tribe is also settled in Marwar, Mallâni, and elsewhere.

Section IX.—Brahmans of Jeypore.

In comparison with other States in Rajputana, Brahmans are most numerous in Jeypore, and are engaged in both secular and religious pursuits. From the greater number of Brahmans residing in Jeypore, we are not to conclude, says Tod, "that her princes were more religious than their neighbours, but, on the contrary, that they were greater sinners" (*c*). Most of the Brahmans of this State are Bâgras, an inferior order, many of whom are agriculturists. Brahmans of a higher rank officiate at temples, or are employed in the public service.

Section X.—Brahmans of Ajmere-Merwara.

These number nearly twenty thousand persons in this province, and enjoy special privileges in the villages, in which they hold lands free from revenue, which they are too proud to cultivate. They are an exclusive race, and as they eat meat, keep themselves apart from other Brahmans.

(*a*) Tod's Rajasthan, Vol. II, p. 262.

(*b*) *Ibid.*

(*c*) *Ibid*, p. 397.

Section XI.—Brahmans of Banswara.

In this small State the Brahmans are well represented, and belong, it is said, to as many as twenty-two separate tribes. The capital has a total population of a little more than six thousand persons, of whom one-fifth are Brahmans.

Section XII.—Brahmans of Bhurtpore.

The Brahmans number about seven per cent. of the entire population of Bhurtpore. Many of them are officials of the Native Government, and in the houses of merchants, bankers, chiefs, and others. The following Brahmanical tribes have their representatives in the State:—

Brahmanical Tribes of Bhurtpore.

1. Gour. These are numerous.
2. Kanyakubja. A few only.
3. Utkal Brahmans from Orissa. A few.
4. Sâraswati. In considerable numbers.
5. Maithala. A few.
6. Nagar Brahmans from Gujerat. A few.
7. Maharashtra. A few.
8. Kashmiri. A few (*a*).

Section XIII.—Brahmans of Bundee.

These are engaged in various occupations, as Government officials, as cultivators, and as headmen of villages; while all are more or less educated. The chief minister of the State is a Nâgar Brahman. The following tribes are represented in Bundee:—

Brahmanical Tribes of Bundee.

1. Sadu.
2. Gour.
3. Sanadhiya.
4. Parikh.
5. Gujar.
6. Daima.
7. Paliwâl.
8. Nâgar.
9. Sâraswati.
10. Sikhwal.

Section XIV.—Brahmans of Dholpore.

In this small State there are thirty-six thousand Brahmans, of whom as many as twenty-seven thousand cultivate upwards of forty-three thousand acres of land. The Golapurah Brahmans occupy twenty-two villages. They profess to be Pâtakh Brahmans, and state that their ancestors entered this district in the middle of the thirteenth century, having come from Palli in Bhurtpore. The Sanadhiya branch of the Kanyakubja Brahmans are the headmen of fifty-one villages.

(*a*) The Rajputana Gazetteer, Vol. I, p. 160.

CHAPTER III.

THE RAJPOOT TRIBES.

I.—CHAUHAN. II—HARA. III.—RATHOR. IV.—JODHA. V.—JOHIYA. VI.—SILKAWAT. VII.—BIRAMOT. VIII.—BIJAWAT. IX.—SISAWAT. X.—KITAWAT. XI.—TENDO. XII.—MOHIL. XIII.—NARBHANA. XIV.—BHADAURIA. XV.—BHAURECHA. XVI.—DHANAIREA. XVII.—BAGRECHA. XVIII.—KOMBAWAT. XIX.—LUNAWAT. XX.—RANAWAT. XXI.—DULAWAT. XXII.—JHALA. XXIII.—BARGUJAR. XXIV.—SISODIYA. XXV.—GAHLOT. XXVI.—SANKLA. XXVII.—ASAYACH. XXVIII.—CHANDRAWAT. XXIX.—SENGAR.

Râjisthân, or Rajputana, is the country *par excellence* of the Rajpoot tribes, in which, for many ages, they have held extensive dominion. In a former work I have written at length on many of these tribes, and therefore shall consider it incumbent on me now, only to furnish such additional information about those inhabiting Rajputana as I have been able to gather (*a*).

It seems to be generally admitted, that the chiefs of Rajputana, "as a class, are superior to the present fruits of our own institutions in India. They are more inclined to mix with Europeans, and enjoy their society and sports, and are freer from prejudice than any other people in India" (*b*). The Rajpoots are fond of excitement, a disposition produced, perhaps, by the feudal system under which they live. Nevertheless, with all their restlessness and turbulence, in the opinion of Colonel Tod, they possess 'in an eminent degree both loyalty and patriotism.'

The Rajpoot tribes in all the States of Rajputana are divisible into three classes: 1, landholders; 2, cultivators, or tillers of the ground; 3, servants, agents, and the like. The landholders include the old hereditary aristocracy.

Among the Rajpoots of Marwar, at the ceremony of betrothal, the young bridegroom and bride partake of opium together. The same pernicious custom also prevails with the Châran tribe.

(*a*) "Hindu Tribes and Castes," by the author—the Kshatriya or Rajpoot Tribes. Vol. I, Part II, Chapters I—XIII, pp. 115—243.

(*b*) History of Mewar, by Captain J. C. Brookes, p. 104.

The social position of these tribes in Rajputana, at the present day, is depicted in these words of Colonel Tod: "The poorest Rajpoot of this day," he says, "retains all the pride of ancestry, often his sole inheritance. He scorns to hold the plough, or to use his lance but on horseback. In these aristocratic ideas he is supported by his reception among his superiors, and the respect paid to him by his inferiors. The honours and privileges, and the gradations of rank, among the vassals of the Rana's house, exhibit a highly artificial and refined state of society. Each of the superior rank is entitled to a banner, kettle-drums preceded by heralds and silver maces, with peculiar gifts and personal honours, in commemoration of some exploit of their ancestors" (*a*).

I. *Chauhân.*

The fort and city of Ajmere were founded, says the local tradition, in the year 145 A. D., by Raja Aja, commonly known as Ajapâl, descended from Anala, the first of the Chauhân race. The Chauhân kings reigned in Ajmere until the end of the twelfth century. In 1193, Mahomed Ghori took possession of the city; but it was not finally annexed to the Mahomedan empire of Delhi until 1195, when the country was once more invaded, and Kutb-ud-dîn Aibeg, viceroy of Mahomed Ghori, fought with the usurper Hemrâj, and having killed him and defeated his army, destroyed completely the remaining power of the ancient dynasty (*b*).

It is very remarkable that although the Chauhâns governed Ajmere for upwards of a thousand years, yet that so few of the tribe are now to be found there. "They must be looked for," says Mr. J. D. Latouche, Compiler of the Gazetteer of Ajmere-Merwara, "in Hârâvati, in Ulwar, and in the desert of Nagar Parkhar, whither they have been pushed by the Râthors, who have occupied their place as the ruling tribe, and who in numbers, wealth, and power greatly preponderate over the other Rajpoot clans who hold land in the district" (*c*).

The Chauhâns have colonies in Marwar, Bhurtpore, Jesalmere, and Mallâni. They have distinguished families in Looe Bah and Sanchore. The Chauhâns of Baidla and Kotario, in the Oodaipore valley, are, says Tod, chiefs of the first rank. The chief of Parsoli is also a Chauhân.

The Gogawat clan is descended from the famous Goga, who defended the Sutlej in the earliest recorded Mahomedan invasion. 'Both Goga and his steed

(*a*) Tod's Rajasthan—Madras Edition—Vol. I, p. 123.

(*b*) General Cunningham's Archæological Survey of India, Vol. II. p. 258.

(*c*) Gazetteer of Ajmere-Merwara, by Mr. J. D. Latouche, p. 28.

Jawadia are immortal in Rajasthan.' The Gogawats are among the most ancient tribes of the desert.

The Narbhans are another clan of this tribe. They formerly had possession of Oodaipore, which they held for a long period.

In Banswara are eleven Chauhân clans, three of which are as follows:—

1. Madawat.—These are of Metwala, and are a junior branch of the Molân family.

2. Hathyot.—This clan belongs to Arthuna, and has also sprung from the Molâns.

3. Keringot.—A clan which came originally from Bankora in Dungarpore. They have possession of the Ganora estate.

The tribe is numerous in Bundee. In Dungarpore eight of the principal landholders are of this tribe.

The Chauhâns succeeded the Tuars in Malwee, and reigned there one hundred and sixty-seven years.

II. Hâra.

The Hâras inhabit the country, called after them, Hârâvati, embracing the two States of Boondi and Kotah, and intersected by the Chumbul. Their founder, according to Tod, was Ishtpâl, descended from Manik Rae, the Chauhân king of Ajmere, who, A. D. 685, "sustained the first shock of the Islamite arms." Ishtpâl was severely wounded in battle while resisting the invading army of Mahmud of Ghizni. "His limbs, which lay dissevered, as the story goes, were collected by Sûrabai; and the goddess sprinkling them with the 'water of life,' he arose. Hence the name Hâra, which his descendants bore, from *har*, or 'bones' thus collected; but more likely from having lost (*hara*) Asi" (*a*). Boondi, the capital of the Hâras, was built by Rae Dewa, about the year 1342, by whom the country received the designation of Hârâvati.

The tribe has the following clans:—

The Hâra Clans.

1. The Kombawat Clan—descended from the famous Aloo Hâra, son of Har-raj. Aloo Hâra had twenty-four castles on the Pathar.
2. The Bhojawat Clan—also descended from Aloo Hâra.
3. The Harpalpota Clan—descended from Harpal, son of Samarsi.

(*a*) Tod's Rajasthan—Madras Edition—Vol. II, p. 420.

4. The Norangpota Clan—descended from Norang, son of the renowned Napûji.
5. The Tharad Clan—descended from Tharad, another son of Napûji.
6. The Meoh Clan—descended from Meoji, great grandson of Hamoo, ruler of Boondî in the fifteenth century.
7. The Sawant Clan—descended from Sawant, brother of Meoji.
8. The Novarmapota Clan—descended from Novarma, grandson of Hamoo.
9. The Jailawat Clan—descended from Jaita, grandson of Hamoo.
10. The Nimawat Clan—descended from Nima, grandson of Hamoo.
11. The Akawat Clan—descended from Ako, great grandson of Hamoo.
12. The Udâwat Clan—descended from Udoh, great grandson of Hamoo.
13. The Chandawat Clan—descended from Chanda, great grandson of Hamoo.
14. The Râma Clan—descended from Râm Singh, son of Arjûn.
15. The Akhirajpota Clan—descended from Akhiraj, son of Arjûn.
16. The Jessa Clan—descended from Kandil, son of Arjûn.
17. The Indarsalot Clan—descended from Indar Singh, who founded Indargurh.
18. The Berisalot Clan—descended from Beri Sal, who founded Bahran and Filodi.
19. The Mokhimsingot Clan—descended from Mokhim Singh, who had Anterdeh.

The Hâras of Kotah, descended from Madhu Singh, the founder of the Kotah State, have the patronymic of Madhani, and are thus distinguished from all other Hâra clans.

III. Râthor.

On the destruction of Kanauj, the capital of the ancient kingdom of the same name, the Râthors abandoned their country, which they had governed with wonderful energy so long, and entering the barren wastes of Marwar, founded a new kingdom there. "The Râthors of Ajmere have the same customs and characteristics as their brethren in Marwar. They are still warlike and indolent, and great consumers of opium. Each man carries at least a dagger, and, except under extreme pressure, none will touch a plough" (*a*). The village of Khori held by the Râthors was once in the possession of the Mers, but was taken from them by these Rajpoots. This tribe has eighty-three Bhumia holdings in

(*a*) Gazetteer of Ajmere-Merwara, by Mr. J. D. Latouche, p. 29.

Ajmere. All the talukdars or great landholders of the district, with few exceptions, are Râthors, descended from Seoji.

The Râthors of Bikaneer have sprung from the Râthors of Marwar, and were established there by Bikâ, the son of Jodhain, in 1459. The Maharaja of Bikaneer claims to be the head of the tribe in that territory. The Râthors of that principality are divided into the following clans :—

The Râthor Clans of Bikaneer.

1. The Bikâ Clan—descended from Bîkâ, the founder of the Bikaneer State, with nine principal families :—1, Rajwi; 2, Ratan Singot; 3, Sringot; 4, Kishan Singot; 5, Umrawat; 6, Nârnot; 7, Bhîmrajot; 8, Gharsiot; 9, Pirthi Râjot. The chief seats of the clan are at Mahajin, Jessanoh, Baie, and Hyadesir.

2. The Bidâwat Clan—descended from Bidâ, Bikâ's brother, with six principal families :—1, Manohardasat; 2, Tejsiot; 3, Khagârot; 4, Pirthi Râjot; 5, Keshodâsot; 6, Mân Singot. Their country extends along part of the Marwar and Shekhawati frontiers. They are especially addicted to plundering. Their chief seats are at Bedasir and Saondwa.

3. The Karmsîot Clan—descended from Karmsî, a less distinguished brother of Bikâ, a small clan. Their chief seat is at Nokho.

4. The Kândhalot Clan—descended from Kândhal, Bikâ's uncle and chief supporter, consisting of three great families :—1, Raolot; 2, Barînrot; 3, Saindasot.

5. The Maudhlâwat Clan—descended from Mandhal, a less distinguished uncle of Bikâ. They have ten villages. Their chief seat is at Saroonda.

6. The Rupâwat Clan—descended from Rûpjî, another uncle of Bikâ (a). They possess ten villages. Their chief seat is at Badilah.

7. The Randhirot Clan—possessing one village.

8. The Mândlot Clan—occupying three villages.

9. The Ranmalot Clan—holding one village.

10. The Jaitmalot Clan—possessing one village.

11. The Kundalia Clan—with two villages.

12. The Udâwat Clan—holding four villages.

13. The Nâthal Clan—occupying two villages.

14. The Patâwat Clan—with one village.

15. The Gohel Clan—with one village.

16. The Benirot Clan.

(a) Gazetteer of Bikaneer, by Captain P. W. Powlett, p. 111.

The ruling chief of Marwar is at the head of the Râthor tribe in that State. There is good ground for the belief that, prior to the conquest of Marwar by the Râthors, that country had been governed at various periods by Jâts, Bheels, and Meenas. The Râthors abandoned Kanauj after the destruction of their capital by Shahab-ud-din in 1194. Some of them migrated westerly, and gradually conquered the small chieftains who formerly ruled over Marwar. The Râthors finally gained possession of Marwar under Rao Chanda, in the year 1382. His grandson, Jodha, founded the present city of Jodhpore, and made it the capital of the Marwar or Jodhpore State.

The Thakurs or great landholders of Ganora and Bednore, in Mewar, belong to the Mairtia clan of Râthors.

Mallâni claims to be the cradle of the Râthors in the west; for, on the downfall of Kanauj, Asthân, the great grandson of the last monarch, abandoning his native country, wandered with his followers to the west, and at the end of the twelfth century, captured from the Gohel Rajpoots the town of Kher, near the Luni, and took possession of the district of Mewo, now called Mallâni. The Gohels had seized the territory from the Bheels twenty years before. On being thus dispossessed the Gohels moved on to Bhaunagar, on the gulf of the Mâhi, where they are still a numerous body. The Râthors increased their principality in the time of Mallinath by the addition of Gûra and Nagar, which they conquered from the Soras. The Barmer District of Mallâni, at the date of the foundation of the Râthor rule under Asthân, was in the hands of the Sanklas, from whom it was taken by the Chauhâns, who, on their turn, were overcome by the Râthors, who annexed the district permanently (*a*).

The Râthors are very powerful in Marwar, where they are divided into the following clans :—

The Râthor Clans of Marwar.

1. The Jodha Clan—holding the chieftainships of Khari-ka-dewa, Chanpur, and Bûdsû.

2. The Champawat Clan—holding the chieftainships of Ahwa, Pokurn, Kâtoh, Palri, Hursola, Degode, Rohit, Jawula, Suttana, and Tingari.

3. The Kûmpawat Clan—holding the chieftainships of Asope, Kuntaleo, Chundawal, Siriari, Kharlo, Hursore, Bulloo, Bajoria, Sûrpura, Dewureo, Buggori, Gujsingpûra, and Roat.

4. The Mandlot Clan—holding the chieftainship of Sârunda.

(*a*) The Rajputana Gazetteer, Vol. II, p. 265.

5. The Pattawat Clan—holding the chieftainships of Kurnichari, Baroh, and Desnokh.
6. The Lakhawat Clan.
7. The Balawat Clan—holding the chieftainship of Dhûnara.
8. The Jaitmalot Clan—holding the chieftainship of Palasni.
9. The Karnot Clan—holding the chieftainship of Lûnawas.
10. The Rûpawat Clan—holding the chieftainship of Chûtela.
11. The Dûngerot Clan.
12. The Sandawat Clan.
13. The Mandnot Clan.
14. The Birot Clan.
15. The Jagmalot Clan.
16. The Hampawat Clan.
17. The Saktawat Clan.
18. The Urivalot Clan.
19. The Ketseot Clan.
20. The Satrosalot Clan.
21. The Tejmalot Clan (*a*).

A branch of the Râthors is settled in Jesalmere, and also in Jhalawar. There are a few also in Bhurtpore.

Talwara and Aorwara, in Banswara, are held by two branches of the Mairtia Râthors. The Talwara Pass is in their hands, and they are responsible for its security.

The chief of Kusalgarh is of this tribe, and is said to be descended from Jodh Singh, the founder of Jodhpore. The appellation of Ranawat is applied to the members of the ruling family of the State. This district has eight principal landholders, all of whom are Râthor Rajpoots. The tribe is also strong in Bundee. It has some representatives in Dungarpore, and one of the principal landowners is connected with it.

IV. Jodha.

The Jodha tribe, descended from Jodha, the founder of the Jodhpore State; is subdivided into a number of clans, as follows :—

The Jodha Clans.

1. The Santal or Satil Clan—having the chieftainship of Satulmere.

(*a*) Tod's Rajasthan—Madras Edition—Vol. II, p. 15.

2. The Mairtia Clan—having the chieftainships of Reah, Gahorah, Mehtri, and Mairta. The Mairtias are descended from Dûdoh, a son of Jodha. The Jaimalot and Jagmalot Clans, says Tod, are descended from Jaimal and Jagmal, two sons of Bîram, a son of Dûdoh.

3. The Bharmalot Clan—having the chieftainship of Bai Bhilara.

4. The Seorajot Clan—having the chieftainship of Dhûnara, on the Lûni.

5. The Karmsot Clan—having the chieftainship of Keonsir.

6. The Raimalot Clan.

7. The Samatseot Clan—having the chieftainship of Dewaroh.

8. The Bîdawat Clan—having the chieftainship of Bîdavati, in the Nagore District (*a*).

Jodha, the first ruler of Marwar, was succeeded by his son, Sûrjoh, or Sûraj Mal, who, through his sons, originated the following clans:—

The Sûrjoh or Sûraj Mal Clans.

1. The Udawat Clan—having chieftainships at Neemaj, Jytarun, Goondochi, Chundawal, Kooahaman, Chundawal, Khada, Marot, Biratea, and Raepore. It has also settlements in Mewar.

2. The Sagawat Clan—with settlements at Burwoh.

3. The Priagot Clan.

4. The Narawat Jodha Clan—a branch is established at Pachpahar, in Harouti (*b*).

V. Johiya.

These are a very ancient tribe, formerly known as Yaudheyas, "who probably contended with Alexander, before whose time they were, it is believed, established on the banks of the Sutlej. Yaudheya coins, as old as the first century of the Christian era, have been found near that river (Cunningham's Ancient Geography, Vol. I, p. 245). The Johiyas are by no means extinct, as Tod imagined. Many of them are Musalmans; but some in the Sirsa District are still Hindus. According to General Cunningham, they formerly held much of the country west and south-west of Bhatner; and their chief places were Kharbara, Sahankot, and Badopul, which the Râhtors took from them. There are three sections of the tribe: 1, the Admera; 2, the Lakvira,—who are settled on the banks of the Sutlej; and 3, the Madhera, who, together with the representative of the house of Madhu, the founder of the clan, are, for the most part,

(*a*) Tod's Rajasthan—Madras Edition—Vol. II, p. 18.
(*b*) *Ibid*, p. 20.

subjects of the Bikaneer State. The boundary of these two divisions is still the bank of the old Sutlej" (a).

VI. Silkawat.

A numerous class of *bhûmias* or landholders in Mehwo and Rardurro, in Marwar, descendants of Siluk or Silks.

VII. Bîramot.

A numerous tribe at Saitroo, Sewandh, and Daichoo, in Marwar, descended from Bîrumdeo, the son of Siluk.

VIII. Bîjawat.

Numerous at Saitroo, Sewandh, and Daichoo, in Marwar, descended from Bîrumdeo, the son of Siluk.

IX. Sîsawat.

A tribe in Marwar.

X. Kîtawat.

A tribe in Marwar.

XI. Tendo.

An ancient tribe in Marwar.

XII. Mohil.

A Chauhân tribe, descended from Manik Rae of Ajmere. The Râthors took Nagore from them in the fifteenth century.

XIII. Narbhana.

A Chauhân tribe, descended from Manik Rae of Ajmere.

XIV. Bhadauria.

A Chauhân tribe, descended from Manik Rae of Ajmere. Their appanage on the Chumbul still bears their name. In the early part of the last century the Bhadaurias under Rajah Kalyan Singh took possession of Dholpore, which they held till 1761, after the battle of Paniput, when they lost it.

XV. Bhaurecha.

A Chauhân tribe, descended from Manik Rae of Ajmere.

(a) Gazetteer of the Bikaneer State, by Captain P. W. Powlett, p. 123.

XVI. Dhanairea.

A Chauhân tribe, descended from Manik Rae of Ajmere. They formerly held Shahabad.

XVII. Bâgrecha.

A Chauhân tribe, descended from Manik Rae of Ajmere.

XVIII. Kombawat.

A tribe of allodial *bhûmias* or landholders in Mewar.

XIX. Lûnawat.

A tribe of allodial *bhûmias* or landholders in Mewar. They are proprietors of lands bordering on Oguna, Panora, and other tracts in the Aravulli. The Lûnawats are like the Dûlawats, descended from Lakha Rana, chief of Chitore in A. D. 1373.

XX. Ranawat.

A tribe of allodial *bhûmias* or landholders in Mewar. The ancestor of the Raja of Shapoora, a descendant of Rana Udya Singh, was of this tribe.

XXI. Dûlawat.

A tribe of allodial *bhûmias* or landholders, in the high lands bordering on Oguna, Panora, and other tracts in the Aravulli. The Dûlawats are descended from Lakha Rana, chief of Chitore, in A. D. 1373.

XXII. Jhala.

The chiefs of Sadri, Dailwarra, and Gogoonda, in Mewar, are of this tribe. It is also found in Jesalmere. The ruling family of Jhalâwâr is of the Jhala tribe. These Rajpoots came originally from Kattywar, of which they were once the rulers.

XXIII. Bargûjar.

An important tribe in Jeypore and Marwar. The Bargûjars are proprietors of twenty-five villages in the State of Dholpore.

XXIV. Sisodiya.

This is properly a branch of the Gahlot or Grahilot tribe. The Rana of Oodaipore or Mewar is a Sisodiya. The Emperor Shah Jehan presented the *pargannah* or barony of Phulia, which was formerly part of Ajmere, to the Raja of Shahpoora, a member of the royal family of Oodaipore.

The tribe also has possession of the *pargannah* of Sâwar, to the south-east of the district, the gift of Jehangir to its ancestor Gokul Dass, who had the reputation of having been wounded eighty-four times in the wars of that emperor.

The Râwals or native chiefs of Banswara have sprung from the Sisodiyas of Dungarpore, from whom they separated in the year 1530. Previously to that period Bagâr or the two States of Dungarpore and Banswara belonged to this tribe. Formerly, in the Banswara State, eight first class nobles of the Sisodiya and Chauhân tribes sat on the right of the throne, and eight Râthors of the same rank sat on the left, of whom only three families are remaining. The Sisodiyas in this State are divided into eight branches. There are a few members of the tribe in Bundee.

The Sisodiyas of Dungarpore, of whom the Maha Rawal is the head, claim to be descended from the elder branch of the Oodaipore family. We learn from Tod that these entered the State as emigrants from Meywar at the end of the twelfth century. Sir John Malcolm states that they came from Meywar about three hundred years ago.

There are also some members of this tribe in possession of lands at Nepoli, in Ajmere (*a*). They occupy four villages in Bikaneer. The tribe has families in Mallâni. Several of the principal chiefs of Oodaipore besides the Maharana, are attached to this tribe. There is also a branch of the tribe at Jaharawar. The principal clans of Sisodiyas in Meywar are as follows :—

Clans of Sisodiyas in Meywar.

1. Chandâwat. In former times the Chandâwats and Sakhtâwats were rival tribes in Meywar, of great power and importance. Their feuds, says Tod, have been the destruction of Meywar. The chief of Saloombra is the present head of the tribe. A few Chandâwats occupy a village in Bikaneer. Two of the chief landholders of Dungarpore are of this tribe.
2. Sakhtâwat. These are fewer in number than the Chandâwats ; but they have the 'reputation of greater bravery and more genius.' The chiefs of Bheendir and Bansi are of this clan.
3. Sangâwat. The chief of Deogarh is of the Sangâwat clan.
4. Megâwat. The Rawat of Beygoo is of this clan.
5. Jagâwat. The Rawat of Amait is a Jagâwat.
6. Sarangdeote. The Rawat of Kanorh is of the Sarangdeote clan.
7. Kishenâwat. The Rawats of Bhynsror and Korabur are of this clan.

(*a*) Gazetteer of Ajmere-Merwara, by Mr. J. D. Latouche, p. 29.

XXV. *The Gahlot Tribe.*

This tribe is descended from a child born in a cave, whose mother, a Ranee of the royal house of Balabhi, was the only person who escaped when that city was sacked. The word *gahlot* means 'cave-born.' The Gahlots are one of the thirty-six royal Rajpoot tribes (*a*).

There is a small community of Gahlots in Bikaneer, Marwar, Mallâni, and Jesalmere.

XXVI. *Sânklâ.*

The mother of Bikâ, the founder of the Bikaneer State, was a member of this tribe. He was the sixth son of Jodha, Rao of Marwar, who originated the State of Jodhpore. The Sânklâs are a branch of the Pramara tribe. They were expelled from Kher in Mallâni by the Chauhâns, who in their turn were subdued by the Râthors. Chiefs of Poogul, and in Marwar, are of this tribe.

XXVII. *Asayach.*

This tribe possesses one village in Bikaneer.

XXVIII. *Chandrâwat.*

The Chandrâwats are landholders in Jeypore. A small number occupy a village in Bikaneer. There is a branch in Jhalawar.

XXIX. *Sengar.*

A few Sengar Rajpoots have established themselves in the village of Kallianpura in Karauli. The chiefs occupy a small mud fort. The Sengars are established at Jagmohanpur, on the Jumna.

(*a*) *See* a detailed Account of this Tribe in the Author's "Hindu Tribes and Castes," Vol. I, pp. 125—135.

CHAPTER IV.

THE RAJPOOT TRIBES—(*Continued*).

XXX. — YADU, JADU, OR JADON. XXXI. — BHATI. XXXII — SODA. XXXIII. — KACHWAHA. XXXIV. — SHEKHAWAT. XXXV. — DEWAL. XXXVI. — SALANKHI. XXXVII. — BHAGELA. XXXVIII.—INDAR. XXXIX.—BIRPURA. XL.—DODHIA. XLI.—BEHILA. XLII.—SIKARWAL OR SIKARWAR. XLIII.—GOYAL. XLIV.—DEORA. XLV.—PARIA. XLVI.—PARIARIA. XLVII.—DHANDU. XLVIII.—DHANDAL OR DHONDAL. XLIX.—BORA. L.—BIDA. LI.—DETA. LII.—SINGARPAL. LIII.—KHIPA. LIV.—JASSOLIA. LV.—PHALSUNDIA. LVI.—SINMAL. LVII.—GOGADE. LVIII. — SAUDI. LIX. — JETANG. LX. — BANDAR. LXI. — KASUMBLIA. LXII.—KARMOT. LXIII.—GAUR. LXIV.—PUAR. LXV.—PUAR, PONWAR, OR PRAMARA. LXVI.—TAWAR. LXVII.—KELAN. LXVIII.—GOGLI. LXIX.—SUGAR. LXX.—MANGALIA. LXXI.—DHAWECHA. LXXII.—KALAEA. LXXIII.—KALAWAT. LXXIV.—UGA. LXXV.—SOR. LXXVI.—JASOR. LXXVII.—SELOT. LXXVIII.—KALA. LXXIX.—BHARAKMAL. LXXX.—MAKWANA. LXXXI. — JHARECHA. LXXXII. — BARECHA. LXXXIII. — KOTECHA. LXXXIV. — KARWA. LXXXV.—BIRAWA. LXXXVI.—JAICHAND. LXXXVII.—KHAWARIA. LXXXVIII.—KARNOT. LXXXIX.—MAHECHA. XC.—TANWAR. XCI.—PARIHAR. XCII.—KHAIR. XCIII.—VIHIL, OR BIHIL. XCIV.—MAIPAWAT. XCV.—KABA. XCVI.—KHICHI. XCVII.—SONAGURRA. XCVIII.—PAWAICHA. XCIX.—BHURTA. C.—KALACHA. CI.—RAOKA. CII.—RANIKIA. CIII.—KHARU-RA. CIV.—TANTIA. CV.—INDAH. CVI.—SINDHIL. CVII.—KHORWA. CVIII.—DHOTI OR DHATI. CIX.—SONDIA OR SONDI. CX.—HADU. CXI.—RAJAWAT. CXII.—SUKHTAWAT. CXIII.—OR. CXIV.—RATHWA. CXV.—DUBIA. CXVI.—TONWAR. CXVII.—TAGARGARI. CXVIII.—MORI. CXIX.—BODANA.

XXX. Yâdu, Jâdu, or Jâdon.

The Jâdu Rajpoots are the dominant tribe of Karauli, which State they have occupied from at least the tenth century, and probably from a much earlier period. The feudal aristocracy of that principality consists entirely of Jâdus. No other Rajpoots possess any rank whatever. They are an exceedingly illiterate people, very few being able to read and write. The Jâdus prefer the affix pâl, 'nourisher of cows,' to the more general Rajpoot affix of Singh, meaning lion. They are said to be brave fighting men, but bad cultivators. Wherever the Jadu "has to compete with cultivators of other castes on equal terms, he manifests his inferiority; and this is remarkably illustrated by the position of the Gonj, Khichri, and Panch Pîr Thakurs in Karauli, who, being out of the caste, are not allowed the advantages enjoyed by respectable Jâdus, and are consequently on a lower level than Meenas and Gûjars "(a).

The principal divisions or *kotris* of the Karauli Jâdus are the following :—

The Principal Jâdu Clans.

1. Hâdoti. This clan usually supplies an heir to the sovereignty of Karauli on the failure of sons in the reigning family. Its chief bears the title of Rao. The original seat of the clan was the neighbouring village of Gareri, which was left for Hâdoti in 1697 in consequence of a dispute with the chief of Fathpur.

2. Amargarh. The first chief of Amargarh was Amar Mân, son of Raja Jago Mân.

3. Inâiti. The first chief of this clan was Bhûp Pâl, son of the Maharaja Chhatr Mân.

4. Râontra. The first chief of this clan was Bhoj Pâl.

5. Bartûn. The founder of this clan was Madan Mân, son of the Maharaja Mukund.

The five nobles representing the above five clans have forts of their own.

6. Hari Dâs. This clan has sixteen divisions, which lie on the western borders of the State.

7. Mukund. The Mukunds have eight divisions, their estates being situated to the north-east of the city (b).

Anjani is the patron goddess of the Jâdus. The ancestors of this race founded Jesalmere, in the year 1157. This city is the present capital of the Bhâtîs.

The Jâdon Rajpoots of Karauli have a tradition that, in the year 1120, their ancestors erected the present fort at Dholpore. It is probable that they held lands in that territory in those days, but they must have been soon dispossessed, especially as we know that in 1194 Shahab-ud-din took possession of the kingdom of Kanauj, of which there is reason to believe that it formed a part.

The Jâdus have considerable possessions in Dholpore, in which State they own forty-nine villages. They have some families also in Dungarpore.

XXXI. Bhâti.

These Rajpoots are said to have established themselves on the Borwa hills of Merwara; and a tradition exists, that a Bhâtî Rajpoot, Ajit Singh, once bore the title of king of Merwara. They are strong to the west of the Bikaneer State, where they are divided into two great clans, namely :—

(a) Gazetteer of the Karauli State, by Captain P. W. Powlett, p. 18.
(b) *Ibid*, p. 46.

The Bhâti Clans of Bikaneer.

1. The Raolot Clans—consisting of nine branches.
2. The Pugalia Clans—consisting of four branches.

These thirteen branches have their chief seats at Poogul, Rajasir, Ranair, Sutasir, Chakarra, Beechnok, Garrialah, Sûrjerah, Rundisir, Jangloo, Jaminsir, Kûdsû, and Naineah.

The Bhâtis of Bhatner are most probably Hindus, who have been converted to the Mahomedan faith. There is a colony of Bhâtis in Marwar, and another in Mallâni.

The Yâdu, Jâdu, or Jâdon Bhâtî Rajpoots claim descent from the ancient Yâdu kings of the Lunar race. The remote ancestors of the Bhâtî Rajpoots came originally from Prayâg or Allahabad, whence they removed to Mathura, from which place, after remaining there for a long period, the tribe dispersed in various directions. The ruler of Jesalmere is of this tribe. The Bhâtis in former times subdued all the tracts south of the Garah; but their jurisdiction has been greatly diminished by the encroachments of the Râthors. Some of the principal branches of the Bhâtis in Jesalmere are the following:—

Bhâti Clans of Jesalmere.

1. The Maldots.
2. The Kailans.
3. The Barsangs.
4. The Pohars.
5. The Tejmatahs.

The Maldots, says Tod, have the character of being the most daring robbers of the desert. They are descended from Rao Maldeo, and possess the fief of Baroo with eighteen villages. The chief seat of this tribe has been successively at Tumoli, Deorawal, and Jesalmere. Deorawal was founded by a Bhâtî chief in the ninth century. He delighted in warfare, and consolidated the Bhâtî rule in this barren region. So great were his exploits that he is regarded as the real founder of the tribe. The city and fort of Jesalmere were built in the middle of the twelfth century by Jesal, the sixth rajah in descent from Deoraj. About the year 1294 Alauddin sent an army against the Bhâtis, which destroyed the city of Jesalmere; but it was afterwards re-built. The Jesalmere princes continued independent for several centuries, and only submitted to the Mahomedans in the reign of Shah Jehan, under Rawal Sabal Singh, the twenty-fifth chief in succession to Jesal. The territory then was more extensive than in any other period of the nation's history, including Bhawalpore, extending northwards to the Sutlej, westward to the Indus, and eastwards and southwards embraced much of the tract subsequently added to Marwar and Bikaneer (*a*).

The Bhâtîs of Marwar hold the chieftainships of Khejurla and Ahore.

The Bhâtî, says Tod, "is not perhaps so athletic as the Râthor, or so tall as the Kachwâhâ, but generally fairer than either."

XXXII. Soda.

A small number of the Soda Rajpoots are in the Bikaneer State, and in Mallâni. This tribe is an offshoot of the Pramaras. In former times, they had possession of the whole of the great desert; and are still found scattered over it. The Umras and Sûmras, now Mahomedans, branches of the Sodas, established Umrakote, where Akbar was born, and Umrasomra. The ruler of Dhât, in the desert, is of this race (*b*). The Sodas have less prejudice than most Rajpoot tribes, and "will drink from the same vessel, and smoke out of the same hookah with a Mussulman, laying aside only the tube that touches the mouth." A Soda may always be known by the peculiarity of his turban.

In the extreme west of Rajputana, on the borders of Scinde, the Sodas display a singular blending of Hinduism and Islamism in their social customs and religious institutions. Their marriages are entirely in accordance with old Rajpoot customs, yet in their religion they conform, for the most part, to Mahomedan rites. Nevertheless, strange to say, they worshipped until very recently the gods of the Hindu pantheon.

XXXIII. Kachwâhâ.

This tribe has its principal seat at Jeypore, which State is mostly in the hands of Kachwâhâ chiefs. A branch of the tribe founded Amber in the tenth century, dispossessing the Meenas and Rajpoots, the former inhabitants of the country. One of the greatest princes of the Kachwâhâs of Jeypore was Rajah Maun Singh, a very distinguished general in the time of Akbar, whose reputation is still fresh among Rajpoot tribes. Another noted chief of the Jeypore family was Jai Singh II, commonly known as Siwai Jai Singh. It was he who erected observatories at Jeypore, Delhi, Benares, Mathura, and Ujain. That in Benares is, on the whole, in excellent preservation, and is an object of curiosity and interest to most European and American travellers visiting that city. This prince was the author of an important treaty between the chiefs of Jeypore, Jodhpore, and

(*a*) The Rajputana Gazetteer, Vol. II, pp. 170—72.

(*b*) Tod's Rajasthan—Madras Edition—Vol. I, p. 85.

Oodaipore, to resist the advancing influence of the Moghul rulers of India. It seems that the Sisodia chiefs of Oodaipore had in no single instance permitted alliances between their family and Moghul nobles, whereas both the Kachwâhâ and Râthor houses had repeatedly consented to such unions, whereby the purity of their Rajpoot blood had been seriously affected. This treaty, however, aimed at establishing a new bond of intercourse between the three tribes on the basis of electing the future chiefs of the two offending tribes from sons by Sisodia mothers and passing over elder sons by wives taken from other tribes. The treaty caused much dissatisfaction and strife, which eventually, instead of strengthening all these tribes, contributed greatly to their weakness (*a*).

In the twelfth century the Kachwâhâs were only great vassals of the Chauhân king of Delhi; and achieved their subsequent greatness with the aid of the Timoors. "Although the Kachwâhâs," observes Colonel Tod, "under their popular princes, as Pujûn, Rajah Mân, and the Mirza Rajah, have performed exploits as brilliant as any other tribes, yet they do not now enjoy the same reputation for courage as either the Râthors or the Hâras. This may be in part accounted for by the demoralization consequent on their proximity to the Moghul Court, and their participation in all its enervating vices; but still more from the degradations they have suffered from the Mahrattas, and to which their western brethren have been less exposed. Every feeling, patriotic or domestic, became corrupted wherever their pernicious influence prevailed" (*b*). "With a proper application of her (the State) revenues," remarks Tod in another place, "and princes like Rajah Mân to lead a brave vassalage, they would have foiled all the efforts of the Mahrattas; but their own follies and vices have been their ruin" (*c*). Most of the Rajpoots of Jeypore are Kachwâhâs, who may be divided into three classes, says Major Bayley, Political Agent of the State, namely, holders of estates, men in service, and cultivators. This last class is small, as Rajpoots are generally too proud to work in the fields, unless compelled by necessity (*d*).

The principal Kachwâhâ clans in the Jeypore State are twelve in number, and are the following:—

Kachwâhâ Clans of Jeypore.

1. Chatharbhojot—having the chieftainships of Pinar and Bhagrû.
2. Kallianot—having the chieftainship of Totwarra.

(*a*) The Rajputana Gazetteer, Vol. II, pp. 136, 137.
(*b*) Tod's Rajasthan—Madras Edition—Vol. II, p. 397.
(*c*) *Ibid*, p. 401.
(*d*) The Rajputana Gazetteer, Vol. II, p. 146.

3. Nathawat—with the chieftainship of Chomû.
4. Balbadharot—with the chieftainship of Acherol.
5. Khangarot—with the chieftainship of Thodrî.
6. Sûltanot—with the chieftainship of Chandsir.
7. Pachâenot—with the chieftainship of Sambra.
8. Gûgawat—with the chieftainship of Dhûnî.
9. Khûmbani—with the chieftainship of Bhanskho.
10. Khumbawat—with the chieftainship of Mahâr.
11. Shiubaranpota—with the chieftainship of Nîndir.
12. Banbîrpota—with the chieftainship of Batko.

The above are the Bârâh Kotrîs, or twelve great Kachwâhâ clans. In addition there are four other clans of the same tribe in the State. These are :—

13. Rajawat—with sixteen fiefs.
14. Narûka—having the chieftainship of Macherri. The chief of Uniârâ belongs to this clan, which has also a few representatives in Bhurtpore.
15. Bhankawat—with four fiefs.
16. Parinmalot—with one fief (*a*).

From the year 1037 A. D., when the Kachwâhâ Rajpoots having taken possession of this country made Amber their capital, down to 1728, Amber continued to be the royal city; but in the latter year the seat of power was transferred to the present city of Jeypore, which was founded by Siwai Jai Singh II.

In the Ajmere District, the Kachwâhâs are principally settled in the villages of Harmâra and Tilornia, in the extreme north of the district, and have *bhûmia* holdings in five villages. The ancestors of the chief of Harmâra narrowly escaped from losing their estates altogether. They were once partially seized by the Râhtors, and altogether by the Mahrattas. The British Government, however, has secured them to the family.

The Kachwâhâs of Bikaneer are divided into four classes, as follows :—

Kachwâhâ Clans of Bikaneer.

1. Girdharjîka.	3. Kachwâhâ.
2. Bhainrujîka.	4. Narûka.

The chief seat of the Kachwâhâs in Bikaneer is at Nynawas. The tribe has lands in Marwar and also in Bhurtpore.

About the middle of the last century, a Kachwâhâ seized a portion of the

(*a*) Tod's Rajasthan—Madras Edition—Vol. II, pp. 403, 404.

Jeypore territory, and formed therefrom the principality of Ulwar, which exists to the present day. The tribe is found also in Dungarpore.

XXXIV. Shekhawat.

The Shekhawats are an offshoot of the Kachwâhâs of Jeypore, and are descended from Balo Ji, third son of the Raja of Udikarn, who became ruler of Jeypore in the year 1389. Balo Ji's grandson, Sheikh Ji, was so named in honour of a Mahomedan Sheikh, through whose prayers, it was believed, the child was born. The Sheikh ordained, says Tod, that, "at the birth of every Shekhawat male infant, a goat should be sacrificed, the *kalma* (Islamite creed) read, and the child sprinkled with the blood. Although four centuries have passed away since these obligations were contracted by Mokul (father of Sheikh Ji), they are still religiously maintained by the little nation of his descendants, occupying a space of ten thousand square miles. The wild hog, which, according to immemorial usage, should be eaten once a year by every Rajpoot, is rarely even hunted by a Shekhawat," out of respect to the memory of the Mahomedan saint (*a*). Balo Ji obtained Amrutsir as an appanage, which district was further increased by Sheikh Ji, so that his territory included three hundred and sixty villages, which in former times had been chiefly in the hands of Chauhân and Tuar tribes. The Shekhawats have the following clans:—

Shekhawat Clans.

1. The Bhojâni Clan.
2. The Sadhâni Clan—in the north of Shekhavati.
3. The Larkhâni Clan. This clan was formerly, says Tod, a community of robbers.
4. The Tajkhâni Clan.
5. Parsrâmpota Clan.
6. The Hurrâmpota Clan.
7. The Nathawat Clan. The chief houses of this clan are Samot and Chomû, the head having the title of Rawal.
8. The Raesilot Clan.

The Shekhawats are also settled in Mallâni, and in other parts of Rajputana.

About a hundred years ago, the Jeypore Government, being jealous of the growing power of the Shekhawatis, forcibly introduced the custom among them of the equal division of all real property among the sons on the death of their

(*a*) Tod's Rajasthan—Madras Edition—Vol. II, p. 359.

father. The result has been a general impoverishment and weakening of all the families of chiefs. Sîkar and Khetrî are the only districts exempt from the custom.

The principal chief of Shekhawati is Raja Ajit Singh, whose territory comprises the *pargannahs* of Khetrî, Bîbai, Singhânâ, and Jhûnjnee. His revenue amounts to about three and-a-half lacs of rupees, of which he pays eighty thousand rupees as tribute to the Maharajah of Jeypore. Other dependencies in Shekhawati, which pay tribute to the same rule, are those of Sikar, Baswa, Nawalgarh, Mandawâr, and Sûrajgarh (*a*). These chiefs govern their own territories with much independence, for although they acknowledge the suzerainty of the Maharajah of Jeypore, yet they are very jealous of any interference in their rule. At certain periods of the year they are obliged to appear at court, and to pay homage to the Jeypore Prince.

XXXV. Dewal.

A tribe in Marwar.

XXXVI. Solankhî, or Châlukya.

The Solankhîs are in Jesalmere, Jhalawar, Bundee, Marwar, and Mallâni. The chief of Roopnagarh is of this tribe. His stronghold, says Tod, "commands one of the passes leading to Marwar." The Solankhis are numerous in the State of Bundee, and a few are in Dungarpore.

XXXVII. Bhagela.

A branch of the Solankhîs. The Raja of Bhagelkhand, and the Raos of Peetapoor, Theraud, and Adaluj are of this tribe. Bhagela families are settled in Mallâni.

XXXVIII. Indar.

These are in Marwar and Mallâni.

XXXIX. Bîrpura.

A branch of the Solankhîs. The Rao of Lunawarra is of this tribe.

XL. Dodhia.

A tribe in Marwar.

XLI. Behila.

A branch of the Solankhîs. The Rao of Kulianpoor, in Mewar, is of this tribe.

(*a*) The Rajputana Gazetteer, Vol. II, pp. 139, 40.

XLII. Sikarwâl, or Sikarwâr.

The small district of Sikarwar, on the right bank of the Chumbul, adjoining Jaduvati, is called after them. They live by cultivating the soil and the chase. There are clans of the tribe in Jeypore. In the small State of Dholpore the Sikarwârs are proprietors of twenty-three villages, and occupiers of eleven more.

XLIII. Goyal.

These are found in Marwar.

XLIV. Deorâ.

In Mallâni and Sirohi. They are a branch of the Chauhâns. The Rajpoot tribes of Mallâni are said to be fifty-two in number.

XLV. Pariâ.

In Mallâni.

XLVI. Pariâria.

In Mallâni.

XLVII. Dhându.

In Mallâni.

XLVIII. Dhândal, or Dhondal.

In Mallâni. Tod says, that the Dhondals are descended from Rao Gango, and are among the most ancient of the allodial chieftains of the desert.

XLIX. Borâ.

In Mallâni.

L. Bidâ.

In Mallâni.

LI. Deta.

In Mallâni.

LII. Singarpâl.

In Mallâni.

LIII. Khipâ.

In Mallâni.

LIV. Jassolia.

In Mallâni.

LV. Phalsundia.

In Mallâni.

LVI. Sinmal.

In Mallâni.

LVII. Gogâde.

In Mallâni.

LVIII. Saudi.

In Mallâni.

LIX. Jetang.

In Mallâni.

LX. Bândâr.

In Mallâni.

LXI. Kasumblia.

In Mallâni.

LXII. Karmot.

In Mallâni.

LXIII. *Gaur.*

The Gaurs are supposed to have come originally to Ajmere from Bengal, while performing a pilgrimage to the famous Dwarka Shrine under Raja Bachraj and Raja Bawan, in the time of Prithi Râja. The former, with his followers, settled in Ajmere, the latter at Kuchâman, in Marwar. Gradually the tribe gained possession of Junia, Sarwar, Deolia, and Srinagar; and in the reign of Akbar built for themselves Rajgarh. Notwithstanding the reverses to which they have been subjected, the city having been twice taken from them, once by the Râthors, and once by the Mahrattas, the Gaurs are still the owners of Rajgarh, and are occupiers of Kotaj, Danta, Jatia, and other places. They also took possession of Srinagar from the Powars, who have entirely left the district. The descendants of Raja Bawan have broad lands at Arjunpura, Tubeji, and elsewhere (*a*).

This tribe is also settled in Marwar. It has five branches or clans, namely, Outabir, Silhala, Tûr, Dûsena, and Bodano. In Ajmere the tribe possesses fourteen villages; and has a few families in Bundee.

LXIV. *Tuâr.*

The Tuârs are in Marwar; but their chief possessions, says Tod, are "the district of Tuârgar, on the right bank of the Chumbul, towards its junction with the Jumna; and the small chieftainship of Pâtun Tuârvati, or Torawati, in the Jeypore State, and whose head claims affinity with the ancient kings of Indraprastha" (*b*), that is, of Delhi. This small territory is to the north of Jeypore, between Kot Putti and Khetri. The Tuâr kings were expelled from Delhi about eight hundred years ago, on its capture by the Ghoris. The Tuârs of Malwa succeeded the Puârs, and reigned there one hundred and forty-two years, when they gave place to the Chauhâns.

LXV. *Puâr, Ponwar, or Pramara.*

These are located in Marwar, Jesalmere, and elsewhere. Although this tribe was once the most powerful of the Agnikulas, and founded great cities, ruling over wide tracts of country, yet little or nothing remains, except ruins, to illustrate its former splendour. The Puârs reigned over Malwa for upwards of a thousand years (*c*). The Rao of Bijolli, in Marwar, is of the ancient Pramaras of Dhâr, and belongs to the Maipawut branch of the tribe. The Pramaras of the

(*a*) Gazetteer of Ajmere-Merwara, by Mr. J. D. Latouche, pp. 28 and 29.

(*b*) Tod's Rajasthan—Madras Edition — Vol. I, p. 80.

(*c*) For a detailed account of the Pramaras, see the Author's "Hindu Tribes and Castes," Vol. I, pp. 145 to 149.

plateau of Mewar, Tod remarks, are of the highest rank. The chief seat of the tribe in Bikaneer is at Jaitsisir.

The tribe has extensive possessions in Dholpore, where they are proprietors of no less than one hundred and three villages. It has also lands in Dungarpore.

LXVI. Tâwar, or Tânwar.

The Tâwars are in possession of two villages in Bikaneer. It has also some families in Marwar and Jesalmere.

LXVII. Kelan.
In Mallâni.

LXVIII. Gogli.
In Mallâni.

LXIX. Sugar.
In Mallâni.

LXX. Mângalia.
In Mallâni.

LXXI. Dhawecha.
In Mallâni.

LXXII. Kalâeâ.
In Mallâni.

LXXIII. Kalâwat.
In Mallâni.

LXXIV. Ugâ.
In Mallâni.

LXXV. Sor.
In Mallâni.

LXXVI. Jasor.
In Mallâni.

LXXVII. Selot.
In Mallâni.

LXXVIII. Kâlâ.
In Mallâni.

LXXIX. Bharakmal.
In Mallâni.

LXXX. Makwânâ.
In Mallâni.

LXXXI. Jharecha.
In Mallâni.

LXXXII. Barecha.
In Mallâni.

LXXXIII. Kotecha.
In Mallâni.

LXXXIV. Karwa.
In Mallâni.

LXXXV. Birâwâ.
In Mallâni.

LXXXVI. Jaichand.
In Mallâni.

LXXXVII. Khâwaria.
In Mallâni.

LXXXVIII. Karnot.
In Mallâni.

LXXXIX. Mahecha.
In Mallâni.

XC. Tânwar.
In Jesalmere.

XCI. Parihâr.

In Jesalmere, and in most of the other States of Rajputana. The capital city of the tribe, in former times, was Mundawur, in Marwar; but they were dispossessed by the Râthors. The Parihârs have now no independent chieftainship in Rajputana. They have a colony, says Tod, "at the confluence of the Cohari, the Sinde, and the Chumbul, which has given its name to a commune of twenty-four villages besides hamlets situated amidst the ravines of these streams" (*a*). The tribe has also one village in Dholpore.

XCII. Khair.

A branch of the Pramaras. Their capital is Khyraloo.

(*a*) Tod's Rajasthan—Madras Edition—Vol. I, p. 92.

XCIII. Vihil, or Bihil.

A branch of the Pramaras. The heads of the tribe are chiefs of Chandravarti.

XCIV. Maipawut.

A branch of the Pramaras. The chief of Bijolli, in Mewar, is of this tribe.

XCV. Kaba.

A branch of the Pramaras. A few in Sirowi.

XCVI. Khîchi.

A branch of the Chauhâns, settled in Gagrown, Ragoogarh, Jesalmere, Boondi, Jhalawar, and elsewhere. They are descended from Manik Rae.

XCVII. Sonagurra.

A branch of the Chauhâns, in Jhalore, Marwar, and elsewhere.

XCVIII. Pawaicha.

A branch of the Chauhâns, settled in Pawagurh.

XCIX. Bhûrta.

A branch of the Solankhîs, in Jesalmere.

C. Kalacha.

A branch of the Solankhîs, in Jesalmere.

CI. Raoka.

A branch of the Solankhîs, settled in Thoda, Jeypore.

CII. Ranikia.

A branch of the Solankhîs, in Daisoori, Mewar.

CIII. Kharura.

A branch of the Solankhîs, in Allote and Jawura, Malwa.

CIV. Tantia.

A branch of the Solankhîs, in Chandbhur Sakunbari.

CV. Indoh.

A branch of the Parihârs, on the banks of the Loony.

CVI. Sindhil.

A branch of the Parihârs, on the banks of the Loony.

CVII. *Kâorwa.*

A nomadic tribe chiefly found in the Thul of Dhât. They move about with their cattle, encamping wherever water or pasturage is to be found.

CVIII. *Dhoti, or Dhâti.*

A pastoral tribe at Dhât. They are a peaceable people, and in their habits resemble the Kâorwas.

CIX. *Sondia, or Sondî.*

These are numerous in the Chaumehla District of the Jhalawar State, where they amount to nearly twenty thousand persons, who are all agriculturists. These Rajpoots are a mixed race, probably descendants of outcasts. For many years they had a bad character as marauders. They were a terror to Sondwara. Before the peace of Mundesar they could muster a force of 1,249 horsemen and 9,250 footmen, all living on plunder. The Sondia has a fair countenance, wears a large white turban, and is readily recognized from all other Hindus. It is very common for Sondia women to marry a second time. These people are rude, robust, and profoundly ignorant. They are held in detestation by other tribes, and yet are greatly feared. All are addicted to the use of opium and to strong spirits, and both men and women are notoriously unrestrained in their sensual appetites. As they are much disunited among themselves, deeds of violence and bloodshed were formerly very common; but a great improvement has come over them in modern times (*a*).

CX. *Hadu.*

A tribe in Jhalawar.

CXI. *Rajawat.*

A tribe in Jhalawar.

CXII. *Sûkhtawât.*

A tribe in Jhalawar. The Sûkhtawât Rajpoots founded the *pargannah* of Awar, five hundred years ago.

CXIII. *Or.*

A Rajpoot tribe of workers in stone in the Jhalawar State. The great tank of Jhalrapatan is said to have been excavated by a Or Rajpoot named Jesu.

(*a*) Malcolm's Central India, Vol. I.

CXIV. Rathwa.

A small tribe in Bundee.

CXV. Dubia.

A small tribe in Bundee.

CXVI. Tonwâr.

This tribe is said to be the first of the Rajpoot tribes which established itself in Dholpore, whither they came, it is supposed, in the beginning of the eleventh century. They are now chiefly to be found in the Rahna Division of Rajakhera. The tribe is in possession of fifteen villages. It has also some families in Dungarpore.

CXVII. Tagargari.

A tribe in Dholpore, where it is the proprietor of half a dozen villages.

CXVIII. Mori.

The tribe has three villages in Dholpore.

CXIX. Bodana.

A tribe settled in Dungarpore.

CHAPTER V.

CASTES.

THE VAISYA CASTES: MERCHANTS, BANKERS, AND TRADERS. THE KAYASTHS. BARDS AND GENEALOGISTS. GOLDSMITHS AND JEWELLERS. AGRICULTURAL TRIBES AND CASTES. HERDSMEN, SHEPHERDS, AND REARERS OF CAMELS. SMALL TRADERS. MANUFACTURERS OF BEADS, BANGLES, AND VARIOUS ARTICLES, WEAVERS, AND DYERS, &c. PHYSICIANS AND SURGEONS. BLACKSMITHS, BRAZIERS, MASONS, CARPENTERS, TINKERS. POTTERS, DIGGERS, &c. DEVOTEES, RELIGIOUS MENDICANTS. SERVANTS AND PERSONAL ATTENDANTS. JUGGLERS, ACROBATS, SNAKE-CHARMERS, BUFFOONS, DRUM-BEATERS. FOWLERS AND HUNTERS. WORKERS IN LEATHER. THIEVES, ROBBERS, AND WATCHMEN. SCAVENGERS AND OTHER LOW CASTES.

THE VAISYA: MERCHANTS, BANKERS, AND TRADERS.

The trading class is found, more or less in all the States. They are divided into numerous branches. Bankers and merchants are mostly Jains, the small traders being generally Hindus.

1. *The Agarwâlas.*

One of the principal trading castes of Ajmere, Marwar, Bikaneer, Mallâni, Jesalmere, Bhurtpore, and Bundee.

They are largely attached to the Jain religion, and are generally wealthy. In Bikaneer the Agarwâlas are the principal traders in English imported goods. They are prosperous in Karauli, and to some extent cultivate the soil.

2. *The Oswâls.*

A leading trading caste in Ajmere, Jesalmere, Marwar, Bhurtpore, Bundee, Dungarpore, and Bikaneer, who, it is said, sprang from Osanaggri, near the Lûni, in Marwar. Like the Agarwâlas, they are chiefly Jains, and are generally well off. The Oswâls have the following clans in Bikaneer:—

1. Dada.	4. Sirono.	7. Bhantia.
2. Kotâri.	5. Sawan Sûkha.	8. Goleha.
3. Sethia.	6. Abani.	

The following are important clans of the Oswâls of Marwar :—

1. Bhandâri.	3. Singwi.	5. Lodha.
2. Mohnot.	4. Muhta.	

Members of these clans have held very high offices in the State of Marwar. Most of the Oswâls of Mallâni are cultivators.

3. *The Maheshwarîs.*

Traders in Ajmere, Jesalmere, Mallâni, Bhurtpore, Bundee, Marwar, and Bikaneer. In the latter territory the Maheshwarîs and Oswâls are the richest Banyas. They are opium traders, contractors, bankers, and the like, and their business is generally far from home. The following are subdivisions of this tribe :—

1. Daga.	5. Bâgri.	9. Mundra.
2. Pugali.	6. Lada.	10. Kotâri.
3. Damâni.	7. Mohota.	11. Râti.
4. Mintri.	8. Sadhani.	

At the marriage ceremony of Maheshwarîs as well as Pancholis, when the bridegroom enters the bride's house, her maternal uncle lifting her up carries her in his arms seven times round the bridegroom.

4. *The Bijaburjis.*

Traders in Ajmere.

5. *The Khandelwals.*

Traders in Ajmere.

6. *The Dhûsars.*

Traders in Ajmere and Bhurtpore.

7. *The Saraogîs.*

These flourish in Karauli, where they belong to the Jain religion. Some of them are cultivators. They are also in Marwar and Bhurtpore.

8. *The Srî Mâls.*

Traders in Karauli, attached to the Jain religion. They are settled also in Marwar and Bhurtpore.

9. *The Palliwâls.*

Jain traders in Karauli, Bhurtpore, Dungarpore, and elsewhere. They came originally from Palli.

10. *The Porwâls.*

Traders in Marwar.

11. *The Sri-sri-mâls.*

Traders in Marwar.

12. *The Vijawargis.*

Traders in Marwar.

13. *The Bhattias.*

Traders in Jesalmere and in the Rajputana desert. They are Rajpoots, who have degraded themselves from their original position. Their habits are like those of the Arorahs.

14. *The Lohanas.*

A numerous tribe of traders and writers in Dhât and Talpoora. They are said to have been originally Rajpoots. Many pursue various callings.

15. *The Arorahs.*

A tribe in the Rajputana desert, addicted to agriculture, trade, and many other pursuits.

16. *Bohra.*

Traders in tin, iron, and other wares.

17. *Khondehwal.*

A trading class in Bhurtpore.

18. *Mahor.*

Traders in Bhurtpore.

19. *Dilwaria.*

Traders in Bhurtpore.

20. *Khestri.*

Traders in Bhurtpore.

21. *Nogdra.*

Traders in Dungarpore.

22. *Narsinghpura.*

Traders in Dungarpore.

23. *Bhutera.*

Traders in Dungarpore.

24. *The Khatris.*

The Khatris are found in the north parts of Bikaneer and in Marwar, and in other parts of Rajputana.

They are chiefly bankers and traders. A few cultivate land. In Mallâni the Khatris stamp dyed stuffs; and those who work for chiefs at this trade are exempt from the payment of taxes. Several clans of Khatris hold estates in Jeypore.

THE KAYASTHS.

There are three clans of Kayasths in Ajmere, some members of which wear the sacred cord. These acknowledge no mutual relationship, and hold no social intercourse with one another. They are as follows :—

1. Ajmere. 2. Ramsar. 3. Kekri.

The Kayasths are accountants and revenue officials over villages and districts. They hold estates free from revenue, and have been hereditary *kanungoes* from the time of the Moghul emperors. The local name for Kayasths in Marwar is Pancholi.

There is a branch of them also in Jhalawar.

The Kayasths of Bhurtpore have the following subdivisions :—

1. Mathur.	5. Suratdhaj.	9. Balmik.
2. Bhatnagar.	6. Amisht.	10. Aithana.
3. Sri Basta.	7. Gaur.	11. Kulshrista.
4. Sakseina.	8. Karan.	12. Nigaen.

The two first of these clans only are found in the Bundee State, each of which is divided into two branches, which do not intermarry.

BARDS AND GENEALOGISTS.

The Chāran Tribe.

The Chârans are a people of great respectability and influence in Rajputana. They are the national bards, which is their chief and most important vocation, especially as attached to great Rajpoot families, whose praises they sing, and whose pedigrees they rehearse. They also perform a number of miscellaneous duties in connection with their high office. The Chârans possess a good many villages in some States. They are a sacred race, and possess many privileges in virtue of their position. In Marwar they hold large grants of land, which have been given to them from religious motives, and for the same reasons enjoy certain immunities as traders (*a*).

The Tirwâris are a kind of Châran in Marwar. The two principal clans of the tribe in that State are :—

1. Bânkedâs.	2. The Chaendâs.

These clans "hold the post of bard ; and it is their duty to collect and preserve the records of each reigning chief, and embody them in their histories, which is done both in prose and verse. They also compose odes commemorative of the most important passing events, which they recite before the Maharaja in Durbar. They receive rich gifts from the chiefs of the courts to which they belong ; and the highest honors are paid to them" (*b*).

A singular and very bad custom prevails among the Chârans of Marwar, of a young man and young woman, when betrothed, eating opium together.

In Mallâni there are two clans of Chârans, namely :—

1. Barath Chârans.	2. Garwi Chârans.

(*a*) Gazetteer of Marwar, by Major C. K. M, Walter, p, 23.

(*b*) *Ibid*, p. 30.

There is a tradition that the Barath Chârans were originally Bhâti Rajpoots. The village of Durmara, in Nagor, is held by the Barath Chârans in *udak*, or rent-free. They worship chiefly Mâthwiji. The Garwi Chârans came originally from Kachh. They are great traders, and do not receive alms like the Baraths. The two clans do not intermarry, or eat and smoke together. Both classes of Chârans consider themselves to be above the law, and pay no dues. Resenting all interference with themselves, they readily commit *chândi* if not left alone, that is, they wound their persons with sharp knives and daggers, and even kill themselves. The Garwi Chârans have always been much respected, and in times of national feud and disturbance have been free from molestation wherever they went.

In Bikaneer an image erected to Karniji, the Châran woman through whose agency it is supposed the State came into the hands of Bika and his descendants, is the chief object of worship, and her shrine is the principal one in Bikaneer.

The Chârans of Central India are divided into two branches :—

1. Kachili.	2. Maru.

The former of these are horse and camel dealers ; but the latter are devoted to the special duties of the tribe.

The Bhât Tribe.

In the North-Western Provinces, Bhâts and Chârans are frequently one and the same tribe ; but in Rajputana they are separate tribes with separate duties. The Bhâts are genealogists, and concern themselves about the pedigrees of great families. They also engage in trade. The tribe has great influence in all the native States, and is held in great awe by the other tribes, in the same way as the Chârans. They possess rent-free estates, and receive presents at weddings.

The Chârans and Bhâts are the chief carriers in the State of Marwar. "Their sacred character," says Tod, "overawes the lawless Rajpoot chief ; and even the savage Kali and Bheel, and the plundering Sahrae of the desert, dread the anathema of these singular races, who conduct the caravans through the wildest and most desolate regions" (*a*). Both these tribes are carriers and traders with pack-bullocks in the State of Bundee.

The Bhâts of Bhurtpore are few in number, and have three branches, namely :—

1. Suth.	2. Bandi.	3. Mangal.

In Bundee, the Bhâts perform the duties of marriage negotiators and reciters of genealogical history at public festivals.

(*a*) Tod's Rajasthan—Madras Edition— Vol. I, p. 602.

GOLDSMITHS AND JEWELLERS.

The Sonârs.

These work in gold, silver, brass, and other metals. In Mallâni they also pursue agriculture. In that State they are divided into two branches,—the Sonârs, and the Mer Sonârs. These do not intermarry, or eat and drink together. They are found in several of the States.

AGRICULTURAL TRIBES AND CASTES.

Lodha.

Cultivators of extensive lands in the eastern districts of Rajputana. In Dholpore they are proprietors of forty-five villages, are occupiers of ninety-one more, and in addition are cultivators of nearly seventeen thousand acres of land.

Mâli.

The Mâlis number upwards of eleven thousand persons in Ajmere, and are good cultivators. They occupy the greater portion of Kusbah, Ajmere, and are scattered about the Rajputana States. They are a very industrious people, and are found in considerable numbers in the eastern districts.

Kâchî.

Laborious cultivators in Rajputana as in other parts of India. They are numerous in the eastern districts, where their lands are extensive. In Dholpore they have a community of fifteen thousand persons, who cultivate nearly twenty thousand acres of land.

Kumbi, or Kurmi.

Cultivators, who are found especially to the south of the Arvalis, having come originally from Central and Southern India. The agriculturists of Dungarpore are chiefly Kurmis.

Kir.

A small tribe in Ajmere, whose employment is the cultivation of melons.

Sirwi.

A class of cultivators in Marwar.

Kalbi.

Cultivators in Mallâni, on estates bordering on the Lûni. They are worshippers of Vishnu.

Pithil.

The principal agriculturists of the desert in Rajputana.

Kirâr.

Landholders and agriculturists in Jeypore, Jhalawar, and other States. Some of them hold large estates.

Bishnawi.

Cultivators in the district of Chahotan in Mallâni.

Mehwâti.

Cultivators in Jhalawar.

Dhâkar.

Cultivators in Jhalawar.

HERDSMEN, SHEPHERDS, AND REARERS OF CAMELS.

Ahir.

Herdsmen and cultivators, especially in the eastern districts, where they possess extensive lands. In Bhurtpore some Ahirs pursue the occupation of coachmen.

Godariya, or Garariya.

Shepherds.

Rebari.

These are properly breeders of camels, but are also growers of rice. They form a small community in Ajmere. In Mallâni the Rebaris keep large herds of sheep and goats as well as cattle and camels. The tribe is scattered about various parts of the Rajputana desert. In Bhurtpore they are cultivators as well as camel-drivers.

SMALL TRADERS.

Tamboli.

Pawn and betelnut-sellers.

Teli.

Oil-crushers and oil-sellers in Ajmere and other districts.

Ghosi.

Milk and butter sellers of Ajmere.

Burbhûnja, or Bhurji.

Grain roasters.

Kulâl.

Spirit-sellers.

Sungâ.

Distillers of spirits in Mallâni, where they style themselves first class traders.

Bisâti.

Pedlars.

MANUFACTURERS OF BEADS AND VARIOUS ARTICLES, WEAVERS, DYERS, &c.

Munihar.

Manufacturers of bangles or armlets.

Lakhera.

Bangle-makers and dealers in lac or sealing-wax. They pay no taxes, but have to repair the bangles of the chief's family.

Odi.

In Jesalmere.

Gwariâ.

Rope-makers in Marwar.

Rangrez.

Dyers.

Chîpî.

Markers of chintz and other fabrics in Ajmere, Jhalawar, and elsewhere.

Patwâ.

Braiders and artizans.

Julaha.

Weavers.

Dabgar.

Manufacturers of leathern jars for holding *ghi*, or clarified butter.

Ghânchâ.

Basket-makers in Marwar. In Mallâni they are oilmen and cultivators.

Koli.

In the States of Karauli, Bhurtpore, and Dholpore, the Kolis are an important class of weavers. They are a low caste race, eaters of the flesh of cows and of carrion, and are consequently regarded with abhorrence by respectable tribes.

The Koli tribes are numerous in the Rajputana desert, where they assume appellations, such as Chauhân Koli, Râthor Koli, Parihâr Koli, and the like, showing their illegitimate descent from Rajpoots and aboriginal Kolis. Their habits are very low. Many are engaged in agriculture.

PHYSICIANS AND SURGEONS.

Baid.

Native physicians. In some places they hold hereditary State pensions.

Bâgri.

In Mallâni they are cattle doctors. They also operate on the human body in cases of lithotomy.

BLACKSMITHS, BRAZIERS, MASONS, CARPENTERS, TINKERS.

Lohâr.

Blacksmiths, distributed in small numbers throughout the States. The Lohârs of Bundee extract iron from the ore by smelting.

Sikligar.

Sharpeners of steel and iron implements, cutlers, knife-grinders.

Thathera.

Braziers.

Râj, or Râjkumhar.

Masons.

Khâti.

Carpenters, and village servants, in Ajmere and other States.

Silâwat.

Stone-masons, builders, and also cultivators. They intermarry with the Khâtis.

Sangtarâsh.

Stone-cutters.

Kalaigar.

Tinkers.

POTTERS, DIGGERS, &c.

Kumhâr.

Potters. The chief custom at the marriage ceremony of the Jâtias of this tribe, is for a thread to be bound round the bride's wrist; which, among most other castes, on exchange of raw sugar and cocoanuts, confirms the betrothal of the parties.

The caste is divided into three great branches, namely :—

1.—The Karsâs, who are cultivators exclusively.

2.—These are potters and cultivators.

3.—Jâtia Kumhârs, called Jâts in Mallâni, workers in wood, rope-makers, and thread-twisters, and also cultivators. The Jâtias do not intermarry with the other two classes. The native chiefs of Mallâni absolve the Kumhârs, when cultivators, from the cultivator's tax of three rupees, and in return are supplied with earthen vessels. They are also excused from the payment of the house-tax of one rupee, and also of the fee paid by all agriculturists on the marriage of their (the Kumhârs') daughters.

There are upwards of eight thousand Kumhârs in Ajmere and Merwara, and between two and three thousand in Dholpore.

Khârwâl.

Men employed on the saltworks of Marwar.

Beldar.

Diggers of tanks and wells.

DEVOTEES, RELIGIOUS MENDICANTS.

The Gosains.

These are professedly devotees. Some are celibates, others marry. They eat flesh, drink spirits, worship Shiva, and at death are buried, some in a sitting posture, others at full length. Many, especially the celibates, subsist on charity. The married Gosains work for their living by cultivating the fields. The tribe has twelve subdivisions in Rajputana, ten of which are found in Mallâni, namely :—

1. Giri.	4. Ban.	7. Parit.
2. Puri.	5. Saraswati.	8. Parghat.
3. Bhârti.	6. Sâgar.	9. Arun.

10. Runkhar.

The Nâths.

Many persons of this caste, especially those in good circumstances, do not marry. These bear the appellation of Nihang. The Nâths are easily recognized by the stone ornament which they wear in the lobes of their ears.

The Nâgas.

Sects of military devotees attached to the various sects, some of whom are employed as soldiers in the native armies of Rajputana. They are vowed to celibacy and to arms, and constitute a sort of military order. They are separated into several sects, as follows:—

The Nâga Sects.

1. Dâdapanthi.	2. Râmnathi.	3. Vishnu Swâmi.

The first sect consists of followers of Dâdu Panth, and the second of followers of Râm Nâth. These sects are replenished by children placed under their charge as disciples by their parents.

Khâki.

Religious mendicants, who go about almost naked, having only a thick cord round their loins, their bodies being smeared with ashes.

Râm Sanehi.

This sect has its head-quarters at Shâhpura. Its members worship no images, and are influenced by love for Râm, as their designation indicates. They wander about in pairs, and are very lightly clothed.

Kabirpanthi.

A sect well known in Northern India, having a few members in Bundee and elsewhere in Rajputana.

Desântari.

A class of beggars in Mallâni. If any Hindu festival happens to fall on an unlucky Saturday, valuable presents are made to the Desântaris, in order to dispel the evil omen, in return for which they worship the God Saturn. They also receive all alms given on a Saturday.

Motesar.

A tribe of beggars peculiar to Marwar. They receive gifts at marriages from Chârans and Bhâts, or through their instrumentality.

SERVANTS AND PERSONAL ATTENDANTS.

Bâri.

A people found in many parts of the North-Western Provinces as well as in Rajputana. They make plates or cups of leaves, stitched together with little wooden pegs, for the purpose of holding food. The Bâris also act the part of servants in respectable Hindu families.

A curious custom prevails in Marwar on the birth of an heir to the throne. An impression of the child's foot is taken by a Bâri on cloth covered with saffron, and is exhibited to the native chiefs, who reward the Bâri liberally for the sight. The Kishnagur chief returns the compliment on the birth of an heir in his family.

Mehra, or Kahâr.

These are in Marwar, Ajmere, Bhurtpore, and elsewhere. They are bearers, palankeen-carriers, water-carriers, day-labourers, and servants. Their occupation seems to differ somewhat in various States.

Chobdâr.

Silver-stick bearers in waiting ; messengers.

Jâti.

Schoolmasters in Mallâni, who are attached to the Jain religion.

Gûrûra.

Spiritual teachers of the Megwâls. They are also cultivators and teachers.

Nâi.

Barbers. Their wives are nurses and wetnurses in Ajmere and elsewhere. The Nâis discharge important duties in the houses of the native chiefs. They enjoy certain special privileges.

Bulâhi.

Messengers and grooms. This tribe numbers twenty-three thousand in Ajmere and Merwara. It has four villages in Beawar.

Darzî.

Tailors.

Dhobi.

Washermen. It would be interesting to know their subdivisions in the several States. They are allowed special privileges granted to some other castes.

JUGGLERS, ACROBATS, SNAKE-CHARMERS, BUFFOONS, DRUM-BEATERS.

Dholi.

Beaters of drums, who are paid by the villagers either in food or clothing, or both, and who receive various other presents.

Jâgri.

Beaters of small drums at dances and festivals.

Nat.

Acrobats, jugglers, and gipsies.

Santhia.

A wandering tribe of Jhalawar.

Kanjar.

Snake-charmers ; a wandering tribe.

Râwal.

Buffoons in Marwar.

FOWLERS AND HUNTERS.

Chiremâr.

Bird-catchers.

Shikâri.

Hunters.

WORKERS IN LEATHER.

Chamâr.

Labourers, tanners, workers in leather, cultivators, and so forth.

These are numerous in some parts of Rajputana, especially in the eastern districts. In Bikaneer they are also called Balâi. Nearly fifty years ago a Chamâr, named Lâlgir, founded a religious sect in that State, to which high officials, Rajpoots, and others have attached themselves. His tenets, which are still those of the sect, are the following :—" He denounced idolatry, and taught his followers to call on the incomprehensible (Alak); and his sole worship consisted in crying 'Alak, Alak !' Charity was to be practised; the taking of life and meat as food was forbidden; asceticism was held profitable to subdue passion; and the sole reward was attainment in this life to purity, untroubled contemplation, and serenity. There was no future state. Heaven and hell (that is, happiness or misery) were within, and may be made independent of external circumstances; but all perishes with the body, which is finally resolved into the elements; and man has no immortal part. Peace in life, and a good name after it, were the sole, but sufficient, inducements to the practice of virtue" (*a*).

The Chamârs are properly workers and dealers in leather; but they are also agriculturists. They likewise perform various menial duties for their employers. In Karauli they often get a certain share in each crop, and certain perquisites, for their labours.

The Gûrûra is the priest of the Chamârs in Marwar. In the State of Dholepore the Chamârs number upwards of thirty-two thousand persons, eighteen thousands of whom cultivate nearly twenty thousand acres of land.

(*a*) Gazetteer of the Bikanîr State, by Captain P. W. Powlett, Political Agent, Ulwar. p 91.

Megwâl.

In Mallâni the tribe is divided into three clans, which can eat together, but not intermarry. They are said to perform the general work of a village in looking after travellers and so forth, and therefore, although of low caste, are of much importance publicly.

1. The Bâmbis. These are said to be the same caste as the Chamârs of the North-Western Provinces. They are workers in leather, weavers, and village servants; and receive the skins of all unclaimed dead animals.

2. The Jâtias. These are the same as Regars elsewhere. Their special occupation is that of dyeing, and of working in untanned leather. They eat the flesh of dead animals.

3. The Bangâras. Cloth manufacturers and cultivators.

The Megwâls of Jesalmere manufacture blankets of sheep's wool, and weave cloth.

Sargarâ.

A kind of Chamâr. They are cultivators and drum-beaters.

Sanjogi Shami.

The offspring of parents of different castes, an ex-communicated race, regarded with much disfavor by Hindus. In Mallâni these persons are cultivators and beggars.

Mochi.

Shoe-makers and workers in leather. "The Thakurs only pay half price for their shoes, some nothing at all; and the Mochis are allowed to cultivate as much land as they can by their own household rent-free." If the Mochis have no lands, they are recompensed in some other way.

Regar.

They are supposed to correspond with the Chamârs of the North-Western Provinces.

Dhanak.

Swineherds and grooms.

Khatik.

Tanners and grooms.

THIEVES, ROBBERS, AND WATCHMEN.

Thori, or Thaori.

A tribe in Ajmere, the Lakhi jungle, and Rajputana desert. They were once notorious robbers.

Chûra.

A tribe in Mewar and the Rajputana desert. They are attached to many chiefs as servants. They guard the barriers of the Rajputana desert. They were once notorious robbers.

Sânsi.

Another class of thieves in Ajmere and other States.

Bâuria and Moghya.

A caste of thieves and robbers in Marwar and elsewhere, professing, like other low tribes in Rajputana, to be descended from Rajpoots. They are employed as village watchmen, but are also well-known professional thieves. These people are styled Bâuria to the north of the Arvali Range, and Moghya to the south. Their villages are on the confines of Tonk, Meywar, and Gwalior, as well as in Nimbahera, Neemuch, and Marwar. They eat flesh and drink spirits.

SCAVENGERS AND OTHER LOW CASTES.

Khâkrob, or Khabrûk.

A sweeper caste in Jesalmere.

Bhangi.

A tribe in Ajmere, Bhurtpore, and elsewhere. The sweeper caste, which has numerous representatives throughout the North-Western Provinces.

Dom.

One of the lowest of the outcast tribes in Rajputana as elsewhere. In the Karauli State the Dom is a marriage negotiator, and gets four seers, or eight pounds, of grain for every marriage performed, as well as ten pounds from every crop grown in connexion with every house in a village.

Baid.

A low people of Marwar.

Satia.

An outcast tribe of Marwar.

Dhânkâ.

The Dhânkâs are a low caste in Marwar.

CHAPTER VI.

THE MAIR, OR MER TRIBES.

I.—THE CHAUHAN MAIRS: 1, THE CHITA TRIBES; 2, THE BARAR TRIBES. II.—THE PRAMAR MAIRS. III.—THE MOTI MAIRS. IV.—THE DAKUL MAIRS. V.—THE GAHLOT MAIRS. VI.—THE PATALIYAT MAIRS. VII.—THE CHAUROT MAIRS. VIII.—THE BHARSAL MAIRS. IX.—THE BUCH MAIRS. X.—THE KHARWAL MAIRS. XI.—THE MAMNOT MAIRS XII.—THE SELOT MAIRS. XIII.—THE BANAT MAIRS. XIV.—THE BANNA MAIRS.

These tribes are the principal inhabitants of Mairwara, or Merwara, from whom the country derives its name. Although they are not supposed to be an aboriginal race, yet they have occupied this tract for a very long period, notwithstanding many efforts to subjugate them. The Mahomedan emperors failed to bring them under their sway. The primitive inhabitants were probably fugitives from other parts of India, who, taking advantage of the impenetrable forests of Merwara, made them their abode. The word 'Mer' means 'hill'; so that the Mairs are in reality hillmen. Mr. LaTouche states that the word 'Mer' or 'Mair' designates not so much a distinct caste or tribe as the inhabitants generally of this portion of the Arvali Range. It is singular, however, if this be the case, that they should be regarded as a separate people.

The Mairs have a bad reputation of being a very dirty people. This may arise from their living in a hilly region, for it is a singular circumstance that all the hill tribes in India are a filthy race. As Hindus, the Mairs are extremely lax, and think little of the orthodox deities worshipped elsewhere. They pay great veneration to the Mâkutji and Goramji hills, and hold a yearly festival in honour of Mâtâ, or the goddess of smallpox.

On occasion of the great Holi festival, a game called Abera is played in every village on the first and last day. It is thus described :—" The whole village turns out into the jungle, each man armed with two sticks, about a yard long, called *pokhri*. Opium and tobacco are provided by the headmen. Having formed a line, the people commence beating for hares and deer, knocking them over by a general discharge of sticks as they start up. A number of hares are killed in this way. If the *mahajans*, or bankers, will pay—and the *mahajans* of Ajmere and Merwara, being Jains, are exceedingly tender of life—the people will not kill on the second day. The festival of the Holi concludes with a game like 'touch in the ring.' The people consume a good deal of tobacco, but very little opium. Tobacco they carry in an oval wooden box called *ghata*, and the principal men append a long wooden handle to this box, which they always carry about with them. The handle signifies that all who ask will get tobacco" (*a*).

Although regarding themselves as Hindus, they are but little affected by strict Hindu usages. They will eat the flesh of most animals, including cows, which all Hindus proper regard as sacred. Even Brahmans in this heterodox State will eat flesh. The people generally are addicted to hero-worship. It is said that at one time they used to sacrifice their first-born sons to Mâtâ, the goddess of smallpox, a disease occasionally very prevalent in Merwara. It is still customary to sacrifice a buffalo on the birth of the first son in a family.

I.—The Chauhân Mair Tribes.

The two chief tribes of Mairs, like many other tribes in Northern India, trace their descent from Prithi Raja, the famous Chauhân king; and their traditions state, that a son of Prithi Raja, named Jodh Lâkhun, married a girl of the Meena tribe, "who had been seized in a marauding expedition near Bundee, supposing her to be a Rajpootani. When he discovered his mistake, he turned away the mother and her two sons, Anhal and Anup. The exiles wandered to Chang, in Beawar, where they were hospitably entertained by the Gujars of that place. Anhal and Anup rested one day under a Bar, or fig-tree; and prayed that, if it was destined that their race should continue, the trunk of the tree might be rent in twain. The instant occurrence of the miracle raised them from their despondency; and the splitting of the fig-tree is a cardinal event in the history of the race, according to the following distich:—

Charar se Chîta bhayo, aur Barar bhayo Bar ghât
Shâkh ek se do bhaye; jagat bakhâni jât.

"The meaning of which is, 'from the sound "charar" (the splitting *noise*) the Chîtas are called, and the Barârs from the splitting *itself* of the fig-tree. Both are descended from one stock. The world has made these tribes famous'" (*b*). From this tradition respecting the origin of the Chauhân Mairs it is plain, if there be any truth in it, that they are partly the offspring of Rajpoots, and partly of Meenas.

(*a*) Rajputana Gazetteer, Vol. II, p. 47.
(*b*) Gazetteer of Ajmere-Merwara, by Mr. J. D. LaTouche, p. 34.

While there are several minor tribes, the Chauhân Mairs are chiefly divided into two principal tribes, the Chitas and the Barârs, each having twenty-four *gotras*, or class subdivisions. The Mers have fifty-one villages in Ajmere, two hundred and forty-one in Beawar, and eighty-eight in Todgarh (*a*).

1.—*The Chita Tribe of Chauhân Mairs.*

These first settled at Chang, to the north-west of Merwara, and after a time destroyed or expelled the Gujars, the former occupants. Gradually they took possession of all the most important towns and villages of Merwara, and built others, such as Jâk, Shamgarh, Lulna, Hattûn, Kûkra, Kot Kirana, and Naî. The Chîtas became the ruling class in the district, and held in subjection at one time as many as sixteen other Mer tribes, from whom they received as tribute one-fourth of the produce of the soil, and of all plundering expeditions (*b*). They are powerful and wealthy, and possess one hundred and seventeen villages in Beawar, sixteen in Todgarh, besides portions of many others.

Some of the principal Chita *gotras* or clans are the following :—

(1.) *The Merât Clan.*

This clan is the chief of the twenty-four. Its members are partly Mahomedans. They sprang from Mera, who flourished about two hundred and fifty years ago. They are divided into two great branches, the Kâtâts and the Gorâts.

i. *The Kâtâts.*

Their ancestor was Harâj, grandson of Mera, about whom the following tale is told :—During a night of terrific rain, Harâj, who was a soldier in the army of Aurungzebe, the emperor of Delhi, remained firm at his post as sentry, with his shield over his head. When the Emperor heard of the circumstance, he exclaimed : "In the Marwar tongue they call a brave soldier Kâtâ ; let this man be henceforth called Kâtâ" (*c*). The Kâtât Merâts are powerful, enterprising, and numerous. They occupy seventy-eight villages in Beawar, and nine in Ajmere, where they have formed for themselves new *gotras*, the Bahâdur Khâni being the most influential. The chief Kâtâts of Hattun Châng and Jâk, in Beawar, are styled Khans, a Mahomedan title, while those elsewhere bear the common Hindu designation of Thâkur. The Kâtâts are a very degenerate kind of Mahomedans.

It is to be regretted that the Kâtâts of Ajmere are beginning to observe some

(*a*) Gazetteer of Ajmere-Merwara, by Mr. J. D. LaTouche, p. 34.

(*b*) *Ibid.*

(*c*) *Ibid*, p. 35.

of the pernicious customs of Mahomedans, especially that of the seclusion of their women, while in Merwara the Kâtât women have the same freedom as the men.

ii. *The Gorâts.*

These are descendants of Gora, a brother of Harâj, and are Hindus. They have spread southwards, and have twenty-one villages in Beawar, Kalinjar and Kabra being the chief of them, thirteen in Todgarh, and one in Ajmere.

The Kâtâts and Gorâts, although belonging to different religions, will eat together all kinds of food.

(2.) *The Laget Clan.*

The Lagets hold six villages in Beawar.

(3.) *The Nanset Clan.*

They possess Bargaon, Palran, Pharkia, Manpura, and Hathibata, in Ajmere, besides lands in other villages.

(4.) *The Rajoriya Clan.*

These hold three villages in Beawar.

(5.) *The Bedariyat Clan.*

This clan has three villages in Ajmere.

(6.) *The Bajriyat Borwara Clan.*

(7.) *The Biladiya Clan.*

(8.) *The Pithrot Clan.*

(9.) *The Balot Clan.*

(10.) *The Nadot Clan.*

The remaining clans are spread over Merwara (*a.*)

2.—*The Barâr Tribe of Chauhân Mairs.*

These are descended from Anup, brother of Anhal. They are only to be found in Merwara. The tribe occupies eleven villages in Beawar, and forty-eight in Todgarh, including the whole of the southern part of this district. "They are more unsophisticated, honest, and straightforward than the Chitas. They call themselves Râwat, a petty title of nobility; and would be insulted by being called Mers. The chief men are called Rao, and they have a multitude of Tikâis, of whom the principal are the Rao of Kukra and the Rao of Barâr" (*b*). The Râwats of Todgarh are exhibiting a strong tendency to adopt Brahminical usages

(*a*) Gazetteer of Ajmere-Merwara, by Mr. J. D. LaTouche. p. 35.
(*b*) *Ibid.*

observed by neighbouring Rajpoots. Since 1874 they have refrained from eating the flesh of kine and buffaloes, and excommunicate those who do so.

The Chîtas and Barârs intermarry, but never marry into their own tribes. Hindus marry Mahomedans, and Mahomedans, Hindus; the ceremony in both cases being performed by a Brahman, who leads the bride and bridegroom seven times round a fire. In some places the Mahomedan Merâts are beginning to adopt Mahomedan usages, and the Brahmanical marriage ceremony is being supplanted by one of an Islamitish character. In Merwara a large portion of the people are tending either to Brahmanism or Mahomedanism. The customs observed on the death of Chîta and Barâr women is curious. A Barâr woman married to a Chîta husband is buried at death; but, on the contrary, a Kâtât woman married to a Barâr husband, is burnt.

The social customs of the two tribes, however, are almost entirely similar. "A sonless widow retains possession of her husband's property till she marries again, or till her death." "Daughters do not inherit when there are sons alive." "All sons inherit equally." "There is no distinction between ancestral and acquired property." "A relation of any age may be adopted; the nearest relation has the first claim, and his children born before his adoption succeed in the adopted family." "Sons by slave girls, who are pretty numerous under the name of *dharmputr*, get land to cultivate, but obtain no share in the inheritance, and cannot transfer the land" (*a*).

II.—The Pramar Mair Tribe.

This tribe is also partly of Rajpoot origin. Both the Pramars and the Motîs are said to be descended from Dhârânâth Powar or Pramar, who built the city of Dharanagar, in Marwar, which, tradition says, was forty-eight miles in circumference. The Pramars were first settled at Rudhâna, to the south of Beawar, whence they spread over the surrounding country, establishing many villages, such as Biliawas, Jawaja, Bahâr, Barkochran, Rawat Mâl, Lusâni, and Akayjitgarh Naloi.

The Pramars are divided into six *gotras* or clans, namely :—

1. Delât. This is the largest of all the clans, and has possession of fourteen villages in Beawar and five in Todgarh. In Ajmere they occupy eleven villages, and have portions of eight others. They appear "to have pushed the other members of the tribe out of Merwara, who thereupon settled near Ajmere, and especially in the *pargannah* of Pushkar" (*b*).

(*a*) Gazetteer of Ajmere-Merwara, by Mr. J. D. LaTouche. p. 36.
(*b*) *Ibid.*

2. Kallât. A small clan in possession of Kalâthân, in Beawar.
3. Doling. These possess Barla, Madarpura, and Gwari.
4. Boya. The villages of Hokran and Gudli belong to this clan.
5. Kheyat. Khwâjpura and Kana-khera are villages in their possession.
6. Pokhariya. These hold the villages of Pushkar, Ganahira, Naidla, and Naulakha.

The Pramars are an industrious people of finer stature than the Chauhân Mairs, whose customs they observe. They are commonly spoken of as Mairs, although they prefer to be addressed as Râwats. Their principal men are styled Gameti. Much social intercourse seems to prevail between them and the Chauhân Mairs, and they intermarry freely with Hindu Chîtas and the Barârs. The Kâtâts of the Chîta tribe will not give their daughters in marriage to the Pramars; but will take Pramar women for their sons (*a*).

III.—The Motî Mair Tribe.

This tribe is descended from an ascetic, named Rohitas, of the family of Dhârânâth, and a Banjârâ woman, who lived together in a cave of the Mâkutji hill. After a time the woman separated from Rohitas, and she and her twin children resided under the roof of Khemchand, a Brahman of Bamunhera. A dispute arising between the boys and their protector, the Brahman expelled them from his house. One of them went to Marwar, the other continued in Bhaelan; and a deadly feud was carried on by his descendants and the Brahmans of the country on account of the treatment of their ancestor by Khemchand, the end of which was that, in the fifth generation, the Motîs, under their leader Makut, destroyed nearly the whole of the Brahmans, and seized the district of Bhaelan. The Mairs pay great respect to the memory of Makut, and worship him as a deity. A cow was yearly offered up in sacrifice at his shrine; and a fair is still held to his honour on the Mâkutji hill every September. The Motî Râwats, as they are called, possess fourteen villages in Bhaelan at the present day. They have estates also in Beawar and Ajmere (*b*).

IV.—The Dakul Mair Tribe.

These have sprung from the union of a Mina woman, of the Dakul Mina tribe, and a Brahman, who escaped from the general destruction of his race in Bhaelan, in the time of Makut, and fled to the village of Burar. He abandoned his caste, and became a Mair. The tribe is divided into several clans (*c*).

(*a*) Gazetteer of Ajmere-Merwara, by Mr. J. D. Latouche, pp. 36, 37.

(*b*) *Ibid*; and also Colonel Dixon's Mairwara, pp. 11, 12.

(*c*) Colonel Dixon's Mairwara, p. 12.

V.—The Gahlot Mair Tribe.

This tribe was founded by two Gahlot Rajpoots, who married two Mina women of Borwa, in Saroth, after the sack of Chitore by Ala-ud-din Ghori. They adopt the title of Râwat, and, notwithstanding their spurious descent, aspire to the dignity of pure Rajpoots, and style themselves Sûrajbansi Rajpoots. Their customs apparently are like those of other Mair tribes, and they intermarry with the Hindu Chauhân Mairs; but the Merâts, while receiving their women in marriage, will not reciprocate the favour by giving wives to Gahlot husbands. The tribe is split up into sixteen clans, the chief of which are the following:—

Gahlot Clans.

1. Godât.	5. Baniyât.
2. Medrat.	6. Lahr.
3. Kâchi.	7. Balot.
4. Pinga.	8. Dhânkal.

The Gahlots possess many villages in Merwara, and also Purbutpura, Ansari, Mayapur, Lakhshmipur, Borâj, and Amba Massena, in Ajmere (*a*). They have eleven villages in Beawar and Kukar Khera, in Todgarh.

VI.—The Pataliyat Mair Tribe.

These are descended from the Bhatti Rajpoots of Jesalmere, and are owners of the village of Baria Nagga.

VII.—The Chaurot Mair Tribe.

The Chaurots profess also to have sprung from the Bhatti Rajpoots of Jesalmere. They possess the village of Kalikankur Kishnpura. Some of the tribe have settled in Mohunpura, in Ajmere (*b*).

VIII.—The Bharsal Mair Tribe.

The Bharsals reside in the village of Ramkhera Dhanâr, and are located also in several villages in Ajmere.

IX.—The Bûch Mair Tribe.

These are found in Rajpur Bûchân, and likewise in two villages of Ajmere.

(*a*) Gazetteer of Ajmere-Merwara, by Mr. J. D. Latouche, p. 37.
(*b*) *Ibid.*

X.—The Kharwal Mair Tribe.

The headman of the town of Beawar is of this tribe, which inhabits Nayanagar and Fathpur.

XI.—The Mamnot Mair Tribe.

XII.—The Selot Mair Tribe.

XIII.—The Banât Mair Tribe.

XIV.—The Banna Mair Tribe.

These last tribes are scattered about a few villages.

CHAPTER VII.

SEC. I.—THE JIT OR JAT TRIBE. SEC. II.—THE GUJAR TRIBES. SEC. III.—THE MEENA TRIBES. SEC. IV.—THE GRASSIA TRIBES. SEC. V.—THE BHEEL TRIBES.

Section I.—The Jit or Jât Tribe.

The Jâts were in possession of the north-western division of Rajputana before the Rajpoots entered the province, and there is good ground for believing that they had been there for a long period. Some persons have formed the idea that the Jâts are a branch of the Indo-Scythian from the banks of the Oxus.

Respecting the physical characteristics of the Jâts, Dr. Brereton makes the following remarks :—"In physique," he says, "the Jâts are generally of fair height, but below the average of Rajpoots or other castes. Their chest measurement and weight are in fair proportion to their height; the extremities, especially the lower, are often disproportionate to their abnormal length. The women are of very strong physique, exceeding the men in this respect, proportionately speaking. They are not remarkable for personal beauty, but some have very fine figures. They are also most industrious and contented, working in the fields, &c., but are said to rule their husbands. The prevailing complexion is fair, and the colour of the eyes, dark; the hair is dark, fine, and straight; beard and moustachios, scanty, and the former not usually worn. The crania are of tolerably fair size and shape, often elongated, altogether a lower type than the Brahman skull. Their intellectual faculties are not brilliant, partaking more of shrewdness and cunning than ability. They are said to possess courage and fidelity, are industrious and persevering in their habits, and are of an agile and muscular frame" (*a*).

This tribe commonly bears the name of Jit in Rajputana. In all the ancient lists of the Rajpoot tribes it is always placed among the thirty-six royal tribes. Now, however, in Rajputana it is never reckoned among them. The Jit and the Gûjars are the original cultivators of the soil in Ajmere-Merwara, and considerably outnumber every other tribe. Their chief possessions are in Ajmere. Tubeji, Suradhua, Makrera, Jethana, Budhwara, Pecholean, and the larger portion

(*a*) The Rajputana Gazetteer, Vol. I, p. 162.

of the Ramsur *pargannah* belong to them; and they have settlements in Kekri and in some of the best villages of the Ajmere and Rajgarh *pargannahs*. The tribe in this tract is divided into three principal clans, namely:—

Jât Clans in Ajmere and Merwara.

1. Puniyo.	2. Seeshuo.	3. Harchitrâl.

These clans have more than a hundred *gotras* or caste distinctions (*a*). They are hardworking, excellent cultivators, and are famous for their wells and their great diligence in improving their lands. None of them are *bhumias*, or occupy land free from revenue. They possess twice as much territory as the Gûjars, and pay three times more revenue. There were more than thirty thousand Jâts in Ajmere-Merwara in 1876. Their headmen are styled Chaudhri or Patel.

In Bikaneer there are, or were formerly, seven clans, as follows:—

Jât Clans in Bikaneer.

1. Godârâ	...	Their principal villages are	Ladhri and Shekhsar.
2. Lâran	...	Their principal village is	Bhândang.
3. Kasvas	...	Ditto	Lidmûkh.
4. Beniwal	...	Ditto	Raisatâna.
5. Puniah	...	Ditto	Bara Lundi.
6. Sihaga	...	Ditto	Sûin.
7. Sodûan	...	Ditto	Dhansi (*b*).

The Godârâ Jâts place the *tikâ*, or sacred mark denoting rank or sovereignty, on the forehead of every successive ruling chief of the Bikaneer State.

The chief object venerated by the Jâts of Marwar, Ajmere, and Kishangarh is Teja Jî. This was a Jât who, according to a legend universally believed, lived some eight or nine hundred years ago, and was bitten in the tongue by a snake, which caused his death. The Jâts have the idea that if a man bitten by a snake tie a cord round his right foot, and repeat the words Teja Ji, he will recover (*c*). A fair is held at Kishangarh, in the month of July, in honour of Teja Jî, and he is worshipped in a temple erected to his memory at Sarsara. Most Jâts wear round their necks an amulet of silver representing Teja Jî on horseback, his sword drawn, and a snake in the act of biting his tongue.

At the marriage ceremony among the Jâts, a rupee and a cocoanut, emblems of wealth and fertility, are sent to the bride. A framework of wood, called *torun*,

(*a*) Gazetteer of Ajmere-Merwara, by Mr. J. D. Latouche, pp. 30, 31.

(*b*) Gazetteer of the Bikanir States, by Captain Powlett, Political Agent, Ulwar, p. 4.

(*c*) Gazetteer of Ajmere-Merwara, p. 30.

is placed over the door of her house, and having been forcibly struck with a sword by the bridegroom when he approaches near, he enters within. This has been considered by some as a remnant of the custom of marriage by conquest (*a*). The marriage ceremony simply consists of the bride and bridegroom, under the direction of a Brahman, going round a fire lit in the centre of the room. The Jâts, as well as all the tribes of Merwara, permit the remarriage of widows. A man may marry the widow of his elder brother, not that of his younger brother. "In all castes, a widow who has no sons retains her deceased husband's property till her death or remarriage." The youngest brother has the first claim to marry the widow of a deceased brother. Widow-marriage is called Nâthâ. At marriages a sum of money is always paid for the wife, a custom which the women seem to like, as it in a fashion denotes their value. Marriages within the same *gotra*, or family order, are regarded as incestuous, and are forbidden.

The Jâts are numerous in the Bikaneer State, where their tribe is twice as large as any other. They are the agriculturists of that country; and are very heavily taxed for the lands they occupy. Before Bikaneer was conquered by Bika, the Jâts possessed the greater portion of the territory. Many are Vaishnavis, and will not take life. They will not even kill game, or sanction or help those who come to their fields for the purpose of doing so. This sect of the Jâts buries its dead.

This tribe had settled in Marwar long before the Râthors acquired possession of that State. Tod says, that in his time they constituted five-eighths of the population of Marwar.

The Jâts are excellent farmers in Mallâni, and have spread over the whole district. Members of this tribe are found throughout Rajputana, where they form the greater portion of the cultivating classes.

Several clans of the tribe are found in the Rajputana desert. Some of these are:

1. The Jakhurs. | 2. The Shiaghs. | 3. The Pooniahs.

The Jâts of Jeypore are some of the principal landholders and cultivators in that State; and some of them have large estates. They have also, with the Gûjars, ten villages in Beawar. In Jeypore they are mostly in the north and west, and in the neighbourhood of the capital.

In the earlier part of the last century the Jâts of Bhurtpore made successful attacks on the Jeypore State, and were able to wrest therefrom a tract of country

(*a*) Gazetteer of Ajmere-Merwara, p. 30.

which was annexed to Bhurtpore. The founder of the State was Churaman, a Jât landholder, who, having erected two forts in the villages of Thun and Sinsiniwar, plundered the country in all directions, which, in spite of the efforts made to destroy him, he gradually gained possession of; and his family, through many vicissitudes, has retained its hold of it to the present day. In consequence of a disputed succession, Bhurtpore was besieged by British troops for six weeks, and was taken by storm by Lord Combermere on the 18th January, 1826.

The Jâts, Gûjars, and Ahirs of Bhurtpore smoke, and, under certain restrictions, eat together. Widows are sold indiscriminately to all three tribes. The Jâts of Bhurtpore number more than one hundred and twenty thousand persons, separated into numerous tribes, some of which are as follows :—

Jât Tribes of Bhurtpore.

1. Sinsiniwar.	4. Nohwar.	7. Aooe.
2. Khuntail.	5. Sogarwar.	8. Naharwar.
3. Chahar.	6. Manga.	9. Pachandra.
	10. Dâgur.	

The first six tribes are highest in rank, and are known by the common designation of Dung. These have peculiar customs of their own. One is, that a Dung, on the death of his brother, does not take his widow to wife, as is the practice among the other tribes. The Jâts, generally, are not at all particular in the choice of a wife, and may take her from any tribe or caste. The Jât women are not secluded, with the single exception of the wives and daughters of chiefs and great landholders. The Jâts are polygamists. They are worshippers of Hindu deities, especially Krishna, and are, for the most part, Vaishnavites.

The head of the small State of Dholpore is a member of the Bamraulia family of Deswali Jâts, who traces his pedigree back to Jeth Singh, who, in the eleventh century, held lands in Bairat, to the south of Ulwar. Afterwards the family settled in Bamroli, and after many vicissitudes, in which it received the aid, first, of the Touwâr Rajpoots, then of the emperors, next of the Mahrattas, and finally of the British, it found itself at the head of Dholpore, Bâri, and Rajakhera, by the treaty of 1805, having lost, however, Gwalior and Gohad, of which it was formerly possessed. The clan of the Rana, or chief, is divided into eight branches or families as under :—

1. Gadi (family of the chief).	3. Pachgaon.	6. Sur Kythoda.
	4. Makoi.	7. Bhagwasi.
2. Ekayuna.	5. Rajpura.	8. Dandrawa (*a*).

The clan next in importance in the State is that of Bidankria.

(*a*) The Rajputana Gazetteer, Vol. I. pp. 249, 250.

Section II.—The Gûjar Tribes.

The Gûjars have long been inhabitants of the tract of country to the north of the Arvalis, stretching on towards the Punjab and along the Jumna, from Bikaneer to Bhurtpore and Jeypore, where they are cultivators, horse-breeders, and herdsmen.

In stature they seem to be somewhat superior to the Jâts, whom they much resemble in social habits. Like them they eat animal food and drink spirits. In Bhurtpore their women do not labour in the fields.

These tribes occupy thirty-five villages in Ajmere, and also villages in the Meywar plain beyond. They are described as careless cultivators, devoting their chief energies to grazing cattle. Their principal deity is Deo Jî, a Gûjar who is supposed to have lived several hundred years ago, and to have worked miracles. Their customs are similar to those of the Jâts, with this important difference, however, that "property is divided according to wives, and not according to sons." The Gûjars and Jâts hold intimate social intercourse with one another, and will eat and drink together (*a*). The Chandela Gûjars are supposed to have settled among the hills surrounding Chang. The headmen of the Gûjars are styled Mihr.

The Gûjars are chiefly cultivators in Karauli, and are most numerous in the northern part of the State. In the south of Karauli Dâng they are the principal inhabitants, and bear a better character than their fellow clansmen of the Dholpore Dâng. Formerly, the Gûjars were notorious for cattle-lifting and stealing ; but they have been led in many places to abandon these bad habits by the severe repressive measures which were adopted against them. The Gûjars are careless cultivators, and do not obtain such good crops as Jâts and Meenas (*b*). They are the proprietors of thirty-eight villages in Dholpore, while Gûjars are headmen of ninety-five more.

In Jeypore these tribes occupy an important position, and are in possession of extensive estates. They possess, with the Jâts, ten villages in Beawar. They chiefly occupy the southern and central districts of Jeypore, and are in the neighbourhood of Jhalrapatan.

The State of Bhurtpore contains nearly fifty thousand Gûjars, divided into two great branches—the Khari and Laur, each of which has a number of tribes.

(*a*) Gazetteer of Ajmere-Merwara, by Mr. J. D. Latouche. pp. 31, 32.
(*b*) Gazetteer of the Karauli State. by Captain P. W. Powlett, p. 19.

The Gûjar Tribes of Bhurtpore.

The Laur Branch.

1. Kumhar.	3. Kisana.	5. Chadri.
2. Madi.	4. Sirande.	

The Khari Branch.

1. Solania.	3. Doralia.	5. Niskaria.
2. Thathwaria.	4. Sipwar.	6. Sua.
	7. Kharia.	

The Laurs occupy a higher social rank than the Kharis, with whom they neither eat nor intermarry. The Kharis are chiefly employed in making and selling butter.

Section III.—The Meena Tribes.

These tribes have played an important part in the history of Rajputana. In former times Rajpoot and Meena chiefs, in subordination to the Tuar kings of Delhi, ruled over a considerable tract of country. Towards the end of the tenth century, the Kachwâhâs dispossessed all of them from what is now the State of Jeypore. The Meenas are more or less connected with most of the tribes of Mairwara, and their clans are found scattered among the neighbouring States. But their character is not the same in all places. For example, in the north-east of Mewar and in Ajmere, the Meenas are a predatory, lawless people, with no settled habits, but passing their lives as robbers and dacoits. In this respect they resemble the Bheels of Rajputana, yet are more civilized than this wild race. They are numerous in the Jahazpore *pargannah*, in Mewar, whence they make their incursions. The agricultural Meenas of Karauli, on the contrary, are a quiet, orderly people.

The Meenas are said to be descended from those Rajpoots who, in the wars between their own tribes, or between them and the invading Mahomedans, were compelled to quit their native country, and to seek refuge in the fastnesses of Rajputana, where they formed alliances with aboriginal families, abandoned many of their caste usages, and established new tribes. It is not to be questioned that this singular people have sprung from unions between the Rajpoot immigrants and the aboriginal inhabitants of the country.

For the last four hundred years the Meenas have been the chief and most important cultivators in the Karauli State. They expelled the Dhangars and Lodhis, the dominant tribes in Karauli five hundred years ago, from a number of villages which they occupied, and have retained possession of them to the present time. These Meenas show their abhorrence of the infamous predatory practices of the Meenas of Kot Pûtti by refusing to intermarry with them. These disreputable Meenas were expelled from the Rajpoot villages of Inâitî Raontra, Sapotra, and Hadoti, where they had established themselves.

In Karauli, the three tribes of Gûjars, Meenas, and Jâts smoke together. "They eat together out of the same pot (degchi), but not out of the same dish (thâli). Their widows are sold to members of the caste, or even to a member of one of the other two. This is called 'daricha,' and is looked upon as an inferior sort of marriage, which gives the woman a position little better than a concubine or slave, but which legitimizes the children she may bear her master" (*a*). Some families of Meenas cultivate lands in Jhalawar.

Probably the Meenas were among the early inhabitants of Marwar. In Jeypore they occupy the highest positions of trust at the native courts. The Meena applies the mark of sovereignty to the forehead of every new chief, showing, says Tod, that the country was obtained from them originally by adoption rather than by conquest. In former times, that is, in the earlier stages of Kachwâhâ power, the Meenas "had the whole insignia of State, as well as the person of the prince, committed to their trust." They are among the principal cultivators of Jeypore, many possessing large estates. Some, however, are village watchmen and professional thieves.

The bards or minstrels of the Meenas are termed Dhâdî, Dholi, Dhom, and Jâegâ.

The tribes are divided into thirty-six sections, which are variously distributed. Some occupy the strongholds and fastnesses of the country, whither, doubtless, their ancestors were driven in earlier times to escape from the Rajpoot invaders. They are powerful in the northern portions of Jeypore and Ulwar, whence they proceed on their great plundering expeditions over Northern India. The tribe is scattered over all the north-eastern States on the banks of the Jumna. As many as twenty thousand are peaceable agriculturists in Bhurtpore and Dholpore, and a great many are employed in several States as village watchmen.

Although the tribes, as stated above, are generally regarded as consisting of thirty-six branches, yet in the Ulwar State it has one hundred and forty-six. The Meenas of Jeypore and Ulwar consider themselves as superior in rank to all other Meenas, and consequently will hold no intercourse with them. Some of them have a tradition that they are descended from an alliance between Brahman and Meena families.

(*a*) Gazetteer of the Karauli State, by Capt. P. W. Powlett, p. 19.

The Pârihar Meenas in the Bundee State and in the north-east of Meywar, were apparently in possession of this part of the country before the Rajpoots arrived, and gradually blended with the invaders. They have the character of being wild and daring plunderers. In the highlands of the country in the south-east of Meywar, in the direction of Neemuch, there are many small Meena villages inhabited by a marauding race. The lowest class of Meenas are those found in the desolate region to the north of Sirohee, occupying the Arvali hills, and being a constant torment to the neighbouring States. Other Meenas will neither eat nor drink nor intermarry with them (*a*).

The Meenas of Bhurtpore eat flesh, drink spirits, and are very superstitious. Their modes of worship are like those of Hindus, and, in taking an oath, they swear by the dagger. They pursue two occupations, and are either cultivators or village watchmen, the latter being prone to theft. The Bhurtpore Meenas are divided into the following tribes :—

The Meena Tribes of Bhurtpore (*b*).

1. Sanadan.	5. Gasika.	9. Bardar.
2. Jhardar.	6. Thorat.	10. Ghilot.
3. Lohara.	7. Bhokira.	11. Goadar.
4. Jordar.	8. Satkal.	

In the Bundee, Meywar, and Jeypore States the Pârihar Meenas inhabit a tract of country called Kerar, close to Deoli, extending for twelve miles from the town of Jahazpore eastwards. They claim to be descended from Shoma, son of Nahar Rao, ruler of Mundor, and a Meena woman. There is an inscription in the Kerar village, showing that they settled originally there in the twelfth century. Every village within a circuit of fifty miles has two or three families of this class of Meenas; but they do not intermarry with Meenas of other districts. The Pârihars adopt the Rajpoot custom of marrying members of clans other than their own. Consequently, as the remaining Meena tribes look down upon them, and refuse to hold social intercourse with them, the Pârihars find it a difficult matter sometimes to find husbands for their daughters, and wives for themselves.

The State of Dholpore has more than ten thousand Meenas, who are proprietors of thirteen villages, and cultivators of nearly twenty thousand acres of land. They are very old inhabitants of Bari and Baseri, and are most excellent landlords and cultivators. The tribe came originally, it is said, from Jeypore.

(*a*) The Rajputana Gazetteer, Vol. I, pp. 72, 73.

(*b*) *Ibid*, p. 163.

Section IV.—The Grassîa Tribes.

The Grassîas of Meywar are said to be descended from Chauhân Rajpoots, from Chainpareen, near Baroda, who were in the country before the Sisodias conquered Chittore. They have lost most of their Rajpoot habits, and are now a wild race associating closely with the aboriginal Bheels, whose daughters they take to wife, and living apart from more civilized people. "None of the Grassîa chiefs have ever been subjugated by Meywar. They voluntarily proffered a nominal allegiance to the Ranas, and hence they hold the *bhûm*, or right of property in the land, over which the Rana has no power. They are not liable to be called on for regular service, to which they are not subject, or to attend at the capital; but they pay a small quit-rent in token of submission. The Bheels and Grassîas obey the orders of these rude chiefs, to whom they are devoted. Every endeavour to dispossess them has only resulted in failure; though it has been constantly attempted by the Ranas, who early conquered the valleys, but were effectually kept out of the hills, in which, however, they always found protection and shelter in times of difficulty" (*a*).

The wilderness of Bhakar, a desolate region of rugged hills, commencing to the south of Mount Aboo, is chiefly in the hands of the Grassîas. They are generally held to be somewhat higher in rank than the Bheels, with whom they associate freely.

The word 'Grassîa,' as used in Gujerat and Malwa, has a different signification from that which it bears in Rajputana. In the former provinces it is applied to the headmen of villages who have a prescriptive right to collect dues from travellers and also certain sums imposed on lands and roads. In Rajputana the word is "becoming applied to a separate set or group of persons associated, though it may be ordinarily taken to denote a halfblood between Bheel and Rajpoot"(*b*).

Section V.—The Bheel Tribes.

The Bheels are a wild, daring, outcast race scattered over Rajputana, of which they are regarded as the aborigines, although this supposition must be taken in a limited signification, inasmuch as in some parts traditions show that they are descendants of Rajpoots. It is exceedingly probable that, while some Bheel tribes have been formed from unions between Bheels and Rajpoots, others are altogether of pure aboriginal Bheel blood.

(*a*) History of Mewar, by Capt. J. C. Brookes, p. 3.
(*b*) The Rajputana Gazetteer, Vol. I, p. 78.

The Bheel country may be said to commence in the north with the Arvali range. They are in greatest strength and most independent in the hills of the south-west of Meywar and Serohi, extending from Serohi to Dungarpore. Their villages are numerous among the forests and hills of Pertabgarh, Banswara, and Dungarpore, and in the Chappan, near Neemuch. There are said to be as many as two hundred thousand Bheels in the Meywar hills, divided into sixteen sub-tribes. Some small chiefs, such as those of Ogna, Panurwa, Jowra, and Jowas, regard themselves as of mixed Rajpoot and Bheel descent. In the wildest parts of the country "there are many powerful villages which own no immediate chief or master whatever, though they may be nominally subject to the State within whose territory they dwell. They live together in *pals*, which appear to be large settlements or collections of hamlets; for a Bheel village is not compact, but a scattered series of isolated huts. They usually follow the lead of some local headman or principal clansman. These *pals* in the small States of Dungarpore, Banswara, or Pertabgarh, are quite strong enough to defy the levies of the ruling chief. In these States, and in the Meywar hilly tracts, and to some degree in the Chappan, the Bheels have for many years given much trouble by their claim to levy blackmail throughout their country, and their inveterate habit of plundering; while it was difficult either to pursue the Bheel himself unto his fastnesses, or to fix the responsibility on the State to which he belonged territorially. The expeditions sent under British officers against the Bheels rarely effected anything permanent, while the native governments were only strong enough to oppress and exasperate without subduing them. In the course of time, however, matters have improved. The Bheels are now fairly pacified, and will be gradually reclaimed by careful management "(*a*).

The Bheel tribes are numerous, and it is much to be regretted that so little is known respecting them. The writers of works on Rajputana seem never to realize the interest connected with the individual tribes, not merely of the Bheels, but also of the other races inhabiting that tract of country; and content themselves, for the most part, with mere generalities and compendious statements. Each writer gives a few details on points which have arrested his attention, but not one, so far as my own acquaintance with their productions extends, has earnestly set himself the task of enquiring into separate clans and their subdivisions, and into their history, customs, manners, and distinctions.

Although the Bheels are not Hindus, yet they practise some of the rites of the Hindu religion. Their deities are chiefly local, they are very superstitious, and

(*a*) The Rajputana Gazetteer, Vol. I, pp. 75, 77.

have great faith in witchcraft. They do not appear to have any separate language of their own, but speak a peculiar Hindi dialect.

The Bheel tribes are sixty in number in Banswara, and are the most numerous of all the tribes of that State. Formerly, they had entire possession of this part of the country. At the present day the Bheel tribes have great power in the State, and are very jealous of the interference of the reigning prince in their affairs. In their villages, indeed, they utterly forbid such interference. They are a dirty race, and their women are small and ugly. The chiefs constantly wear swords, and all others always appear with their bows and arrows. They drink spirits, eat meat, and are passionately fond of quarrelling and fighting (*a*). The Bheel landholders exercise both civil and criminal jurisdiction over their lands.

These people live not so much in villages as in detached houses congregated together, "each built on separate hillocks at some distance from one another. The cultivation belonging to a family surrounds the homestead, and each congregation, or *pal*, thus covers a large extent of ground. This mode of living, by preventing surprise, gives the wild race greater security from the troops of the native States, who treat them rather as enemies than subjects. The jungle on the larger hills near the *pal* is allowed to grow; and, in case of attack, the Bheels flee into the cover with their families and cattle. Each homestead is complete in itself, consisting of several houses for grain and cattle within a single enclosure. Many of the Bheel houses in Meywar are well built, capacious, and tiled; and far superior to the habitations of the same class elsewhere. The Bheels lived originally in independent communities, each acknowledging its own leader. Those that were conquered by the Meywar sovereigns or chiefs, transferred their allegiance to them; whilst the greater portion, who coalesced with the Grassîas, before the entry of the Udaipore family into the country, still remains faithful to these allodial or *bhûmia* chiefs" (*b*).

The Bheels and Grassîas are much intermingled, the latter freely intermarrying with Bheel women. They obey, to some extent, the chiefs of the States in which they are settled; but the lands they occupy are their own, and no force has yet proved sufficiently strong to dispossess them.

The Bheels may be regarded as one of the aboriginal races of Marwar. They are found scattered about the Rajputana desert, where they are very degraded in their habits, even more so than the Kolis. They feed on foxes, jackals, rats,

(*a*) The Rajputana Gazetteer, Vol. I, p. 117.

(*b*) History of Mewar, by Capt. J. C. Brookes, p. 3.

guanas, snakes, and other vermin. Some Bheels are scattered about Ajmere, Merwara, and are addicted to thieving.

The tribe has some good cultivators in Mallâni, and also gives excellent servants to the chiefs. They form body-guards at marriage festivals, and are too prone to engage in village disputes.

One excellent custom in regard to marriage prevails among the Bheels in some districts. Girls are not betrothed in childhood, as is common among Hindus. Frequently it happens that a girl is not married until she is twenty or twenty-five years of age. The father of a girl can do nothing of himself to promote her marriage, but must wait, as in civilized countries, until a proposal is made on the part of a young man seeking a wife. When such a proposal is made, the question then comes, how much money is to be paid for the girl? (*a*).

The Bheels of Banswara erect stone tablets, with the figure of the deceased carved upon them, to the memory of their male dead. The figure is represented on horse-back, and sometimes on foot, with sword and shield, or a lance, in his hands. Deceased boys are honoured with tablets, on which a hooded snake is sculptured.

The principal inhabitants of the small State of Kusalgarh are Bheels. They have many clans also scattered about Dungarpore, of which State they are said to be the earliest or aboriginal inhabitants.

Respecting those tribes which are partly of Bheel and partly of Rajpoot descent, Sir John Malcolm remarks that they exhibit in their lives the defects of both, and are a proud, thievish, and debauched race. These Bhilalas, as they are termed, are, says Mr. Aberigh-Mackay, "descended from Rajpoots who have mingled their sacred blood with that of the abased people of the jungle They are half Rajpoot, half Bheel, but take the name of the Rajpoot clan to which they trace their origin. Nearly all the chiefs of the Bheel States on the Vindhyan slopes belong to this class. They affect to ignore their Bheel taint, and desire to be regarded as an ancient Rajpoot clan. But the forest lineage is deeply impressed on every line of their faces, and on every feature of their character"(*b*).

(*a*) The Rajputana Gazetteer, Vol. I, p. 118.

(*b*) The Chiefs of Central India, by Mr. G. R. Aberigh-Mackay, Vol. I, pp. xxxii, xxxiii.

CHAPTER VIII.

THE MAHOMEDAN TRIBES.

1.—SAIYID. 2.—KAIM-KHANI. 3.—KATAT MERAT. 4.—RATH. 5.—DAMMAMI. 6.—HAIWASI. 7.—PATHAN. 8.—DARAS. 9.—SAMEJA. 10.—SAMA. 11.—RAHAMA. 12.—NUHRI. 13.—ARISAR. 14.—MANGLIA. 15.—MALLAYA. 16.—BAKIYA. 17—JONIJA. 18.—HALIPOTRA. 19.—ABRA. 20.—BHAMSARA. 21.—MHER. 22.—CHAMA. 23.—JANJ. 24.—BHYA. 25.—SAUD. 26.—SANGRASI. 27.—KALLAR. 28.—CHICHAR. 29.—SAHTA. 30.—DAL. 31.—RAJAR. 32.—GAJJU. 33.—JHAKRA. 34.—THABA. 35.—RAMDAWA. 36.—BHATI. 37.—KATI. 38.—TALOZI. 39.—DEWAT. 40.—HINGORA. 41.—SARAI. 42. DHANDAL. 43.—CHOPAN 44.—SUMRA. 45.—PANU. 46.—RIND. 47.—JESAR. 48.—SARWANI. 49.—LOWANI. 50.—KURURWANI. 51.—BAIDWANI. 52.—TOGRU. 53.—BRIKU. 54.—BARAHA. 55.—SEHRAE. 56.—KOSSA, OR KHOSSA. 57.—CHANDIA. 58.—SADANI. 59—SAMAICHA. 60.—OMAR. 61.—KALLORA. 62.—TALPURA. 63.—NUMRI, LUMRI, OR LUKA. 64.—MAIR, OR MER. 65.—MOHOR, OR MOR. 66.—TAWURI, THORI, OR TORI. 67.—JOHYA. 68.—DAHYA. 69.—BAIRAWI. 70.—KHAIRAWI. 71.—JANGRIA. 72.—UNDAR. 73.—BAGRIA. 74.—SHEIKH. 75.—AFGHAN. 76.—DESWALI. 77.—BANJARA. 78.—MEO. 79.—PIRADAS. 80.—RAHAT. 81.—MEWATTI. 82.—BOHRA.

Mahomedans are fewest in the States lying to the west and south-west, and perhaps fewest of all in Meywar. The influence of the great Moghul rulers of India in former times was powerfully felt in some parts of Rajputana, leading to the conversion to Islamism of many families connected with the Rajpoot tribes. The tribes situated nearest Delhi, such as those of Ulwar, Ajmere, and of the States bordering on the Jumna, were especially affected.

In Bhurtpore the Mahomedan population numbers one hundred and thirteen thousand persons, or eighteen per cent. of the entire community. Some hold high positions in the native court, while others are found in the army and police. They are in greatest numbers in the villages of Paharsar, Saidpura, Helak, and Rara. The Sunni sect preponderates greatly over the Shiah.

Many Mahomedans are found in Rajputana, especially in Ajmere and the eastern States, and not a few are in the employment of native chiefs. In Jesalmere one-third of the people are Mahomedans belonging to seventy-six tribes. In Merwara the Kâtât Merwâts, a degenerate class of Mahomedans, are numerous ;

but in Bikaneer, Mahomedans form only a small community. The following classes of Mahomedans are scattered about the States of Rajputana:—

1. *Saiyids.*

In Bikaneer there are many Saiyid sepoys. In Karauli the Saiyids have a mosque, and hold various offices of respectability. There are more than three thousand Saiyids in Ajmere. There are some also in Bundee and other States.

2. *Kâim-Khâni.*

In Bikaneer, Mahomedans descended from Chauhân Rajpoots. They are settled about Futtehpoor Jhoon-joonee, and form a numerous class in Shekhawati. These last were originally Chauhân Rajpoots, and are said to have once possessed the Shekhawati District, but were dispossessed by Sheikh Jî, the founder of the Shekhawat tribe. The ancestors of the Kâim-Khânis were Rajpoots, who fought against Baber in 1528.

3. *Kâtât Merât.*

Degenerate Mahomedans of Merwara. They are intimately associated with the Hindu Mer tribes, from whom they originally sprang. Until lately the Mers and Merâts intermarried.

4. *Râth.*

Mahomedans in Bikaneer of Rajpoot extraction. They belong to four clans, two descended from Chauhâns, one from Tuars, and one from Saroas.

5. *Dammâmi.*

Mahomedan kettledrum-beaters in Bikaneer.

6. *Haiwâsi.*

Converts from the Haiwâsi Brahmans of Marwar.

7. *Pathâns.*

Pathâns are the most important Mahomedans in Karauli, and are regarded as the most trustworthy of the troops of the durbar. There are a few in Ajmere and Bundee.

8. *Daras.*

In Mallâni.

9. *Sameja.*

In Mallâni.

10. *Samá.*

In Mallâni.

11. *Râhamâ.*

In Mallâni.

12. *Nuhri.*

In Mallâni.

13. *Arisar.*

In Mallâni.

14. *Manglia.*

In Mallâni and the Rajputana desert. Rajpoot proselytes to Islam.

15. *Mallaya.*
In Mallâni.

16. *Bakiya.*
In Mallâni.

17. *Jonijá.*
In Mallâni.

18. *Hâlipotra.*
In Mallâni.

19. *Abra.*
In Mallâni.

20. *Bhamsara.*
In Mallâni.

21. *Mher.*
In Mallâni.

22. *Châma.*
In Mallâni.

23. *Janj.*
In Mallâni.

24. *Bhyâ.*
In Mallâni.

25. *Sâud.*
In Mallâni.

26. *Sangrâsi.*
In Mallâni.

27. *Kallar.*
In Mallâni.

28. *Chichar.*
In Mallâni.

29. *Sahta.*
In Mallâni.

30. *Dal.*
In Mallâni.

31. *Râjar.*

In Mallâni, the Rajputana desert, and the borders of Jesalmere; they are said to be descended from the Bhâtî Rajpoots. They are, says Tod, "cultivators, shepherds, and thieves, and are esteemed the very worst of the converts to Mahomedanism."

32. *Gajju.*
In Mallâni.

33. *Jhakrâ.*
In Mallâni.

34. *Thâbâ.*
In Mallâni.

35. *Râmdawa.*
In Mallâni.

36. *Bhâti.*

In Mallâni and Bikaneer; converts from Hinduism.

37. *Kati.*
In Mallâni.

38. *Tâlozi.*
In Mallâni.

39. *Dewat.*
In Mallâni.

40. *Hingora.*
In Mallâni.

41. *Sarai.*
In Mallâni.

42. *Dhândal.*
In Mallâni.

43. *Chopân.*
In Mallâni.

44. *Sumrâ.*

In Mallâni and the Rajputana desert, they are converts from the Pramara Rajpoots.

45. *Panu.*	46. *Rind.*	47. *Jesar.*
In Mallâni.	In Mallâni.	In Mallâni.

The Mahomedans of Jesalmere are divided into seventy-six classes or clans.

48. *Sarwâni.*

A branch of the Chauhân Rajpoots, settled in Shekhawati.

49. *Lowâni.*

A branch of the Chauhân Rajpoots, in Shekhawati.

50. *Kururwâni.*

A branch of the Chauhân Rajpoots, in Shekhawati.

51. *Baidwâni.*

A branch of the Chauhân Rajpoots, in Shekhawati.

52. *Togru.*

A branch of the Solankhî Rajpoots, in the Punjnud.

53. *Briku.*

A branch of the Solankhî Rajpoots, in the Punjnud.

54. *Baraha.*

A tribe of Rajpoot converts to Islam in the Raputana desert.

55. *Sehrâe.*

One of the most numerous of the tribes in the Rajputana desert. They are notorious robbers, and are the terror of that wilderness.

56. *Kossa, or Khossa.*

A branch of the Sehrâes, with similar habits.

57. *Chandia.*

A branch of the Sehrâes.

58. *Sadani.*

A branch of the Sehrâes.

These Sehrâe tribes are chiefly found in the southern part of the desert, about Noakote, Mittie, to Buliari. Formerly, they were very notorious for their depredations.

59. *Samaicha.*

Proselytes to Islam from the Soda Rajpoots, inhabiting the Rajputana deserts. Tod observes respecting them, "that they never shave or touch the hair of their heads, and consequently look more like brutes than human beings. They allow no animal to die of disease, but kill it when they think there are no hopes of recovery. The Samaicha women have the reputation of being great scolds, and never veil their faces" (*a*).

60. *Omar.*

A branch of the Pranava Rajpoots, in the Rajputana desert.

61. *Kallora.*

A Belooch tribe, in the lower part of the Rajputana desert. See the chapter on the Scinde tribes.

62. *Tâlpura.*

A Belooch tribe, in the lower part of the Rajputana desert. See the chapter on the Scinde tribes.

63. *Nûmrî or Lûmrî, or Lûka.*

A Belooch tribe, in the lower part of the Rajputana desert. See the chapter on the Scinde tribes.

64. *Mair, or Mer.*

A branch of the Bhâtî Rajpoots, in the lower part of the Rajputana desert.

65. *Mohor, or Mor.*

A branch of the Bhâtî Rajpoots, in the lower part of the Rajputana desert.

66. *Tawuri, Thori, or Tori.*

On this tribe Tod has the following remarks: "These engross the distinctive epithet of *bhût*, or evil spirits, and the yet more emphatic title of 'sons of the devil.' Their origin is doubtful, but they rank with the Bawurîs, Khengârs, and other professional thieves scattered over Rajputana, who will bring you either your enemy's head, or the turban from it. They are found in the Thuls of Dâûdputra, Beejnote, Noke, Noakote, and Udar. They are proprietors of camels, which they hire out, and also find employment as convoys to caravans" (*b*).

67. *Johya.*

Rajpoot proselytes to Islam, in the lower part of the Rajputana desert.

68. *Dahya.*

Rajpoot proselytes to Islam, in the Rajputana desert.

69. *Bairawi.*

A Belooch tribe, in the Rajputana desert.

(*a*) Tod's Rajasthan—Madras Edition—Vol. II, p. 294.

(*b*) *Ibid*, p. 295.

70. *Khairawi.*

Rajpoot proselytes to Islam, in the Rajputana desert.

71. *Jungria.*

Rajpoot proselytes to Islam, in the Rajputana desert.

72. *Undar.*

Rajpoot proselytes to Islam, in the Rajputana desert.

73. *Bagria.*

Rajpoot proselytes to Islam, in the Rajputana desert.

74. *Sheikh.*

There are upwards of three thousand Sheikhs in Ajmere-Merwara. The Sheikhs are found in several States.

75. *Afghan.*

Upwards of seven thousand Afghans are resident in Ajmere-Merwara.

76. *Deswâli.*

Rajpoots converted to Mahomedanism. They hold two villages in the north of Ajmere. The tradition is, that their ancestors changed their faith in the reign of Shahâb-ud-dîn.

77. *Banjâra.*

Converted to Mahomedanism, it is stated, at the same time as the Deswâlis. There are some in Ghegul.

78. *Meo.*

An indigenous tribe, converted to the Mahomedan faith, inhabiting Ulwar and Bhurtpore in large numbers. They retain, however, a good many Hindu religious customs. While they make pilgrimage to tombs of Mahomedan saints, they, at the same time, observe the Hindu idolatrous festivals of the Holi and Diwâli. Like the Rajpoots, the members of one clan do not intermarry, but marriages are invariably contracted between members of different tribes. They intermarried with Meena families until lately. The names of some of the Meena and Meo clans are the same. The Meos are now an agricultural people.

The chief territory in the occupation of the Meos is called Mewat, and lies partly in Bhurtpore, partly in Ulwar, and partly in lands under British jurisdiction. It is one hundred miles from north to south, and eighty from east to west. They are divided into twelve *pâls* or clans, some of which are as follows:—

Meo Clans.

1. Singal.	4. Dondolote.	7. Ratawat.
2. Nae.	5. Chirglote.	8. Darrawal.
3. Doolote.	6. Sundawat.	9. Khosa.

79. *Pîradâs.*

Descendants of a Mahomedan saint, occupying the lands between Anupgurh, Pugal, and Marot, in Bikaneer.

80. *Rahat.*

A small tribe of converts to Islam in Bikaneer.

81. *Mewâtti.*

These Mahomedans are found in the State of Bundee.

82. *Bohra.*

A small community of traders in Bundee.

PART II.

THE TRIBES AND CASTES

OF THE

MADRAS PRESIDENCY.

CHAPTER I.

INTRODUCTION—BAIDS OR PHYSICIANS; PUJALIS OR PRIESTS; THE TENGALAS AND VADAGALAS; THE LINGAYETS OR JANGAMS; THE SATANIS OR SANATANAS; THE SAKTIS; THE CHRISTIAN POPULATION, PROTESTANTS AND ROMAN CATHOLICS. THE JEWS OF COCHIN; THE SYRIAN CHRISTIANS; THE JAINS; THE MAHOMEDANS; CASTE—THE VEDANGEI, OR RIGHT-HANDED CASTES, AND THE IDANGEI, OR LEFT-HANDED CASTES.

SECTION I.—THE BRAHMANICAL TRIBES.

THEIR NUMBERS; THEIR PURSUITS. THE OORIYA BRAHMANS. THE NAMBURI BRAHMANS. THE SHAIVA TAMIL BRAHMANS. THE VAISHNAVA TAMIL BRAHMANS.

SECTION II.—THE KSHATRIYA, KETHREE, OR RAJPOOT TRIBES.

THE PAIK TRIBES.

SECTION III.—THE VAISYA CASTES—CHETTIES OR SETTIES.

THE VAISYAS OF VIZAGAPATAM.

INTRODUCTION.

IN Northern India there is a large and distinct class of Hindus, called Baids, who follow the profession of medicine. Some of these are much respected, and exhibit no little skill in the practice of the healing art, while all exert great influence over the minds of the people generally. In the Madras Presidency, however, no one caste or section of Hindus follows this pursuit. "Barbers practise rough surgery; and potters are employed now and then to set broken bones; while women of the barber and chuckler castes officiate as midwives; but a man of any caste may practise as a native doctor"(*a*). Many Mahomedans are employed in this profession. The Hindus of Southern India have greater confidence in magicians, exorcists, devil-drivers, and workers of spells, than in doctors (*b*).

In this Presidency there are about twenty-eight thousand *pujâlis*, or priests, and ten thousand 'church or temple servants.' There are also one

(*a*) The Madras Census Report, Vol. I, p. 182.

(*b*) *Ibid.*

hundred thousand mendicants, many of whom are devotees and ascetics, and belong to various religious orders.

The worshippers of Vishnu in Southern India are divided into two great sects, the Tengalas and Vadagalas, between whom there is an incessant feud. Both acknowledge themselves to be disciples of the famous Râmânuj. The Tengalas follow Manavala Manumi or Râmyaja Matri; and the Vadagalas, Vedântachâri or Vedânta Desika. The rites observed by these sects are nearly the same. Their religious differences and dissensions, which are sometimes very bitter, do not prevent them, as they would do in Northern India, from holding social intercourse with one another, for they attend the same festivities, eat and drink together, and even intermarry. As the two words designating these sects bear philologically the meaning of 'Southern and Northern Veda' respectively, it is not improbable that the disputes between them sprung from the rivalry of two great religious bodies separated originally by geographical boundaries. However, the chief subject now on which their mutual anger is expended, is of a very childish character, and is no more than, whether the middle stroke of the trident, the badge of Vishnu represented on the forehead, should commence from the upper part of the nose, or at its root (*a*).

The small sect of the Lingayets is scattered over various provinces of Southern India. They are worshippers of Shiva, and are consequently opposed in principle to the Vaishnavas. Nevertheless, they are a mild and peaceable people. They wear upon their persons the *lingam*, or emblem of Shiva, called 'Jangama Lingam,' or locomotive image, in contradistinction to the Lingas erected in Shiva temples, called 'Sthavara Linga,' or the stable image. Hence they are commonly designated Jangams. These people discard the modern phases of Hinduism. They also reject the Bhâgavat and Râmâyana as sacred writings, and with them Brahmanical authority, the efficacy of pilgrimages, austerities, self-mortification, and caste, while they pay great respect to the Vedas and to the doctrines of the celebrated teacher Sankara Achârya. The sect was originated by Basava, a Brahman, who flourished in the twelfth century, and was prime minister to the king of Karnataca, a Jain (*b*). 'He taught that all men are holy in proportion as they are temples of the Great Spirit—that by birth all are equal'—that women should be treated with the same respect as men—that widows may remarry, and should she

(*a*) The Madras Census Report, Vol. I, pp. 97, 98.
(*b*) *Ibid*. pp. 98, 99

not do so, may wear her jewels and appear in society with the same privileges as she possessed in her married state (*a*).

The Satanis or Sanatanas are a Vaishnava sect in Southern India, corresponding, in the tenets which they hold, very closely to the Chaitanyas of Bengal. They abolish all caste distinctions. Most of them are Telugus; and all assume the distinctive badge of the Vadagalas, or the Vaishnavas of the northern part of the Madras Presidency.

Modern Hinduism as existing in Southern India as well as in Northern is, in the main, the same, and is evidently a compromise between the religion of the Hindu tribes and that professed by the aboriginal races. The religion prevailing among the masses of the population, is of Tantric origin, and embodies the peculiar rites connected with Sakti worship, or the worship of power as represented by female fecundity. There are two great branches of Sakti religionists, the Dakhshinachâris, or right-hand worshippers, and the Vâmachâris, or left-hand worshippers. The former are comparatively innocent in their religious celebrations; but the latter plunge into all the licentious and cruel rites associated with the worship of the wife of Shiva in one or other of her numerous disguises, or practised at some of the religious festivals held in her honour. "No respectable Hindu," says the compiler of the Madras Census Report, "will admit that he is a Vâmachâri, or follower of the left-hand ritual, in which flesh is eaten, wine and spirits drunk, castes are promiscuously mingled, and a naked female, the personification of the vital power, is adored"(*b*). "It is difficult to ascertain to what extent Sakti worship prevails in the present day in Southern India. The hideous and filthy carvings on idol cars and temple walls in the south, show but too clearly that lewdness and indecency enter largely into the religious life of the people"(*c*).

The Christian population of Southern India numbers five hundred and thirty-three thousand, seven hundred and sixty persons, of whom forty thousand, eight hundred and seventy-nine are Europeans and East Indians, the rest being natives. The Protestant Native Christians are ninety-three thousand, two hundred and twenty-eight; and the Roman Catholic, three hundred and ninety-nine thousand, six hundred and fifty-three.

(*a*) Essay on the Creed, Customs, and Literature of the Jangams, by Charles P. Brown, Esq., Madras Civil Service.

(*b*) The Madras Census Report, Vol. I., p. 103.

(*c*) *Ibid.*

A thousand years ago a few Jews settled at Cochin. Their descendants are partly black and partly white. The former have become black, it is conjectured, by intermixture with the natives, or, as some suppose, from long residence in the country. The white or pale-faced Jews, however, have retained their complexion, it is rightly imagined, by keeping themselves apart from the Hindus, and only intermarrying among members of their own community. They are even said to be fairer than the Jews of Europe.

The Syrian Christians of Malabar have a tradition that their ancestors embraced Christianity under the teaching of St. Thomas.

There are upwards of twenty-one thousand Jains in the Madras Presidency. They are chiefly found in North and South Arcot and Canara.

The Mahomedan population in the Presidency consists of one million eight hundred and fifty-seven thousand persons. More than one million six hundred and fifty thousand of these are Sunis. Three-fourths of the Mahomedans of Southern India are, it is conjectured, converts from aboriginal tribes.

Under British rule the lower castes being, for the most part, free to act as they choose, instead of repudiating caste, and emancipating themselves from its fetters, display a singular anxiety to raise themselves in the opinion of the better castes, and in doing so, to tighten the chains which bind them. "So far from caste distinctions dying out, there probably was never a time when the great bulk of the people of Southern India were so pertinacious in the assertion of the respectability and dignity of their castes" as they have been of late years.

There has been a much greater fusion of races in Southern India than in Northern. "The fair complexioned Aryans have, for the most part, disappeared in the presence of the more numerous dark races, to whom India is a soil on which they can prosper and multiply. The fair Northern Brahmans are delicate exotics in Southern India. The plains of Southern India never could have supported a pure Aryan stock" (a).

The Hindu castes of Southern India are divided into two widely separated branches, the Vedangei, or right-handed, and the Idangei, or left-handed, a distinction not traceable elsewhere. The Sakti worshippers are also divided in the same manner. The origin of this peculiar feature of Southern Hinduism is unknown. Tradition and the literature of the people throw upon it no clear light. Many feuds have arisen between the rival hands, some of which have only

(a) The Madras Census Report, p. 29.

been allayed by the energetic interference of the Government. "Whatever the origin of the dispute, it seems certain that the castes of the 'right-hand' fraternity claim certain privileges which they jealously deny to those of the 'left-hand.' For instance, the right-hand castes claim the prerogative of riding on horseback in processions, of appearing with standards bearing certain devices, and of erecting twelve pillars to sustain their marriage booths; while the left-hand castes may not have more than eleven pillars, nor use the standards and ensigns belonging to the right-hand fraternity. The quarrels arising out of these small differences of opinion, were so frequent and serious in the seventeenth century, that in the town of Madras it was found necessary to mark the respective boundaries of the right and left-hand castes, and to forbid the right-hand castes, in their processions, from occupying the streets of the left-hand, and *vice versâ*. The following list shows the more important of the castes which take part in the disputes of the rival hands:—

Left-hand Castes.	*Right-hand Castes.*
Chetties.	Vellâlars.
Artisans—The Panchala, of five sorts of smiths.	Kavaries.
	Komities.
Oilmongers.	Accountants.
Weavers.	Silk Weavers.
Patnavars.	Pullies (males).
Leather-workers (males).	Pariahs.
Pullies (females).	Leather-workers (females).

"It is curious that the females of two of the inferior castes should take different sides from their husbands in these disputes. The wives of the agricultural labourers side with the left-hand, while their husbands help in fighting the battles of the right; and the shoemakers' wives also take the side opposed to their husbands." Certain castes, as Brahmans, Kshatriyas, Shepherds, and the Satanis or mixed castes, take no part in these disputes (*a*). The right-hand castes occupy, for the most part, a higher social position than the left-hand; to which circumstance may be ascribed the feuds and jealousies which spring up between them. The Pariahs bear the designation of Valangei mattar, or friends, in their relation to other right-hand castes.

The Rev. J. F. Kearns has communicated to the "Indian Antiquary" an important extract from the work of Von Philipp van Mokern, entitled 'Ostindien seine Geschichte, Cultur, und seine Bewohner,' concerning the right-

(*a*) The Madras Census Report, pp. 129, 130.

hand and left-hand castes of Sriringapatam. "The left-hand," he says, "consist of the following nine castes:—

Left-hand Castes of Sriringapatam.

1. The Panchâlar, which includes the five classes of mechanics or artificers.
2. The Chettis, or merchants, who say they belong to the Vaisya caste.
3. Weavers.
4. Oilmen, who drive their mills with two bullocks.
5. The Gollûr caste, people employed to carry money.
6. The Paliwanlu caste. } Both cultivators, but not belonging to the
7. The Palavantu caste. } Karnâtaka.
8. Hunters.
9. Tanners and shoemakers.

"The Panchâlar command the entire body; but the Tanners are their warmest supporters in all difficulties, because in matters of dispute they are very adroit.

"The right-hand division consists of eighteen castes.

Right-hand Castes.

1. The Bangaru caste. This embraces many occupations and many Hindu sects. They are mostly traders and shopkeepers.
2. The Wodigaru caste—Sudra cultivators.
3. Oilmillers, who drive their mill with but one ox.
4. The Tailors.
5. The Sandara caste—Mahomedan artisans.
6. The Gujerati caste—Merchants from that district.
7. The Kamâtigâru caste—People of the Vaisya caste.
8. The joiner or Jaina.
9. Shepherds and Weavers, especially weavers of woollen blankets.
10. Potters.
11. Washermen.
12. Palankeen-bearers.
13. The Padma, equal to the Shalayavârû caste, a class of weavers.
14. The Barber caste.
15. The tank-diggers.
16. Painters.
17. The Gullâra caste—People who herd cows and buffaloes.
18. The Whalliâru caste. These are the warriors of this division. They

commonly speak of themselves; in the Tamil country, as Vallangais, but are the well-known Pariahs.

"The origin of the division of the Hindus into right and left-hand, is overlaid with fable. The oldest Hindu account attributes it to the goddess Kâli, at the founding of Kancheveram; and it is said that the pagoda there contains a copperplate, having upon it an inscription that accounts for this division of castes. Both sides refer to this plate, but neither side has ever produced it, and therefore its existence may be doubted.

"The castes of which both sides are composed are in no way bound by any mutual obligation of religion or of relationship. The great idea that keeps them together appears to be, to attain more dignity. The right-hand claim exclusive right to have a *pandâl* under which to perform their marriage ceremonies; and they maintain that the left-hand have no right in their marriage processions to ride a horse, or to carry a flag upon which there is an image of Hanuman. The left-hand assert a right to all these, and appeal to the copperplate already mentioned; and they further assert, that to them belongs the higher rank, because the goddess placed them on the left side, which in India is the place of honour" (*a*).

Section I.—The Brahmanical Tribes.

The Brahman population of the Madras Presidency is small, compared with that existing in Northern India. In 1871, according to the Census then taken, there were in the whole Presidency one million, ninety-five thousand, four hundred and forty-five Brahmans, who were nearly equally divided between the two sexes. They are most numerous in Canara, and in the regions of the north, approaching the Presidency of Bengal. Thirteen per cent. of the Hindus of South Canara are Brahmans, while not two per cent. are in Madura, South Arcot, Coimbatore, and Salem, and less than four per cent. in Chingleput, Trichinopoly, and Tinnevelly.

The religious creed of the Brahmans, and of the other Hindu tribes, is three-fold,—namely, 1. Shaivite; 2. Vishnavite; 3. Lingayet.

The philosophical tenets of the Brahmans are also three-fold,—1. The Smârtâ; 2. The Mâdhûâ; 3. The Sri Vaishnava. The Shaivites, who are, for the most part, disciples of the famous Sankara Achârya, adhere to the Smârtâ. The Vishnavites either hold to the views of Mâdhûâ Achârya, or to those of

(*a*) The Indian Antiquary. Vol. V, p. 354.

Râmanuja, the founder of the Sri Vaishnava system. The Lingayets are a small community, and are attached to the Arâdhya sect of Jangams.

In Madras, the Brahmans are chiefly engaged in agricultural and professional pursuits. Some, however, are employed as servants, or in trade, or in industrial occupations. Dr. Cornish, in his Report on the Census of 1871, says that "the Brahmans have gradually shifted their position from that of mere priests, teachers, and beggars, to the more substantial one of a landed aristocracy. All other occupations fade into insignificance in comparison with that of landholders. As a rule, Brahman cultivators have secured for themselves the best lands in the country. By the proceeds of the land, tilled by serf labour, they have increased in substance, and grown wealthy; but they have contributed little or nothing by their own exertions, or foresight, to this result" (*a*). The mendicant Brahmans in the Presidency number less than sixteen thousand persons.

These Brahmans carefully abstain from worshipping the village deities whom the aboriginal tribes venerate, and are also free from many of the gross and degrading superstitions which the latter observe. For further particulars respecting the Brahmanical tribes of Southern India, see the chapters in this work on the races scattered over that tract of country, and likewise the author's "Hindu Tribes and Castes," Vol. I, Part I, Chaps. XII—XVI, pp. 77—101.

The Ooriya Brahmans are numerous in the north. There are fifteen subdivisions of the tribe in the Vizagapatam district. They eat meat of various animals, especially game; and will 'drink water drawn by the shepherds.'

In Travancore, Cochin, and Malabar, the Nambûri Brahmans are numerous. They are described in the chapter on the tribes of Travancore. In Malabar they keep themselves entirely separate from the Pullars or Tamil Brahmans, who are foreigners, and numerically much exceed the Nambûris in that province. Only the eldest son of a Nambûri is permitted to marry.

The Tamil Brahmans of Madura, according to Mr. Nelson, are divided into two great branches, the Shaivas and the Vaishnavas, each of which has its separate and peculiar tribes. The Shaivas number ten tribes. These, with some of their clans, are as follows :—

The Shaiva Tamil Brahmans.

I. The Vadabâl Tribe.

(*a*) Report on the Census of the Madras Presidency for 1871, Vol. I, p. 135.

Principal Clans.

1. Vadadesa.
2. Choladesa.
3. Tendubi.
4. Tannayira.
5. Jyyuni.
6. Márgati.
7. Karuvîra.

II. The Brahatcharana Tribe.

Principal Clans.

1. Kandaramânika.
2. Malaganûr.
3. Malagasûr.
4. Mângudi.
5. Maruthan-cheri.
6. Lattiyamangala.

III. The Ashtasahasra Tribe.

Principal Clans.

1. Aruva-padai.
2. Attiyûr.

IV. The Thilli Mûvâyiratthâl Tribe.
V. The Savaiyân Tribe.
VI. The Mukkaniyâr Tribe.
VII. The Nambûriyar Tribe.
VIII. The Vatthiyamâl Tribe.
IX. The Kâniyâlar Tribe.
X. The Kesiyar Tribe.

The Vaishnava Tamil Brahmans.

I. The Vadagalei Tribe.
II. The Thengalei Tribe.
III. The Soliâr Tribe.

These are the principal tribes; the names of the rest have not been ascertained. Each tribe, both among Vaishnavas and Shaivas, is subdivided into a number of clans (*a*).

All the great divisions of the Drâvira Brahmans, with the exception of the Gûjars, are found in Nellore. Members of the Sarwariya and Kanyakubja Brahmans of Northern India are also settled there.

Section II.—The Kshatriya, Kethree, or Rajpoot Tribes.

The Rajpoots of Southern India are less than two hundred thousand in number; and are chiefly found in the city of Madras, and in the districts north and west, in North Arcot and in South Canara. Several thousands

(*a*) Manual of the Madura Country, by J. H. Nelson, Esq., Madras Civil Service, Part II, Chap. 1, p. 23.

colonize the tract of Tinnevelly known as Strivilliputtur; but it is uncertain whence they came, and how long they have resided there. The Rajpoots of this presidency contrast very unfavourably with the same fraternity in Northern India, where they are a stalwart race, of noble physique, and of fine martial appearance. Their degeneracy in the south seems to arise mainly from a greater intermixture with inferior tribes of Hindus than is practised in the north. Moreover, in the latter region they were the dominant ruling power for many ages, whereas in the former they never gained a stable footing, and never rose to the exercise of much authority or influence.

The following curious list of the Rajpoot tribes of Southern India is furnished by the Madras Census Report; yet the Kethrees are said to have sixteen subdivisions:—

	Names of Tribes.	*Occupation or Condition.*
1.	Arasar (Tamil)	The king's caste.
2.	Ooriya Kshatriya	Kshatriyas of the Ooriya country.
3.	Bondiliar	Rajpoots of spurious origin.
4.	Bhat Rajah	Bards who sing the praises of kings.
5.	Manu	Name implying descent from Manu.
6.	Pândyakulam	Descendants of Pândiyas.
7.	Râjavar (Telugu)	The king's caste.
8.	Nandamandalum Râjulu ...	Of the Nandamandala country.
9.	Murikinâti Rajah	Named from the locality.
10.	Sûryavamsapu Râjulu	Of the Solar Race (*a*).

The same authority states, that the most numerous of these tribes are the Bondiliar or Bondili, and the Bhat Rajah. The former tribe is apparently that of the Bundelas of Bundelkhand. The Shaivite Bondilis bury their dead, but the Vaishnavite Bondilis burn them. This difference of custom, however, only appertains to certain localities. As to the Bhat Rajah Rajpoots, it is questionable whether they are properly Rajpoots at all. In Northern India, the Bhats are a distinct race; and although they sing the praises of Rajpoot chiefs, and are constantly seen as minstrels attached to Rajpoot families, are nevertheless an entirely separate tribe. Their amalgamation with the Rajpoots of Southern India furnishes another proof of the deterioration of the latter.

It is singular that the compiler of the Report alluded to above should have omitted from his list the Gahlot tribe, to the Sisodiya branch of which the most distinguished Rajpoot of the Madras Presidency belongs. This is His

(*a*) Madras Census Report for 1871, Vol. I, p. 140.

Highness the Maharajah of Vizianagram, K.C.S.I., who is descended from the Ranas of Udaipûr, one of the most ancient and illustrious of Hindu families. Some account of this nobleman, and of his lineage, is given in the author's "Hindu Tribes and Castes," Vol. I, pp. 128—135.

The Kethrees of Vizagapatam are divided into sixteen branches.

A native gentleman, Bomma Teperumal Chettiar, writing on the castes of Nellore, affirms, that just as there are ten great divisions of the Brahmanical tribes, five Gaur and five Drâvira, so there are ten of the Kshatriya tribes, five Gaur and five Drâvira. I presume he refers to the Madras Presidency, or perhaps only to that part about which he was specially writing. It would have been interesting had he named the ten tribes of Kshatriyas, and pointed out their exact localities.

The Paik Tribes.

These are traditionary fighting tribes, which, in more unsettled times, were exclusively devoted to war. 'They are a fine race, and brave; and are good shots with the matchlock.' These tribes are settled in the Vizagapatam district, and are now engaged in agriculture, trade, and other peaceable pursuits. They are ten in number, as follows :—

1. Suathro.
2. Bellama.
3. Noula.
4. Kampu.
5. Kalingu.
6. Kunu.
7. Uriya.
8. Binakurya.
9. Bosuntea.
10. Guri (a).

The Paiks were formerly a very numerous body, but have greatly reduced of late years. Their widows are not permitted to remarry, but are supported by the younger brothers of their husbands—a custom practised also by the Brahmans, Kethrees, and Karnams, or writer castes of the Vizagapatam district.

Section III.—The Vaisya Castes—Chetties or Setties.

These are, for the most part, similar to the Vaisya castes of Northern India, but differ from them in the names they bear. The members of all these castes number in the aggregate less than one million of persons. They are included under the generic term of Chetti, or Setti, a word probably allied to the Set or Seth, of Northern India, which title many bankers and merchants assume.

(a) The Madras Census Report, Vol. I, p. 219.

Although the designation of Vaisya is placed at the head of this section, as representing the castes commonly supposed in Madras to be embraced by the third great division of Hindu tribes, nevertheless it is extremely doubtful whether any pure Vaisya castes exist in Southern India at all. There are certainly none to the north of the Nerbuddha, from Calcutta to Lahore. All more or less of the professedly Vaisya castes, throughout that extensive region, are open to the suspicion of having, in former times, if not in later, formed marriage alliances with the Sudras. Some are purer than others; yet it would be absurd for any one to lay claim to an unsullied lineage, like that which many Brahmans, and not a few Rajpoots, with undoubted right, can claim for themselves. Notwithstanding the assertion by Dr. Cornish, the Compiler of the Madras Census Report, that the trading classes of that Presidency are generally admitted to be Vaisyas, it is not for a moment to be imagined that they better deserve to be so reckoned than the same classes in the north, which are known everywhere as Banyas. Indeed, some of the Chetties, as, for example, the Vaniyars, or oil-pressers and oil-dealers, similar to the Telis of the North-Western Provinces, would never be regarded as Vaisyas in Northern India, but as Sudras, although evidently admitted into their fellowship in Southern India.

No order or classification has been observed in that Report in the arrangement of the Chetti tribes with their subdivisions and branches, which are described as numerous. "They are entered under about ninety designations; but most of these refer to the localities inhabited. The greater part of these people are classified as Chetties, or Beri Chetties, and Komaties (in Bellary and other localities), Banyas, Marwaris, Vaniyars or oilmongers, Kâsikkârâ or bankers, and even some of the less fortunate traders as Bankrupt Chetties" (*a*). They are more numerous, in proportion to other classes, in Kistna, Nellore, Cuddapah, Kurnool, Madura, Coimbatore, and, most of all, in the town of Madras. Every town has a proportion of them. The Chetties are few in number in South Canara district only; and here the trade of the country seems to have fallen into other hands,—*i. e.*, Brahmans, Mussulmans, and others. In Canara and Malabar, where few of them figure as traders, a larger proportion are described as cultivators; and the reason appears to be that they advance money on growing crops of pepper, ginger, turmeric, and other produce, superintend the cultivation themselves, and ultimately obtain possession of the land" (*b*). Unfortunately, the Report affords no information on the relation

(*a*) The Madras Census Report for 1871, Vol. I, p. 143.

(*b*) *Ibid*, pp. 142, 143.

subsisting between the Chetti tribes and their clans, and gives scarcely a hint respecting them of ethnological or historical value.

The Nâttukotai Chetties of Madura form a peculiar class of local traders. Some of them are wealthy, yet live in no better style than the rest. As a class they are rapacious and hardfisted. But they display excellent business qualities, and have acquired a character for honesty and good faith. They have a tradition that their ancestors came from the town of Kâveri-pattanam a thousand years ago. There are three classes of Chetties or Setties in Madura, namely:—

1. The Nâttukotais.
2. The Ariyûrs.
3. The Eriyûrs (*a*).

The Vaisyas of the Vizagapatam district are divided into three branches, namely:—

1. Gaura Komati.
2. Traivarnikulu.
3. Kalinga Komati.

The Gaura Komatis are traders and agriculturists; and are attached to the Smârtâ, Râmanuja, and Shaiva sects.

The Traivarnîkulus are goldsmiths and jewellers; and belong to the Râmanuja sect.

The Kalinga Komatis are much inferior to the other two, and hardly rank as Vaisyas at all. They eat flesh and fish, from which the others refrain. The northern parts of Vizagapatam, and the district of Ganjam, are inhabited by them.

These three classes hold no social intercourse with one another, and do not intermarry (*b*).

(*a*) Nelson's Manual of Madura, Part II, p. 68.
(*b*) Manual of Vizagapatam, by Mr. D. F. Carmichael, Agent of the Governor of Fort St. George, pp. 62, 63

CHAPTER II.

SECTION I—THE AGRICULTURAL TRIBES—VELLALARS.

SECTION II.—THE AGRICULTURAL LABOURING TRIBES.

SECTION III.—THE IDAIYAR OR SHEPHERD TRIBE.

SECTION I.—THE AGRICULTURAL TRIBES—VELLALARS.

The agricultural population of the Madras Presidency numbers nearly eight millions of persons, and constitutes more than one-fourth of all the Hindus of the entire Presidency. In Cuddapah and Coimbatore they form more than forty per cent. of the inhabitants. In some districts 'forty-nine per cent. of the males are cultivators' (*a*). These tribes are sometimes spoken of under the generic term of Vellâlar, although in fact the Vellâlars are only one, albeit a very large one, of the agricultural tribes.

I.—Vellâlar.

These profess to have been originally introduced into the country they now inhabit by the Pandya kings, and speak Tamil, and no other language. Some are proprietors of land, while others are cultivators. There are, however, a few here and there who are engaged in trade, or who, having received a better education than the rest, are employed in Government offices, or in other positions, for which their superior attainments have fitted them. But, as a body, the Vellâlars are devoted to agricultural pursuits. They follow the usages and observances of their caste with great strictness, and, consequently, are regarded by

(*a*) Madras Census Report, Vol. I, p. 146.

Hindus generally as occupying a high social status, approaching in honour to that held by the Brahmans, whose customs in relation to eating and drinking, and the treatment of widows, they strive to imitate. Indeed, it is said, in reference to them, that 'there is not that hard line of separation between Brahman and Sudra in Southern India which obtains still in the North-West.' The Vellâlars are mostly worshippers of Shiva. They are a laborious people, of frugal and peaceable habits. In South Arcot they form more than fourteen per cent. of the entire population.

The Vellâlars of Madura, where they are called Vellâlans, were originally ranged under seven divisions, when they entered that territory, namely:—

The original Vellâlars of Madura.

1. The Siru Malalei clan.
2. The Ukantha Muttûr clan.
3. The Patthiyâna Arumbûr clan.
4. The Parama Thokurûr clan.
5. The Muttamilsera Kodamalur clan.
6. The Muthumei Thirukkâna clan.
7. The Selugei clan (*a*).

The Siru Malalei clan is referred to in an ancient inscription of the period of Kûn Pândea, probably of the eleventh or twelfth century. The inscription itself leads to the supposition that the Vellâlars were in the eleventh century one of the principal castes in the Madura kingdom (*b*).

The Vellâlans in Madura at the present day are divided into the following five clans:—

Existing Vellâlan clans of Madura.

1. The Arumbû-kutti clan.
2. The Kârakattu clan—In Madura and on the Palani hills, where they have been settled for many generations.
3. The Konga clan—Found in the western division of the district.
4. The Chola clan.
5. The Kadikkâl, or Betel-vine clan, cultivators of the betelnut. A very numerous body, found all over the district (*c*).

The Vellâlans are a proud people, and, although agriculturists, will not

(*a*) Nelson's Manual, Part II, p. 28.

(*b*) *Ibid*, p. 29.

(*c*) *Ibid*, p. 30.

themselves handle the plough, but employ labourers to do the work of their fields. They strictly adhere to the Shaivite form of Hinduism. They abstain from animal food, sanction early marriages, forbid the remarriage of widows, and bury their dead. There is a tradition prevalent among them that they came originally from Benares, in the reign of Kula Shekhara Pândya, in order to introduce into Madura the worship of Shiva (*a*).

II.—Kavare.

This is a very extensive tribe with at least eighteen branches, some of which are so important and numerous as to deserve to rank as separate tribes. The Kavares were originally entirely devoted to agriculture, in the capacity of land-owners, while their lands were cultivated by inferior races; but, although most are still engaged in their hereditary calling, uniting with it the tilling of the soil, there are several clans which pursue other avocations, and are sailors, small traders, pedlars, and the like. They are properly a Telugu people, which language nearly all of them speak ; yet some, having settled in the Tamil country, now commonly carry on the business of life in the latter tongue. Two branches of the Kavare tribe are the following:—

1. The Baligis. Chiefly petty traders, hawkers, and so forth.
2. The Tottiyars, Tottiyans, or Kambalattârs. The Tottiyars are said to be split up into nine clans, differing considerably from one another. They are very industrious and energetic as cultivators, and in other pursuits. Many of them occupy an important position in the city of Madras.

Several clans of Tottiyars entered the district of Madura as colonists four or five hundred years ago, where they have distinguished themselves as agriculturists, especially in reclaiming waste lands. They are fond of cock-fighting and hunting, and have a character for dissoluteness beyond that of other castes. The worship of Vishnu is popular among them, and they have great reverence for relics, are very superstitious, and are peculiarly addicted to the practice of magic. The people generally regard them with awe, because of their mystical rites, which are said to be singularly successful in curing snake-bites. In feature the Tottiyars have a distinctiveness of their own, separating them in a marked manner from neighbouring tribes. The men wear a bright coloured head-dress; and the women cover themselves with ornaments, neglecting to clothe the upper part of their persons. The marriage ceremonies of the Tottiyars are curious. Polyandry in reality, though not professedly, is practised by them. They never

(*a*) Nelson's Manual, Part II, p. 32.

consult Brahmans, as they have their own spiritual guides, called Kodangi Nayakkans, who direct their religious ceremonies, preside at their feasts, cast their horoscopes, and enjoy many privileges in return, some of which are not of the most reputable character (*a*).

III.—Kâpû, Kâpalu, Reddi, or Naidu.

This tribe is known by all these different appellations. They are cultivators of Nellore, Cuddapah, Kurnool, the Ceded districts, and throughout a large portion of the Telugu country, in some places in which they form a preponderating element among the Hindu population. Most are engaged in agriculture, either as farmers or cultivators; but some of them are traders. They have a character for energy and thrift. In physique these agriculturists are a finer race than Tamil cultivators. The relations of the sexes are much too lax. In Nellore the Kâpûs are divided into the following thirteen clans:—

1. Desuri Kapalu.
2. Pakanati do.
3. Panta do.
4. Pedakanti do.
5. Motati do.
6. Are do.
7. Palle do. { i. Aviri Pallelu. ii. Vanne do.
8. Challakuti Kapalu.
9. Konide do. Found at Atmakur.
10. Rachu Kapalu. Found in the North.
11. Yerra Kapalu } Both found in the west.
12. Velama do. }
13. Neratu do. (*b*).

IV.—Velama.

The Velamas as agriculturists are considered to hold the same relation to the land in the Telugu country as the Vellâlars in the Tamil provinces. They originally held their lands on military tenure, and in social rank claim the equality with Kshatriyas. The Velamas are divided into three great branches, namely:—

1. Arava Velamalu. 2. Tenugu Velamalu. 3. Gona Velamalu.

V.—Kammavâr.

Cultivators in the Northern districts, divided into two branches:—

1. Gumpakammelu. 2. Illellanikammelu.

VI.—Kammâ.

Cultivators in the Northern districts.

(*a*) Nelson's Manual of Madura, Part II, pp. 81—83.
(*b*) The Nellore Manual, pp. 207, 208.

VII.—Bhuttar.

Cultivators in Canara.

VIII.—The Nairs.

Land-owners and cultivators in Malabar. For a detailed account of these tribes, see the chapter on the Tribes and Castes of Travancore.

IX.—Kappilian.

A respectable class of Canarese farmers, bearing the title or designation of Kaûndan.

X.—Muthali.

It is supposed by Mr. Nelson that this tribe has sprung from the Vellâlars of Madura, especially as the customs of the two tribes are very similar. The Muthalis are described as a "small but highly respectable and influential agricultural caste. They are strict followers of the Shiva faith; and appear to have come into the country in very recent times." The word Muthali means 'leading or principal man.'

These agricultural tribes are partly of Aryan and partly of non-Aryan origin. The darkness of complexion and peculiarity of features of some of them point to the supposition that they are largely connected with the aboriginal tribes. An additional argument leading to the same conclusion, is furnished by the laxity of marriage and of marriage relations, and of the prevalence of polyandry among several of these tribes. The Brahmans act the part of priests in the villages and families of all the agricultural classes.

For information respecting the Agricultural Tribes of Northern India, see the author's Hindu Tribes and Castes, Vol. I, Part III, Chap. X, pp. 323—331.

Section II.—The Agricultural Labouring Tribes.

These are personally engaged in the cultivation of the soil, in contradistinction to the tribes already described, who are chiefly land-owners, and only labour with their own hands in tilling the ground when compelled by necessity or other circumstances to do so. The term Vunnia or Pulli designates the largest of these tribes; and hence is often used as generic of them all. Nearly four millions of persons are thus represented, among whom the females slightly exceed the males. They are most numerous to the south and west of Madras, but are very few in number, in no case not more than three per cent. of the population, in the Telugu country. They are, for the most part, worshippers of Shiva, only twenty-two per cent. of them being of the Vishnavite form of Hinduism. Some are village servants, policemen, small traders, and the like; but the great majority are cultivators. One per cent. of the whole, perhaps, are proprietors of land. Formerly, before the British rule commenced in India, nearly all these tribes were in a condition of slavery. They do not all occupy the same social rank, some being much lower than others. Several indeed might properly come in the list of low caste and aboriginal tribes, but are placed here because they are chiefly engaged in agriculture.

I.—Vunnia or Pulli.

The great agricultural labouring class of the southern districts. The Madras Census Report says of them, that "before the British occupation of the country, they were slaves to the Villâlar and Brahman cultivators; but a large number of them are now cultivators on their own account, or else work the lands of the higher castes, on a system of sharing half the net produce with the proprietor. Others are simply labourers; and many of them, by taking advances from their employers, are still practically serfs of the soil, and unable to extricate themselves from the bondage of the landlord. In all respects, these people have the characteristics of aboriginal tribes. As a rule, they are a very dark-skinned race, but good field labourers, excellent farm servants and cultivators. They abound largely in the Tamil districts of Trichinopoly and Tanjore" (*a*). Many of the Vunnias claim the honorary title of Naick. The Pullies are divided into thirty clans, which can all eat together, and, in some cases, intermarry. Formerly, it is supposed, the tribe held a position of influence and respectability in Southern India. The Ceylon records frequently allude to armies of Vunnias.

Between the Pareiyas and the Pullâs a feud exists respecting precedence, which has lasted for ages, and seems never likely to be settled. The Pareiyas, in virtue of their position as 'right-hand' castes, consider that they are superior to the Pullâs, which the latter, who belong to the 'left-hand' castes, are altogether unwilling to allow. In the great disputes of the 'right-hand' and 'left-hand' castes, which have occasionally occurred, the most active and noisy partizans of the two sides have been the Pareiyas and Pullâs. The two races occupy a servile position in relation to the higher castes, and it is difficult to perceive any real distinction in their social rank.

(*a*) The Madras Census Report, Vol. I, p. 157.

II.—Kallan.

A dark race, of small stature, and of many distinctive peculiarities, pointing them out as having sprung from an aboriginal tribe. The word *Kallan* means thief or robber in several of the South Indian languages, and may have been applied to this people originally as representing their violent and lawless habits. Before the British entered the country, they were in constant warfare with their neighbours. The eastern division of the tribe in Madura, who occupy what is termed the Kil Nâdu, and are separated from the western division of the Mel Nâdu, and do not intermarry with them, were once in subjection to the Vellâlan land owners; but gradually encroaching on the prerogatives of their masters, they eventually gained the upper hand, and took possession of their estates. Therefore they bade defiance to the rulers of Madura, and remained for a time in a *quasi*-independent condition. The Kallans in the west by different means accomplished the same ends, and gained extensive lands stretching to the extremity of the great Dindigal Valley. In the early period of British rule in India, the Kallans gave infinite trouble to the authorities; but since the year 1801, when the province of Madura was annexed to the Company's territories, they have changed their habits, and although still a bold and high-spirited people, have abandoned their turbulence and submitted to order.

The Kallans are spread over a wide tract of country, and are found more or less throughout the whole of the southern part of the Madras Presidency. Even now their children are brought up in the olden fashion as though intended to gain their livelihood by preying on their neighbours' property. "The boyhood of every Kallan," says Mr. Nelson, who had unusual opportunities of acquiring a knowledge of this strange race, "is supposed to be passed in acquiring the rudiments of the only profession for which he can be naturally adapted, namely, that of a thief and robber. At fifteen he is usually entitled to be considered a proficient; and from that time forth, he is allowed to grow his hair as long as he pleases, a privilege denied to younger boys. At the same time, he is often rewarded for his expertness as a thief by the hand of one of his female relations" (*a*).

The custom of marriage among the Kallans is very peculiar. "It constantly happens that a woman is the wife of either ten, eight, six, or two husbands, who are held to be the fathers jointly and severally of any children

(*a*) Nelson's Manual of Madura, Part II, p. 55.

that may be born. And when the children of such a family grow up, they, for some unknown reason, invariably style themselves the children not of ten, eight, or six fathers, as the case may be, but of eight and two, six and two, or four and two fathers" (*a*).

Many Kallans practise the rite of circumcision, which has been observed in the tribe from very ancient times. As a people they profess to be worshippers of Shiva, although in reality they are, for the most part, merely devil-worshippers. They both bury and burn their dead. The dress of the men consists of a coarse cloth or blanket. Their houses are generally mean and poverty-stricken.

III.—Oddar, or Wuddava.

An aboriginal race of strong well-formed bodies, ignorant, debased, eating flesh, especially pork and rats, drinking spirits, and living in curious conical huts gathered together in separate villages. Though born and bred to husbandry, they readily undertake manual labour of other kinds, such as making roads, wells, tanks, and the like. They are professedly worshippers of Vishnu, and generally bear upon their breasts and foreheads the trident of that god, yet in reality pay greater reverence to a malicious demon called Yellamma. The Oddars have a character for great industry. They object to work separately, however, but readily work in union with their families and friends. Polygamy is largely practised, chiefly because each additional wife is an additional source of income from the labour she is able to perform. The wives seem to be as easily divorced as married.

IV.—Upparava.

Although properly cultivators, yet many of the tribe are employed in the manufacture of salt and saltpetre.

V.—Vallamban.

A tribe in Madura reputed to have sprung from the union of a Vellâlan with a Valiya woman. They are an insignificant people, yet claim to have been once the proprietors of the land.

VI.—Arasa Palli.

A small tribe of cultivators and coolies in Madura.

(*a*) Nelson's Manual of Madura, Part II, p. 54.

VII.—Padeiyâtchi.

Poor ryots of Madura. Some call themselves Nâyakkans; and the men of the caste are usually styled Palli Padeiyâtchis.

VIII.—Pallan.

These are very numerous throughout Madura, where they are regarded by all classes with the utmost contempt. "Their principal occupation is ploughing the lands of more fortunate Tamils. Though nominally free, they are usually slaves in almost every sense of the word, earning by the ceaseless sweat of their brow a bare handful of grain to stay the pangs of hunger, and a rag with which to partly cover their nakedness. They are to be found in almost every village, toiling and moiling for the benefit of Vellâlans and others; and with the Pariahs doing patiently nearly all the hard and dirty work that has to be done. Personal contact with them is carefully avoided by all respectable men; and they are never permitted to dwell within the limits of a village; but their huts form a small detached hamlet, removed to a considerable distance from the houses of the respectable inhabitants, and barely separated from that of the Pariahs" (*a*). The Pallans are probably an aboriginal race. They were formerly slaves of the Vellâlans.

The customs of this people are rude and degraded. Divorce is common. The marriage tie is lightly regarded. They prefer to bury their dead. Demon-worship in its grossest forms prevails among them.

IX.—Nathambâdiyan.

A respectable class of cultivators of Madura, who in modern times have immigrated into that country. They are a fine manly race. Many have become Roman Catholics.

X.—Urâli.

A numerous class of Tamil cultivators, mostly poor and of little consideration.

SECTION III.—IDAIYAR, OR SHEPHERD TRIBE.

The Idaiyars seem to represent two distinct tribes of Northern India, the Ahîrs or Herdsmen, and the Garariyas or Shepherds. The Telugu term for the Idaiyars is Golla, and the Canarese, Gollam, both being a corruption of Gopâla,

(*a*) Nelson's Manual of Madura, Part II, p. 58.

the Hindustani for cowherd, a word often employed in the north for the Ahîrs, especially in reference to their occupation.

This caste is a very important one in the Madras Presidency, and numbers upwards of one million seven hundred thousand persons, most of whom are settled in Bellary, Kurnool, Cuddapah, and Nellore, while scarcely any are found on the western coast, 'where the climate is inimical to sheep and goats, and the breed of cattle is inferior.'

Three-fifths of the tribe are Vaishnavas; the remainder being Shaivites. In reality, however, they are all mostly addicted to the worship of local deities. It is singular that while the Ahîrs and Garariyas of Northern India everywhere burn their dead, the Idaiyars should in many cases bury them. They agree, however, in one very important feature of marriage relation, that of a husband's brother marrying the widow, on the death of the former. In the south, the sexual intercourse between the members of a clan or sub-caste, are of a somewhat loose character (*a*).

The Idaiyars occupy an honourable position socially in the estimation of other castes, and even Brahmans will receive milk and curds from them. They are generally addressed by the word *pillai*, in token of the respect due to their order. In Bellary and Salem some of the sub-castes are weavers.

The tribe has many clans; but its principal branches are the following :—

1. Uridaiyar.
2. Mattidaiyar.
3. Attidaiyar.
4. Tambidaiyar.
5. Karithatidaiyar.
6. Tolia Idaiyar.
7. Kâtu do.
8. Vadugu do.

Each of these branches is divided into eighteen clans, which hold little social intercourse with one another (*b*).

Some of the Telugu divisions of the tribe are as follows :—

1. Puni Gollalu.
2. Yerra do.
3. Arava Gollalu.
4. Peddeti do.

For information respecting the Herdsman and Shepherd's tribes of Northern India, see the author's "Hindu Tribes and Castes," Vol. I, Part III, Chapter XI, pp. 332—338.

The Idaiyars of the district of Cuddapah are chiefly cultivators and labourers, only sixteen per cent. of them being engaged in pastoral pursuits.

(*a*) Madras Census Report, Vol. I, p. 150.
(*b*) *Ibid*, p. 149.

The lands of Madura are ill-adapted for grazing purposes, and consequently the Idaiyars generally devote themselves to cultivation, or to trade, or to other occupations not of a degrading character.

This people, it is said, commonly bury their dead; and therein, if this be true, resemble the aboriginal tribes. The Idaiyars assume the title of Konan, which may perhaps be connected with *koenig* and *kohen*, the Saxon and Hebrew words for king. Yet there are no traditions showing that the tribe ever exercised rule in the country.

CHAPTER III.

SEC. I.—THE KAMMALAN, OR ARTISAN TRIBES. SEC. II.—THE KANAKKAN, OR WRITER TRIBE. SEC. III.—THE KAIKALAR, OR WEAVER TRIBES. SEC. IV.—THE SATANI OR SANATANA, THE JANGAM OR VIRASAIVA, AND OTHER RELIGIOUS SECTS AND TRIBES—MIXED CASTES. SEC. V.—THE KUSAVEN, OR POTTER TRIBES. SEC. VI.—THE AMBATTAN, OR BARBER TRIBES. SEC. VII.—THE VANNAN, OR WASHERMAN TRIBES. SEC. VIII.—THE POTHARAVANNAN TRIBE. SEC. IX.—THE VANIKAN TRIBE. SEC. X.—THE UPPILIAN TRIBE. SEC. XI.—THE KUNNUVAN TRIBE. SEC. XII.—THE MARAVAR TRIBE. SEC. XIII.—THE AHAMBADIYAN TRIBE. SEC. XIV.—THE SEMBADAVEN, OR FISHERMEN AND HUNTER TRIBES. SEC. XV.—THE PALM CULTIVATING TRIBES: 1. THE SHANARS AND ILAVARS; 2. TIGAR; 3. BILLAWAR; 4. IDIGA. SEC. XVI.—LOW-CASTE TRIBES: 1. OTTAN, TANK-DIGGERS; 2. ILLUVAKAN, DISTILLERS; 3. CHAKKILIAN, DEALERS IN LEATHER; 4. METHAKARAN, BASKET-MAKERS; 5. SIKILKARAN, KNIFE-GRINDERS; 6. SEMMAN, LIME-BURNERS; 7. KUTTHADI, STROLLING PLAYERS AND DANCERS; 8. DASI, WOMEN ATTACHED TO PAGODAS.

Section I.—Kammâlan, Kammâlar, or Artisans.

These are five in number, referring to five species of technical labour, namely, the Goldsmith, Blacksmith, Coppersmith and Brass-smith, Carpenter, and Stonecutter tribes. They bear the designation of Kammâlar, in Tamil, and Kamsâla and Pâuchâla, in Telugu. A radical difference of caste regulations subsists between these castes of Southern India and their counterparts in Northern India. In the latter they are all separated by impassable barriers, and so rigid is caste prejudice that even their subdivisional clans, generally numbering seven in each tribe, do not intermarry, or hold close social intercourse with one another. Moreover, the Goldsmiths caste is far higher in rank than any of the rest, and some of its branches affect to be allied even to the Brahmans. In Southern India, on the contrary, although the Goldsmiths are most respected, nevertheless all these five castes and tribes are practically united and gathered together into one, for they associate together on a perfect equality, eat and drink together, and intermarry. As they all wear the sacred thread, and as some of them speak of themselves as Visva Brahmans, it would appear that several of these tribes, for instance the Blacksmith, Carpenter, and Stonecutter, occupy a higher grade socially than the corresponding tribes in Northern India. In Ceylon the Goldsmiths are in the third rank of inferior castes; and next in succession are the Carpenters.

There is evidently a restless ambition cherished by the Artisan castes in Madras such as is not known among the same castes in the Bengal Presidency. The Madras Census Report takes special notice of this. "The Artisan castes in Southern India have always maintained a struggle for a higher place in the social scale than that allotted to them by Brahmanical authority. Here, they wear the thread of the 'twice-born' castes; and some of them style themselves Achâri, or religious teacher. The origin of the quarrel between the Southern Artisans and Brahmans, it is not easy to trace; but there is no doubt as to the fact that the members of this great caste dispute the supremacy of the Brahmans, and that they hold themselves to be of equal rank with them" (a). The Artisans belong to the left-hand castes.

The Kammâlars are mostly worshippers of Shiva, and bury their dead. A few only worship Vishnu; but these burn their dead. They are much stricter as Hindus, in not permitting their widows to marry again, than most of the Artisan castes in the north. The Kammâlars of South Arcot form little more than two per cent. of the whole population.

For information respecting the Artisan tribes of Northern India, see the author's "Hindu Tribes and Castes," Vol. I, Part III, Chapter IX, pp. 314—322.

Section II.—Kanakkan, or Writers.

This is a small caste in Southern India, where it has neither the wealth nor the social status and influence which the Kayasths of Northern India have acquired. In some places, they are village accountants, but this occupation is now largely in the hands of Brahmans and Vellâlars. They are most numerous in Ganjam, North and South Arcot, and Chingleput. The word Kanakkan is Tamil. Its correlative in Telugu is Karnam. In Canara, the Writer caste has the designation of Shambogue; and in Malayalim, of Adigâri.

The tribe has four subdivisions in the Madras Presidency, as follows:—

1. Sir Kanakkan.
2. Saratu do.
3. Minadu Kanakkan.
4. Mattuvali do.

M. A. Esquier, in his work on the Castes of India, especially on those in the French Settlement of Pondicherry, gives a different list, namely:—

1. Sircanaka.
2. Haratticanaka.
3. Saraloucanaka.
4. Nattucanaka (b).

The last three of this list differ from those of the former list, which is that

(a) Madras Census Report, Vol. I, p. 151.
(b) *Ibid*, p. 153.

supplied by the Madras Census Report. None of these names, however, is given to any of the twelve and-a-half clans, into which the Kayasths of Northern India are divided (*a*).

The Kanakkans are somewhat strict as Hindus, and do not permit their widows to remarry. They worship village deities, as well as Shiva and Vishnu; and in some cases burn, and in others bury their dead. When addressed, they commonly receive the honorary title of *pillai.* The entire tribe numbers one hundred and seven thousand persons, of whom about twenty per cent. are employed as writers and accountants, the remaining four-fifths being engaged as cultivators, servants, and in other pursuits. Formerly, the Kanakkans were interpreters, agents, brokers, and the like, to the East India Company; and were much more important persons, and held much more important posts, than now (*b*).

Section III.—Kaikalar, or Weavers.

The Weaver castes in Madras seem to be an entirely different race from those in Bengal and the North-Western Provinces. Not only so, but the Telugu weavers are distinct from the Tamil, and hold no social intercourse with them. They bear separate names, as may be seen by examining the lists of the two classes of weavers given below. Even when the Telugu weavers remove from their own country and settle among the Tamils, or *vice versâ*, they keep themselves entirely apart from the weaver tribes among whom they are located. All the weavers are addicted to drinking spirits, and have the character of indulging to great excess. Their habits generally are said to be non-Aryan, and to be similar to those of aboriginal tribes. Some are Shaivites, and others Vaishnavas; the former burying their dead, the latter burning them. They are found in largest numbers in the cotton-producing districts of the Presidency, such as Vizagapatam, Godavery, Kistna, Cuddapah, Bellary, Coimbatore, Salem, and Tinnevelly. There are few, however, in South Arcot, Tanjore, Trichinopoly, South Canara, and Malabar (*c*).

The Tamil weavers are split up into six subdivisions or clans; and the Telugu weavers into five, as follows:—

Divisions of Tamil Weavers.

1. Kaikalar.	3. Jendravar.	5. Sedan.
2. Seringar.	4. Saliyar.	6. Silupan.

(*a*) Hindu Tribes and Castes, Vol. I, Part III, Chapter VIII, pp. 305—313.

(*b*) Madras Census Report, Vol. I, p. 154.

(*c*) *Ibid.*

Divisions of Telugu Weavers.

1. Salay.
2. Jendra.
3. Padmay Salay.
4. Thokata.
5. Devangalu.

Maharathi Clan.

Jawai.

Clan of Silk Weavers.

Patnûlkar.

The Silk weavers came originally from Gujerat, and speak the language of that country. They have a fair skin, and expressive features; and their women are beautiful, but they do not bear a very reputable character; and the wealth which they accumulate is spent in self-indulgence and excess.

The Madras Report has the following observations on the present condition of cloth manufacturers in the Madras Presidency: "The weaving business," Dr. Cornish remarks, "has, for many years past, been in a decaying state. Manchester floods the country with cheap piece-goods, loaded with China clay; and if the fabrics imported would only wear, the weaving trade in India would decay faster than it is now doing. But the Lancashire manufacturers have not yet attained the secret of producing machine-made cloth equal in strength and price to the products of the hand-looms of India; and, consequently, there is still a demand for hand-woven cloth, and occupation for a large number of hand-loom weavers. While the weaving trade is but a poor industry, it affords employment to a large number of persons, probably half a million in all, as the women and children of weavers' families all work at the looms. The yarns and twists used by the Indian weavers, except for the coarser qualities of cloths, are all imported. There are as yet (1871) no cotton spinning mills on this side of India in use" (*a*).

Section IV.—The Sâtâni or Sanatana, the Jangam or Virasaiva, and other religious sects and tribes—Mixed castes.

These two great antagonistic religious sects are composed of persons who, for a religious object, have abandoned their own castes and have attached themselves to the one or the other of these communities which, although starting with the renunciation of caste, have in reality formed themselves into two separate castes or tribes, with their own laws and usages. They number in all about three-quarters of a million of persons, who are nearly equally divided

(*a*) Madras Census Report, Vol. I, pp. 155, 156.

between the two sexes, there being a few more women than men. They are numerous in Trichinopoly, where they constitute more than ten per cent. of the entire Hindu population. They are common also in Coimbatore and Bellary, but are rare in Malabar.

The Sâtânis or Sanatanas are disciples of the great Vaishnava Chaitaniya, who flourished in the fifteenth century, and espoused strongly the cause of Vishnu. The Sâtânis, therefore, are rigidly and exclusively devoted to the worship of this deity. Their founder was Sanatana, a man of low social position, but famous for the enthusiasm of his attachment to Chaitaniya, and the skill and energy with which he enunciated his doctrines. The Sâtânis are "frequently religions mendicants, priests of inferior temples, minstrels, sellers of flowers for offerings, and the like. Many prostitutes join this sect, which has a recognised position among Hindus. This they can easily do by the payment of certain fees, and by eating in company with their co-religiouists; and they thus secure for themselves decent burial, with the ceremonial observances necessary to ensure rest to the soul" (*a*). This sect is much smaller than the Jangam, and numbers less than two hundred thousand persons. They are generally worshippers of Krishna, an incarnation of Vishnu. The Sâtânis of South Arcot are numerous, but are for the most part poor. They are flower-sellers, servants in temples, and religious mendicants.

The Jangams or Vîrasaivas are Shaivite reformers, obeying the doctrines of Basava. Many of the Pandârams, or inferior priests of Shiva, have the same characteristics as Jangams in the abandonment of caste prejudices, and in separating themselves from caste ties.

These mixed castes bear a multitude of designations, two hundred of which are given in the Census Report. The following are a few of them :—

1. Andi.	6. Jangam.	12. Satadavan.
2. Bairagi.	7. Jogi.	13. Satatan.
3. Dasaradi.	8. Lingadhari.	14. Tambiran.
4. Dasari.	9. Ochan.	15. Virasaiva.
5. Gosayi.	10. Pandaram.	16. Bogam (*b*).
	11. Rama Jogi.	

Section V.—Kusaven, or Potters.

The Potters in the Presidency are about a quarter of a million in number, and are scattered about in small numbers all over the country. They chiefly

(*a*) Madras Census Report, Vol. I, p. 159.

(*b*) *Ibid*, p. 160.

consist of two divisions:—1. The Tamil Potters; 2. The Telugu Potters. These tribes do not intermarry, and in fact do not hold any social intercourse with each other. They are mostly worshippers of Shiva; yet some of them are attached to the Lingayet sect. Their favourite objects of religious veneration, however, are demons and inferior deities. The Kusavens bury their dead (*a*). They are proverbial for their ignorance and stupidity.

Section VI.—Ambattan, or Barbers.

This caste in Southern India seems to pursue the same kind of miscellaneous occupations as in Bengal (*b*). The Ambattan, or Nâû, and Hajam, as he is called in Northern India, not merely discharges the duties of a barber, but together with his wife, attends at public festivals, which he, to a large extent, superintends. He arranges for marriages and funerals, and other ceremonies. He acts the part of a surgeon. He is occasionally a musician. Indeed, in many matters he is called in as a most useful practical personage; and occupies an important position in Hindu families. The women are generally employed as midwives. This caste, therefore, is, everywhere in India, of influence socially, although it may not secure much respect. In Madras some are polygamists; and all worship the local deities. They are called Ambattan by the Tamils, Mangalus by the Telugus, and Hajâms by the Canarese and Mahrattas.

Section VII.—Vannân, or Washermen.

There are upwards of half a million members of this tribe in the Presidency, who are called Vannân, in Tamil; Sâkalu, in Telugu; Agasa, in Canarese; Asavun, in Malayâlim; and Dhobî, in Hindustani. There are apparently no subdivisions of the caste in Southern India, whereas in the North-Western Provinces there are nearly a dozen, which are separated socially from one another, and do not intermarry (*c*). Two-thirds of the caste in Madras are worshippers of Vishnu. The Vannâns seem to occupy a lower rank in Southern India than the corresponding caste of Dhobîs in Northern India.

Section VIII.—Pothara-Vannân.

The members of this tribe wash the clothes of Pariahs, Pallans, and other low castes, and therefore are regarded as much lower in the social scale than the Vannâns, who only wash for the respectable castes.

(*a*) Madras Census Report, Vol. I, pp. 158. 159.
(*b*) Hindu Tribes and Castes, Vol. I, Part III, Chapter XII, pp. 341, 342.
(*c*) *Ibid*, pp. 342, 343.

Section IX.—Vânikan.

These extract oil from vegetable seeds, which they generally purchase from the farmer, instead of cultivating the plants themselves. They are also traders in oil.

Section X.—Uppilian.

This tribe manufactures salt and saltpetre. The word *uppilian* is derived from *uppu*, salt.

Section XI.—Kunnuvan.

The Kunnuvans formerly inhabited the plains of Coimbatore, and migrated thence to the Palani hills, it is conjectured, from three to four centuries ago, where they formed connexions with the Kârakattu Vellâlans, and hence are sometimes designated as Kunnuva Vellâlans. The customs of the two tribes differ considerably; and indeed the eastern Kunnuvans and the western Kunnuvans differ greatly from each other. In both divorce is very common, mere disagreement or contrariety of feeling being regarded as sufficient reason for separation. Poleiyans are predial slaves of this tribe.

Section XII.—Maravar.

In former times, the Maravars, as a great fighting or warrior tribe, held the same position in the south that the Rajpoot tribes held in Northern India, only they did not rise to the same rank and powers which the latter attained. They were a wild, lawless, unmanageable race, and were a perpetual terror to quiet and peaceable tribes. But their character has undergone a great and radical change for the better. The Maravars are found in greatest numbers in Madura and Tinnevelly. They eat flesh and drink spirits, and the form of religion of which they are most fond, is demon-worship. The tribe is divided into seven principal clans. These are as follows:—

1. Sembu-nâttu.
2. Kondayan-kottei.
3. Apanûr-nâttu.
4. Agatâ.
5. Orûr (Oreiyûr?) -nâttu.
6. Upu-kottei.
7. Kurichi-kattu (*a*).

There are other clans besides these, but of inferior rank. The highest of all is the Sembu-nâttu. The Maravans, as they are termed in Madura, were once very numerous and powerful in that district; but compared with ancient times their numbers have been greatly reduced. They were formerly notorious for turbulence and lawlessness, and eighty years ago gave much trouble to the

(*a*) Nelson's Manual of Madura, Part II, p. 39.

British authorities of the district; but they have settled down, for the most part, to peaceable habits, exhibiting, however, a bolder and more determined spirit than their neighbours. Some of their customs are peculiar. For instance, cousins on the fathers' sides may intermarry, contrary to Hindu usage. Divorce is easy and frequent; and widows may remarry.

The head of the Maravans, styled the Sethupati, who is the hereditary ruler of Ramnad, is entitled to extraordinary honour from some of the nobles of the Dekhan. "The Rajah Tondiman of Puthu-kottei, the Rajah of Sivagangei, and the eighteen chiefs of the Tanjore country, must stand before him with the palms of their hands joined together and stretched out towards the presence. The chiefs of Tinnevelly, such as Kataboma Nâyakkan of Panjâla Kuriechi, Serumali Nâyakkan of Kudal Kudei, and the Tokkala Tottiyans, being all of inferior caste, should prostrate themselves at full length before the Sethupati, and after rising must stand, and not be seated. But the Sillavas, and others, of Ettiyapuram, the Marava chiefs of Vadagarei, Shokkampatti, Uttumalei, Settûra, Sarandei, and other tracts, and the Vanniya chiefs of Sivagiri of seven thousand fields, and of Dalavan Kottei—all these make no obeisance of any kind to the ruler of Ramnad"(*a*).

The Maravans wear their hair exceedingly long, and both sexes hang heavy ornaments on their ears, thereby lengthening the lobes several inches. The men eschew the turban, the national covering for the head, and in its place tie a cloth round their heads. The ears of the women are sometimes so enormously elongated that they rest upon the neck. The features of the Moravans are quite different from those of the races and tribes in their neighbourhood (*b*). They are tall, well made, and of somewhat striking physique.

Section XIII.—Ahambadiyan.

The Maravans and Ahambadiyans of Madura intermarry, and have, for the most part, the same customs and habits. The former, however, occupy a somewhat higher social position, and are a little more numerous in that district than the latter. Some of the tribes are household servants, and many are poor ryots and field-labourers. They are divided into three branches:—

1. Ahambadiayns.
2. Raja-bâsha do.
3. Kottei-pattu do. (*c*).

(*a*) Nelson's Manual of Madura, Part II, p. 41.
(*b*) Pharaoh's Gazetteer of Southern India, p. 392.
(*c*) Nelson's Manual of Madura, Part II, p. 43.

Section XIV.—Sembadaven, or Fishermen and Hunters.

The fishermen and hunters of Southern India are associated together indiscriminately in the same tribes, but in Northern India they are entirely distinct tribes. The Tamil fishermen, however, keep apart from the Telugu. In the Madras Presidency they number nearly a million of the Hindu population, while there is a large community of Mahomedans and out-cast races pursuing the same occupation. The Sembadavens are mostly of a non-Aryan stock. They eat flesh and fish, marry several wives, and generally bury their dead. The term Sembadaven is Tamil. Its counterpart in Telugu is Besta; and in Canarese, Mukkava or Mogiva.

The principal tribes are as follows:—

1. Boi or Boya.
2. Besta.
3. Châpakulam.
4. Patnâvar.
5. Mogivlu.
6. Parava.
7. Valaiyân.
8. Makwar.

The Boi tribe of Telugu fishermen are extensively employed as palankeen-bearers and domestic servants. Many of the Paravas of Tinnevelly and Madura became Roman Catholics when the Portuguese exercised authority and influence over the rulers of those countries. The Bois of Kurnool and Bellary are largely employed in cultivation and manual labour. A distinction prevails in Madura between the Sembadavens and Savalakârans, the former fishing in tanks and streams, the latter in the sea. Traditions exist respecting the great antiquity of the Paravas. They are said to have been the earliest navigators of the Indian Ocean, and to have been once divided into thirteen clans. The Makwars are a numerous class of fishermen in Malabar.

For information respecting the Fishermen and Hunter tribes of Northern India, see the author's "Hindu Tribes and Castes," Vol. I, Part III, Chapter XIII, pp. 346, 347; and Chapter XIV, pp. 352, 353.

Section XV.—Palm-cultivating Tribes.

The date palm, the cocoanut palm, the areca palm, and the palmyra trees grow abundantly in various parts of the south, and numerous families connected with various tribes are interested in their cultivation. The date palm grows wild; the palmyra tree does not require much attention, and grows luxuriantly in the dry and rainless parts of Tinnevelly; but the cocoanut tree is always cultivated, and will not flourish far from the sea. The tribes engaged in this branch of industry, are the following:—

1. *Shânârs and Ilavars.*

This tribe numbers upwards of one million six hundred thousand persons, who form an important section of the population of Malabar, Canara, and Tinnevelly. In the last province they are divided into five clans, which, however, intermarry; and are called Ilavars in the north, and Shânârs in the south. For a further account of this tribe, see the chapter on the Tribes and Castes of Travancore.

The Shânârs are a laborious people, eat flesh and fish, and drink strong toddy. Their notions on marriage indicate greater degradation than they otherwise exhibit. Many of them have become christians, and have thereby made great progress in intelligence, civilization, and morals. The Shânârs of Tinnevelly and Canara are, for the most part, devil-worshippers. The Sâṇâns of Madura, who are petty traders as well as palm cultivators, belong apparently to the same tribe.

2. *Tiyar.*

Palm cultivators in Malabar and Travancore. They practise polyandry, one wife being the common property of several brothers. Physically, they are a fine and well developed race. Their women are fair and handsome. Many Tiyars are in the service of the Government, or engaged in trade. They are a despised race, and are not allowed to come within sixteen feet of their superiors in caste (*a*). In the north of Malabar they may come within five feet. Many are servants to Europeans. They are a good looking people.

The Tiyars are properly Pariahs. See number 5 in the list of the Pariah tribes.

3. *Billawar.*

Palm cultivators in Canara.

4. *Idiga.*

Palm cultivators of the Telugu districts in the north.

Section XVI.—Low-caste Tribes.

1. *Ottan.*

An itinerant caste of Telugu tank-diggers and earthworkers, who are supposed to have migrated southwards in the time of the Nayakkans. "They are a strong, hardworking race, but also drunken, gluttonous, and vicious; and

(*a*) Madras Census Report, Vol. I, p. 350.

but little faith can be placed in their most solemn promises. They will take advances from half-a-dozen employers within a week, and work for none of them if they can possibly help it" (*a*).

2. *Iluvakan.*

Distillers of arrack, regarded as infamous by Hindus of the stricter sort.

3. *Chakkilian.*

The Chakkilians are similar to the Châmârs of Northern India, and are dealers in leather and in all things made of leather. They are of drunken, dirty, licentious habits. Their women are said to be both beautiful and virtuous.

4. *Meṭhakâran.*

Basket-makers. The materials they use are bamboos, bamboo leaves, cane, and the like.

5. *Silkilhâran.*

Knife-grinders, the same as the Sikilgars of Northern India.

6. *Semmân.*

Lime-burners and sellers.

7. *Kutthâdi.*

These are strolling dancers, players, performers, and so forth.

8. *Dâsi.*

The Dâsis are disreputable women attached to pagodas, and form a distinct and recognized caste. They are numerous in every town or large village in which are endowed temples. "Their ranks are recruited by the purchase of female children of any caste, and also by members of certain Hindu castes vowing to present daughters to the temples on recovering from illness, or relief from other misfortune. The female children of the dancing-women are always brought up to the mother's profession, and so are the children purchased by them, or assigned to the temple service by the free will of the parents" (*b*). Superfluous daughters in families of certain castes are presented to the pagodas, to be brought up as Dâsis.

(*a*) Nelson's Manual of Madura, Part II, p. 88.
(*b*) The Madras Census Report, Vol. I, p. 167.

CHAPTER IV.

ABORIGINAL AND LOW-CASTE TRIBES.

THE PARIAH, OR PAREIYAN TRIBES:—1. VALLUVA. 2. TATHA. 3. TANGALANA, OR TONDA. 4. DURCHALI. 5. TIYA. 6. MARASU. 7. AMBU. 8. VADUGA. 9. ALIYA. 10. VALEI. 11. VETTIYAN. 12. KOLIYA. 13. PERUM. 14. EGALI. 15. TAMILA. 16. KUDI PILLEI. 17. POLA. 18. TAVALEI-TINNUM. 19. MANNAL-KADEI-TINNUM. 20. ARUTTU-KATTATHA. 21. EIYA AND AMMEI. 22. TOTTI. 23. OTAGA-KARAN. 24. KOTTAGA-KARAN. 25. SANKU. 26. SOLAGU-KATTI. 27. ARIPPU-KARAN. 28. SALIYA. 29. UPPAREIYAN. 30. MALEI. 31. CHUCKLER. 32. CHERMAR.

ABORIGINAL AND OUTCAST TRIBES.

THE PARIAH, OR PAREIYAN TRIBES.

The common designation of these tribes in Tamil, is Pariah or Pareiyan; in Telugu, is Mala; in Canarese, is Holia; in Malayalim, is Poliyar; and in Mahrâthi, is Dhed. They are regarded by the Brahmans as defiling their presence; and are not allowed to dwell in villages inhabited by Hindus, but live in their outskirts. They perform service of a very menial character, and although much despised, are an exceedingly useful people. In their own estimation they constitute a fifth great caste, in contradistinction to the four Hindu castes.

Formerly, these tribes were in a condition of slavery to the superior castes. "There were," says Dr. Cornish, "fifteen species of slaves recognized, namely:—

1. Those born of slaves.
2. Those purchased for a price.
3. Those found by chance.
4. Slaves by descent.
5. Those fed and kept alive in times of famine.
6. Those given up as a pledge for money borrowed.
7. Those binding themselves for money borrowed.

8. Those captured in battle.
9. Those unable to pay gambling debts.
10. Those becoming slaves by their own wish.
11. Apostates from a religious life.
12. Slaves for a limited period.
13. Slaves for subsistence.
14. Those who for love of slave women became slaves.
15. By voluntary sale of liberty.

"Of these fifteen descriptions of slaves the first four could never obtain their liberty without the consent of their owners. The other kinds of slaves might obtain their freedom under stipulated conditions" (*a*). No Brahman could ever be subjected to slavery.

The Pariahs are a dark-skinned race, eating every species of food, hard-working, thriving, yet intensely ignorant and debased. "In public passenger boats, a Pariah dare not show his face; and in Government schools, or schools helped with public money, it is pretty much the same." The Madras Presidency contains nearly five millions of these industrious and contemned people, in nearly equal proportions of the two sexes. They are most numerous in Chingleput and South Arcot, where they comprise twenty-six per cent. of the Hindu population. In the latter district they number nearly four hundred and fifty thousand persons.

These tribes pursue many kinds of occupation. A considerable number are agricultural labourers. Others are servants, village watchmen, workers in leather, scavengers, and so forth. Their habits are low; they have a lax idea of the marriage tie; and most of them are addicted to intemperance. For the most part, they are worshippers of demons and local deities. They belong to the 'right-hand' castes, of which, in the periodical disputes which occur, they are among the principal supporters, especially in opposition to the Pallans, a low agricultural people already described. They live in the Parei-chari, a quarter set apart for themselves.

In regard to the origin of the Pareiyas, Dr. Caldwell considers that the balance of evidence is in favour of their being Dravidians. "Nevertheless," he remarks, "the supposition that they belong to a different race, that they are descended from the true aborigines of the country—a race older than the Dravidians themselves—and that they were reduced by the first Dravidians to

(*a*) The Madras Census Report, Vol. I, p. 169.

servitude, is not destitute of probability" (*a*). He mentions the traditions, that the Canarese Pareiyas were once an independent people, and that the Tamil Pareiyas were formerly the most distinguished caste in the country. He also states, that in certain parts the Pareiyas 'enjoy peculiar privileges, especially at religious festivals.' The strongest argument which, Dr. Caldwell says, can be adduced in favour of their pre-Dravidian origin, is, "that the national name of Tamilians, Malayâlis, Kannadis, &c., is withheld from them by the *usus loquendi* of the Dravidian languages, and conferred exclusively upon the higher castes. When a person is called a Tamiran, or Tamilian, it is meant that he is neither a Brahman nor a member of any of the inferior castes, but a Dravidian Shudra. As the lower castes are never denoted by this national name, it would seem to be implied that they do not belong to the nation, but, like the Tamil-speaking Brahmans and Mahomedans, to a different race" (*b*).

Mr. Nelson, in his Manual of Madura, gives the completest account of these numerous and interesting, though degraded, tribes with which I am acquainted. It is as follows:—

1. *Valluva Pareiyan.*

The Valluvans are by far the most respectable of the Pariahs, inasmuch as they act as *gûrûs* or spiritual pastors to the others; and cannot be reproached to the same extent as other Pariahs, on account of the filthiness of their lives and habits. Tiru-valluvan, the celebrated Tamil poet, belonged to this family.

2. *Tatha Pareiyan.*

These often wander about as religious beggars of the Vaishnava sect, and subsist entirely on alms given to them by all classes of people.

3. *Tangalâna, or Tonda Pareiyan.*

This is perhaps the most numerous group, and, with the exception of the Valluvans, the most respectable. They are usually employed as cultivators and predial slaves; but some of them are petty traders, artisans, domestic servants, horse-keepers, and the like.

4. *Durchâli Pareiyan.*

The Durchâlis are said to be distinguished from others as being eaters of frogs, mussels, jackals, &c.; but the name does not appear to be well known in Madura.

(*a*) Dr. Caldwell's Grammar of the Dravidian Languages, App. IV, p. 546.
(*b*) *Ibid*, p. 549.

5. *Tiya Pareiyan.*

This tribe belongs properly to Malabar. I am not aware that any families of them are fixed inhabitants of the district of Madura.

6. *Marasu Pareiyan.*

These play on a kind of tom-tom.

7. *Ambu Pareiyan.*

The Ambus, as the name implies, live properly by hunting wild animals with bow and arrow. They act as *shikâris* or beaters to zemindars or land-owners, and others, when engaged in hunting in the jungles.

8. *Vaduga Pareiyan.*

The Vadugas belong properly to the Telugu country, and to the Vaishnava sect, and are said to be hippo-phagists. They are often employed as palankeen bearers.

9. *Aliya Pareiyan.*

These appear to be a tribe whose sole peculiarity consists in addressing their fathers by the title of *âlei*, and their mothers by that of *âlâ*. Many of them are employed in dressing skins for exportation, &c.

10. *Valei Pareiyan.*

The Valeis, as their name implies, live properly by netting birds, and works of a similar nature.

11. *Vettiyân Pareiyan.*

The members of this tribe properly beat tom-toms, and act as undertakers at funerals. They also attend as tom-tom beaters when other ceremonies are performed; and eke out a living by hawking goods, and doing odd jobs of various kinds. Some of them are to be found in every large village, their services being indispensably necessary wherever Hindus live in numbers.

12. *Koliya Pareiyan.*

These weave cloths of a coarse description.

13. *Perum Pareiyan.*

The Perums are a better sort of Pariahs, employed principally as gentlemen's servants, &c.

14. *Egâli.*

The Egâlis are washermen by profession. As they wash only for Pariahs, and have to handle the filthiest and most disgusting of rags, the contempt with which they are regarded can be readily understood.

15. *Tamila Pareiyan.*

These are usually merchants, and are regarded as men of some substance and respectability.

16. *Kudi Pillei.*

Barbers who shave Pariahs. Their occupation must be a most unpleasant one; and they are viewed with special abhorrence.

17. *Pola Pareiyan.*

These make mats, baskets, &c., of bamboo, rushes, osiers, and similar materials.

18. *Tavalie-tinnum Pareiyan.*

So called because they eat frogs. Possibly this is only the local name of the Durchâli tribe.

19. *Mannal-kâdei-tinnum Pareiyan.*

Eaters of the mannal kâdei, a large, coarse kind of frog or toad, which buries itself deep in the soil.

20. *Aruttu-kattâtha Pareiyan.*

So called because their widows are not allowed to remarry. The observance of this high caste custom causes them to be somewhat respected.

21. *Eiya and Ammei Pareiyan.*

These are in the habit of addressing their fathers and mothers by these two titles respectively.

22. *Totti Pareiyan.*

The Tottis are found in every village. They are the village scavengers and messengers; and a certain number of them are paid for their services by Government.

23. *Ottaga-kâran.*

Spinners of cotton thread. When work is slack, they till the soil, and do other kinds of work.

24. *Kottaga-kâran.*

Mostly rough-riders and grooms.

25. *Sanku Pareiyan.*

Wear shells on the left arm, and are thereby readily distinguished. They blow conches (large shells) at ceremonies, and do various kinds of work.

26. *Solagu-katti Pareiyan.*

Live chiefly by winnowing paddy and other kinds of grain.

27. *Arippu-kâran.*

These wash sand for gold, where gold is procurable. It is said that they find very minute particles of the precious metal in the Veigei, but not in sufficient abundance to repay their exertions.

28. *Saliya Pareiyan.*

Generally hawkers of cheap wares.

29. *Uppareiyan.*

Scavengers.

30. *Malei Pareiyan.*

Hill Pariahs, a tribe who cultivate lands on the Palani, and other mountains. The Virupâkshi Paleiya-kâran (Poligar) settled a number of Pariahs, Poleiyans, and others of the lowest caste on the Palanis about two hundred and fifty years ago, and so laid the foundations of the present hill colony (*a*).

In addition to these tribes enumerated by Mr. Nelson, are two others also well known, yet not found in his list. These are—

31. *Chuckler.*

32. *Chermar.*

These are regarded as very degraded persons. They are not permitted to approach the Nair nearer than thirty-two feet, or the Brahman nearer than sixty-four feet; and should they be travelling on the same road as either of these personages, must run into the neighbouring jungle to let him pass.

There are many other tribes of Pariahs, but those given above are among the most numerous and important. As a class they are composed of aboriginal races intermingled more or less with outcasts of various tribes, who have from time to time joined their ranks.

(*a*) Nelson's Manual of Madura, Part II, p. 76—78.

CHAPTER V.

ABORIGINAL AND LOW-CASTE TRIBES,—(*Continued.*)

1. IRULAR, OR PUJARI. 2. MUCHI. 3. YARAKALA. 4. SUKALI, SUGALI, OR LAMBADI. 5. WUDDUR, OR WODDEVANDLU. 6. PAMULAVANDLU. 7. MUTTARACHAVANDLU. 8. DASARIVANDLU, OR DONGADASARLU. 9. PICHIGUNTAVANDLU. 10. YENADI. 11. CHENTSU, CHENCHU, OR CHENCHUWAR. 12. MALAYALI. 13. MULCER. 14. SHOLAGAR. 15. KADER. 16. BRINJARI. 17. DOMMARA. 18. TAKKUVADLAJATI. 19. KURUMAR. 20. PIRAVAY. 21. KORCHA. 22. BUDUBUDUKAR. 23. GADALA. 24. JETTI. 25. KORAVAR. 26. KUMARI. 27. PYELAVAR. 28. PAMBATTAR. 29. TOMBIRAN. 30. VILLI. 31. KOYA. 32. VALIYAN. 33. VEDAN. 34. KURUMBAN. 35. PULEIYA. 36. POLEIYAN. 37. KANIYAR. 38. PALLIYAR OR PALLIYAN. 39. KARCHAYAR. 40. NAGADI OR NAYADI. 41. VILLIYAR.

1. *Irular, or Pujari.*

These are a wild, untutored race inhabiting the jungles of several districts, "gathering forest produce, and living upon roots and whatever they can manage to kill. They are by no means particular as to what they eat, and do not object to snakes, lizards, rats, and so forth. They are simple and superstitious to a degree, and, among the people of the plains, have the reputation of being sorcerors. They seldom if ever come out of the jungles ; and their headmen, who, in their own way, are little kings, act as the middle-men in dealings with the Chetties, who barter grain, salt, condiments, and petty trinkets for jungle produce. Money has little or no value in their eyes ; and they would far rather have tobacco or a sheep than a handsome present in money. They seem to intermarry very much, and a plurality of wives is permitted. They have large families, but the children die off in great numbers from fever. They are singularly well-conducted and quiet" (*a*).

The Irulars are excessively fond of eating tobacco. "They will chew this drug without expectorating, and having masticated it for some time, swallow it. Their theory is, that it improves the wind, and gives strength ; and they are certainly wonderfully active in the way of climbing" (*b*). In Arcot

(*a*) Report of Mr. Price, Collector of Salem. Madras Census Report, Vol. I, p. 59.

(*b*) *Ibid.*

the Irulars mostly subsist on the sale of jungle produce, although a few are now taking to agriculture.

The Irulars of Nellore intermarry with the Villis. They live in huts on the outskirts of villages. Their clothing is very scanty; the women wearing nothing above the waist. They bury their dead.

2. *Muchi.*

These are evidently connected in some way with the Mochis, or workers in leather, of Northern India. Both the Telugus and Hindustanis, because of their trade, are held in disrepute. Everywhere in India those who handle skins or leather are regarded contemptuously by respectable Hindus.

3. *Yarakala.*

An aboriginal tribe of Nellore, leading a precarious life by wandering about the country and selling wood and leaves, carrying salt and grain, making baskets, telling fortunes, hunting, and the like. But they are notorious for their thieving propensities on a large scale, especially for dacoity, highway robbery, and robbery. These people are usually of a very dark-brown colour, though not of so deep a shade as the Yenâdis. They are muscular and hardy, exceedingly dirty, and almost naked. Both the Yarakalas and the Yenâdis wear their hair tied in a knot on the forehead. The tribe is said to have many subdivisions; but these refer chiefly, if not exclusively, to the various occupations they follow. They are not so wild as the Yenâdis, but are said to be more determined criminals.

The Yarakalas are akin to the Koravers, the former being a Telugu word, the latter a Tamil. Some persons regard the two tribes as really the same; but a distinct account is furnished of them. The Yarakalas are found in the northern districts of the Madras, and the Koravers in the southern. Professor Wilson, in his Glossary, affirms that Yerukulavar is the Telugu probably of Erukvada; and that the people are the same as those corruptly termed Yerkelwanloo, Yerakedi, Yerakelloo; and are also 'said to be called Koorshewanloo and Yerkelvanlu; but to be known among themselves as Kurra.' In Nellore they undoubtedly speak of one another as Kurra and Kola. Yar or Yara may be merely a prefix (*a*).

The tribe practises polygamy freely, but is not addicted to polyandry. Child marriages are not allowed. A bride is purchased from her parents for

(*a*) Manual of the Nellore District, by J. A. C. Boswell, Esq., p. 157.

about twenty pagodas. A singular custom prevails in the tribe whereby the maternal uncle may claim the two first daughters of a family as wives for his sons.

4. *Sukali, Sugali, or Lambadi.*

A small roving tribe in Nellore of similar occupations to those of the Yarakalas. They like to encamp in jungles at a distance from villages. In complexion the Sukalis are of a dark reddish brown. Their staple food is a course cake made of wheat or maize; and they are fond of strong drink. The women are tall and of good figure; and the men are robust. At the marriage ceremony a string is tied round the neck of the bride. The dress of the women is striking, and consists of a 'kind of petticoat of patchwork of very bright colours,' and they have the appearance of gipsies (*a*).

The Sukalis are more numerous in Canara. They call themselves Mahrattas, and as they speak a Mahratta dialect, there can be little doubt that they have sprung from this race. They are notorious for cattle-stealing (*b*). These people are well clothed. The men wear trousers, and the women a short jacket. In Bellary they are a gipsy tribe, and are carriers of salt and grain from one part of the country to another.

5. *Wuddur, or Woddevandlu.*

A tribe chiefly employed in digging tanks, who have emigrated originally, it is supposed, from Orissa, and now wander about the country, remaining temporarily in those places where they obtain work. They speak a peculiar dialect, but worship Telugu deities. Being accustomed to severe labour, it is not surprising that they are a muscular and hardy people (*c*).

6. *Pamulavandlu.*

A tribe of snake-charmers and itinerant showmen, notorious for robbery and dacoity. They are chiefly, it is said, of Tamil origin.

7. *Muttarachavandlu.*

These call themselves Nayudus, and are hereditary watchmen. They have permanent abodes, and are not addicted at all to roving about (*d*).

(*a*) Manual of the Cuddapah District, by J. D. B. Gribble, Esq., p. 36.

(*b*) Manual of the Nellore District, pp. 162, 163.

(*c*) The Nellore Manual, p. 166.

(*d*) *Ibid.*

8. *Dasarivandlu, or Dongadasarlu.*

Mendicants and thieves. 'They usually practise what is known as scissor-theft,' and are very clever in their unlawful profession. The tribe is found scattered about the Telugu and Canarese countries (*a*).

9. *Pichiguntavandlu.*

Mendicants, doctors, herbalists, and the like. "They beat the village drums, relate stories and legends, and are apparently a kind of heralds, being learned in family history, and giving names, it is said, to the Kapu families."

10. *Yenâdi.*

An aboriginal tribe of primitive habits inhabiting the jungles and wild tracts to the south of the Kistna river. The Government has long taken special interest in the civilization of a small number of this tribe inhabiting the island of Sriharikota. Previously to 1835, "the Yenâdis, who dwelt in the jungles, were rarely seen, and were in a state of complete barbarism. They lived on fruit, roots, and other-jungle produce. In order that they might be induced to adopt the use of rice and clothing, these commodities were supplied to them instead of money (in exchange for the jungle products which they collected for the Government), of the use of which they were entirely ignorant. To restrict their wandering habits, a system of registration was introduced, which has been continued to the present time. All marriages were also registered, and premiums on births were given at the rate of two annas and six pies (three pence three farthings) for male, and one anna and three pies (two pence) for female children"(*b*).

The Yenâdis in Nellore dwell in huts scattered over the whole town. "In their wild state they are a wretched set of people. They are small in stature, with poor attenuated frames, and have no regard for human life. One of them admitted that he saw no difference between killing a sheep and killing a man. They live upon roots, and what grain they can get in exchange for honey and medicinal herbs. They will carry off sheep from stocks grazing on the hills when they can, effecting their purpose by violence, if necessary. When inducements offer, they readily take to a civilized life, and rarely return to their old habits after they have found employment on the plains"(*c*).

(*a*) The Nellore Manual, p. 167.

(*b*) Extract from Mr. Boswell's Nellore Manual. The Madras Census Report, Vol. I, p. 249.

(*c*) Report of Mr. Horsley, Collector of Cuddapah. Madras Census Report, Vol. I, pp. 44 and 45.

The language of the Yenâdis is a corrupt form of Telugu. "Their type of features is Mongolian, broad about the cheek-bones, which are also more or less prominent, with a pointed chin, a scanty moustache, no whiskers, and a scanty, straggling beard over the fore part of their chins. Among them are a few in whom the Caucasian type of features predominates over that of the Mongolian, which latter, though greatly masked, is never entirely absent. Some of them are tolerably well featured, more especially a few of the women. The men are generally dark coloured; but the women vary from a dark to a brown bamboo (*a*)." They are very filthy in their habits; and the skin of some of them emits a foul musty odour.

11. *Chentsu, Chenchu, or Chenchuwar.*

An aboriginal tribe similar to the preceding, and found in the same region. In the Kurnool district they inhabit the Nallamalas, and seldom visit the plains. They subsist, for the most part, on the products of the jungle, and on the chase; and are an inoffensive and peaceable people. Their weapons are the dart, which they throw by hand, the bow and arrow, the bill-hook, and the match-lock. They are almost naked. These people live principally by hunting, by breeding cattle, and by the sale of jungle products. Their huts are small and round, the walls being about a yard in height. They are a finer race than the Yenâdis, but resemble them in their social habits.

The Chenchus are very dark. Their hair is tied up in a knot on the head. Some of them wear a cap made of skin. Those in Nellore call themselves Bentachenchuvandlu. There is a clan in the deep jungle which is represented as wearing an apron of leaves stitched together, and never quitting the dense jungle (*b*).

12. *Malayali.*

A tribe of cultivators, woodmen, and shepherds spread about the hills of Salem, Malabar, South Arcot, Trichinopoly, and other districts. Some of them hold little intercourse with people on the plains. There is a small community of this tribe in two hamlets above Papanassam, in the mountains dividing Tinnevelly from Travancore. The Malayalies are not so uncivilized as many of the hill tribes.

(*a*) Account of some rude tribes in Southern India, by Dr. Shortt. Transactions of the Ethnological Society, New Series, Vol. III, p. 374.

(*b*) The Nellore Manual, p. 164.

13. *Mulcer.*

An aboriginal race of ancient traditions, found among the hills of Coimbatore, Malabar, and Canara, living on roots and herbs, and the products of the chase.

14. *Tholagar.*

A degraded tribe dwelling in the jungles of Collegal in the Coimbatore district. As cultivators they turn the soil with a hand-tool in the place of a plough.

15. *Kader.*

Another aboriginal tribe of similar characteristics as the Mulcers, inhabiting the Anamalay hills of Coimbatore. They cultivate patches of ground on the hills.

16. *Brinjari.*

A tribe of gipsies and grain carriers.

17. *Dommara.*

A tribe of jugglers. They are somewhat similar in their habits to the Karawars; and wander about in gangs, performing athletic feats, and thieving (*a*). The tribe is variously designated as Dommara, Dombari, and Domber; which words are doubtless forms of Dom, the term by which the very numerous outcast race of Northern India is known.

The Dombers are more or less scattered over Southern India. They are tall and well-made, with a complexion varying from different shades of copper colour to very dark. Dr. Shortt considers that the predominant type of countenance which they exhibit is Mongolian, "somewhat pointed chin and absence of whiskers, large eyes, and prominent cheek-bones." In addition to their conjuring tricks, rope-dancing, and the like, they hunt, fish, make mats, tend donkeys and pigs. They worship the goddess Polariamah (*b*). They eat all kinds of flesh, including cats, pigs, and game. Like the Sukalis, they are usually well clothed. The Dombers marry only one wife, but keep concubines at pleasure. The marriage string is always tied round the bride's neck.

18. *Takkuvadla Jati.*

A wandering mendicant tribe of Bellary.

(*a*) The Madras Census Report, Vol. I, pp. 165 to 167, to which I am indebted for the information respecting these tribes given above.

(*b*) Transactions of the Ethnological Society, New Series, Vol. III, p. 391.

19. *Kurumar.*

A low-caste people of Malabar.

20. *Firavay.*

A low-caste people of Malabar.

21. *Korcha.*

An aboriginal tribe in the Bellary district, leading a wandering life, and of habits similar to those of the Lambâdis.

22. *Budubudukar.*

Wandering mendicants.

23. *Gadala.*

A branch of the Jat tribe.

24. *Jetti.*

Boxers, wrestlers, shampooers.

25. *Koravar.*

A tribe of thieves and vagabonds, wandering about the districts of the Carnatic. This tribe is common to several districts. Among the Tamils these people are called Koravars; but by the Telugus, Yerakalas. In North Arcot they mortgage their unmarried daughters to their creditors when unable to pay their debts. In some districts they obtain their wives by purchase, giving a sum varying from thirty to seventy rupees. The clans into which they are divided, do not intermarry. In Madura and South Arcot the Koravars are hawkers, petty traders, dealers in salt, jugglers, box-makers, breeders of pigs and donkeys ; and are a drunken and dissolute race.

26. *Kumari.*

Jungle cultivators.

27. *Pyelavar.*

A tribe of jugglers.

28. *Pâmbattar.*

A tribe of snake-charmers.

29.—*Tombiran.*

A tribe of jugglers.

30. *Villi.*

A tribe inhabiting the jungle country of Nellore. Their countenance is of a Mongolian type. The lips and chin of the men have little hair upon them; and their faces are entirely destitute of whiskers. They lead a precarious life by selling medicinal herbs and drugs gathered in the jungles. They are very superstitious, but do not practise image worship (*a*).

31. *Koya.*

Hill tribes of the Godavery district, employed chiefly in agriculture.

32. *Valiyan.*

A numerous tribe of low and degraded people in the Madura district. A Valiya woman is supposed to have been the primitive mother of the Vallambans, an agricultural tribe already described. This circumstance would indicate that the Valiyans are an ancient people. They pursue various occupations, such as fishermen, iron-smelters, labourers, coolies, and the like; but their proper vocation is that of fishermen. The word *valei* means net; and hence the term *valiyan* has been, it is conjectured, applied to the tribe as denoting the netting of fish by which they obtain their livelihood (*b*).

33. *Vedan.*

One of the most debased tribes of Southern India, the same probably as the Veddahs of Ceylon. They are despised and loathed by all classes of natives. Not long since they were naked savages, roaming about the jungles; but even they have felt the beneficent influence of British rule, and have become somewhat civilized. Some suppose them to be the most primitive race in Southern India, and to have been subdued by the Kurumbans. There is an outcast tribe of Veds living in the jungles of Northern India, whose habits resemble in some respects those of the Vedans in the south (*c*).

34. *Kurumban.*

An insignificant tribe notorious for senselessness and folly, so that the stupidity of the race has become a proverb among the tribes in Southern India. They are spread over the immense tract of country in which the Telugu, Tamil, and Canarese languages are spoken. Properly, the Kurumbans are

(*a*) Transactions of the Ethnological Society, New Series, Vol. III, pp. 383 and 384.

(*b*) Nelson's Manual of Madura, Part II, p. 63.

(*c*) The Author's "Hindu Tribes and Castes," Vol. I, Part IV, Chap. VI, p. 404.

shepherds and goatherds in wild and dense jungles; yet some of them cultivate the soil, and most of them occasionally indulge in pursuits of a disreputable character. "They are probably," remarks Mr. Nelson, "the descendants of one of the first castes that settled in the south; and are supposed to be a branch of the Idaiya caste" (*a*).

35. *Puleiya.*

A small, black, and degraded race on the coast of Malabar.

36. *Poleiyan.*

These are stated to be the aborigines of the Palani hills. They have always been predial slaves of the Kunnuvans, as already stated. Their marriage ceremony is simple enough, and consists of a mutual declaration of consent at a family feast. Their treatment of small-pox is peculiar. The person affected is left to his fate, and a line being drawn round the village, all communications with neighbouring villages is rigidly prohibited. The isolated villagers quit their houses, and encamp in the open fields until the disease disappears. This tribe buries its dead after the fashion of other aboriginal races (*b*).

37. *The Kaniyar Tribe.*

A degraded people who are not permitted to approach within twenty-four feet of persons of the higher castes.

38. *Palliar, or Palliyan.*

A wandering tribe in Warsanad and the jungles of Madura, of a type far below that even of the Poleiyans. They are described by Mr. Nelson as "savages, who decline to adopt the most simple usages of ordinary men, having neither houses, clothes, nor any kind of property. Roaming the hills they satisfy hunger with such roots and fruits as they can find by search, and occasionally a little wild honey. They carefully shun the society of civilized men, and will never approach a stranger except upon the offer of a piece of tobacco or a strip of cloth, for both which commodities they show a great natural fondness. They are gentle in disposition, and show no inclination to rob their neighbours." "The Palliyans," he adds, "are so like ordinary Tamils in physiognomy and physique, that it is difficult to believe that they belong to another and earlier type" (*c*).

(*a*) Nelson's Manual of Madura, Part II, p. 64.

(*b*) *Ibid*, p. 65.

(*c*) *Ibid*, pp. 65, 66.

39. *Karchayar.*

A rude people in Wynaad, expert in the use of the bow and arrow, and noted for their dexterity in destroying wild animals.

40. *Nâgâdi, or Nâyâdi.*

The Nâgâdis are among the lowest types of humanity. Without land or property of any kind, without implements to till the soil, or weapons to defend themselves or hunt the wild animals of the forest, with no occupation but that of begging, they pass their lives in the utmost misery and destitution, subsisting on offal and roots, and on the alms which they occasionally receive. "They do not, like the hillmen, live away from the sight of others; but are to be seen in the open country howling and yelling from a distance after passers-by, running after him until something is thrown down in charity, which they will come and pick up after the traveller has passed on. They are not allowed to approach within ninety-six feet of Hindus; but so degraded are they, that they generally observe a much greater distance from all other human beings. They enter no town or bazaar, but deposit their money on some stone at a distance, and trust to the honesty of the bazaar man to give what goods, and what quantity, he thinks fit in return" (*a*). The Nâgâdis are scattered about Malabar. They are small in stature, of the deepest black in colour, ugly and brutish in feature, with hair bushy and generally curly, and their habits are said to be more like wild animals than men. It is a singular circumstance in regard to these wretched creatures, that they bear the names of Brahmans, and that a tradition exists respecting them, that they are descended from excommunicated Brahmans. Many have embraced the irregular Mahomedan faith professed by the Moplahs, and have entered their fraternity.

41. *Villiyar.*

A tribe of hunters in South Arcot.

(*a*) Pharaoh's Gazetteer of Southern India, p. 521.

CHAPTER VI.

TRIBES AND CASTES OF MYSORE.

I.—THE BRAHMANICAL CASTES: 1, THE SRI VAISHNAVA TRIBE; 2, THE MADHUA TRIBE; 3, THE SMARTHA TRIBES. II.—THE KSHATRIYA TRIBES. III.—THE VAISYA CASTES. IV.—THE SUDRA CASTES. V.—THE MARKA CASTE. VI.—THE LINGAYAT TRIBES. VII.—THE PANCHALA, OR ARTISAN CASTES. VIII.—SECTS OF DEVOTEES AND RELIGIOUS MENDICANTS. IX.—THE INFERIOR CASTES. X.—WANDERING TRIBES. XI.—TRIBES INHABITING THE JUNGLES. XII.—THE MAHOMEDAN TRIBES.

The population of Mysore, at the close of 1871, was 50,55,412, which is 186 for every square mile of territory. Of these more than three millions are Sudras, and a little less than one hundred and seventy thousand are Brahmans. The natives recognize one hundred and one castes; but according to the recent census they number four hundred and thirteen. The agricultural, artisan, and trading communities are divided into the Bala-gai and Yeda-gai, or Right-hand and Left-hand castes, which, as given by the Gazetteer of Mysore and Coorg, newly published, are as follows :—

Right-hand Castes.

Banajiga	... Traders.
Wakkaliga	... Cultivators.
Gâniga	... Oilmen, who yoke only one bullock to the mill.
Rangâre	... Dyers.
Lâda	... Mahratta traders.
Gujerâti	... Gujerât traders.
Kâmâti	... Labourers.
Jainas.	
Kuruba	... Shepherds.
Kumbâra	... Potters.
Agasa	... Washermen.
Besta	... Fishermen, or palankeen-bearers.
Padmasâle	... A class of weavers.
Nainda	... Barbers.
Uppâra	... Salt-makers.
Chitragâra	... Painters.
Golla	... Cowherds.
Holaya, the lowest right-hand caste.	

Left-hand Castes.

Pânchâla, comprising—	
Badiga	... Carpenters.
Kanchugâra	... Copper or brass-smiths.
Lohâra	... Ironsmiths.
Waddar	... Stonemasons.
Akasâla	... Goldsmiths.
Bheri	... A class of Nagarta traders.
Devânga	... Weavers.
Heggâniga	... Oilmen, who yoke two bullocks to the mill.
Golla, or Dhanapâla	Cowherds.
Beda	... Hunters.
Yâkula	... Cultivators.
Palli, or Tigala.	
Mâdiga, the lowest left-hand caste (*a*).	

(*a*) A Gazetteer of Mysore and Coorg, by Mr. Lewis Rice, Director of Public Instruction, Mysore and Coorg, Vol. I, pp. 316–318.

The principal Right-hand castes are the Banajigas and Linga Banajigas; and the principal Left-hand, the Pâuchâlas and Nagartas. The Right-hand castes "claim the exclusive privilege of having twelve pillars in the pandal, or shed, under which their marriage ceremonies are performed (allowing to the Left only eleven); of riding on horse-back in processions; and of carrying a flag painted with the figure of Hanumân" (*a*). Brahmans, Kshatriyas, and the greater part of the Sudras take no share in the disputes of the rival factions.

I. The Brahmanical Castes.

The Brahmans of Mysore divide themselves into three great tribes, the Sri Vaishnavas, the Vaishnavas or Mâdhuâs, and the Smârthas. These hold no social intercourse with one another. They not only do not intermarry, but decline to eat and drink together. Should it so happen that they meet at a public festival, or in travelling, or on any occasion are found preparing their food in each other's neighbourhood, they separate widely from one another, so that the accusation may not possibly be made of their sitting in company and uniting in the same repast.

First.—Sri Vaishnava.

These are connected with the Sri Vaishnavas of Northern India, and are properly the disciples of Vishnu Swâmi, one of the four *sampradyas*, or sects, of Vaishnavas among the Bairâgis (*b*). They are in creed closely allied to the followers of Râmanuj, the famous disciple of Râmanand, the celebrated founder of the order of Bairâgis, devotees or ascetics, so much so that they are often spoken of as Râmanujis, and even regard themselves as belonging to this sect. They are worshippers of Vishnu; and speak the Tamil language. They are scattered about Mysore and along the Coromandel Coast, from Trichinopoly to Cape Comorin.

The Sri Vaishnavas bear the mark of a trident on their foreheads. They are divided into three branches:—1, the Mai-nâd, or up-country; 2, the Mores-nad, or middle-country; and 3, the Kil-nad, or low-country (*c*).

Second.—Mâdhuâ.

The Mâdhûâs are followers of Mâdhû Achârya, and are in reality one of

(*a*) Gazetteer of Mysore and Coorg, Vol. I, p. 319.

(*b*) See the author's "Tribes and Castes of India," as represented in Benares, Vol. I, pp. 260, 261.

(*c*) Gazetteer of Mysore and Coorg, Vol. I, p. 324.

the four sects of Vaishnavas, although, strange to say, they call themselves Vaishnavas in contradistinction to the Sri Vaishnavas, another sect of the same religious order, as stated above. They are divided into six branches, three speaking the Mahrathi language, and three the Canarese:—

1. Deshastha. 2. Hydrabâdi. 3. Uttarâdi.	Speaking Mahrathi.
4. Karnata. 5. Badagunâd. 6. Kambâle.	Speaking Canarese.

The three classes speaking Mahrathi differ greatly from those speaking Canarese, and are bold, energetic, and determined, while the latter are of a gentle and yielding spirit.

The Mâdhûâ Brahmans bear a perpendicular black streak upon their foreheads, divided by a red spot.

Third.—Smârthâ.

These are both Vaidika, or such as are devoted to a purely religious or studious life, and Lokika, or those who are, for the most part, engaged in secular pursuits. Some of these Brahmans are Shaivites, and some Vaishnavites; they may be separated according to the languages which they speak, and are divisible into twenty-six branches, as follows:—

Speaking Telugu.

1. Velnâd.	6. Vangipuram.
2. Veginâd.	7. Arvelu.
3. Kâsalnâd.	8. Nandavaidik.
4. Murikinâd.	9. Gundhadrâvid.
5. Telagânlu.	10. Konashimadrâvid.

Speaking Mahrathi.

11. Deshashta.

Speaking Canarese.

12. Badagunâd.	15. Huls-kamme.
13. Sirinâd.	16. Babbur-kamme.
14. Huyishanig.	17. Kanva.

Speaking Tamil.

18. Vadama.	20. Sanketi.
19. Brihach-charana.	

Others—Shaivite Brahmans.

21. Shaiva.	24. Gânâpatya.
22. Shaktiya.	25. Saura.
23. Kâpâlika.	26. Arâdya.

The last six tribes of Brahmans have been many years in Mysore, and are of a darker complexion than the rest.

The Smârthâ Brahmans are marked on the forehead by three horizontal lines of powdered sandal-wood, with a red spot in the middle.

II.—The Kshatriya Castes.

These are said to be divided into five branches,—namely, Are or Mahratta, Râjpinde, Râchevâr, and Rajpoot, as follows:—

1. Mahrattas—subdivided into the following clans:—
   Bhaniya, Baruva, Kine, Kshatribhânu, Lankekâra, Manga, Râvuta, Bhussa Mahratta, and Kumari Mahratta.
2. Râjpinde—divided into the Arasu and Komarapatta clans.
3. Râchevâr—whose clans are:
   Telugu Arasu, Jatti, Ranagâra, Mallâru, Chitragâra or Bannagâra, Meda, and Sarige.
4. Rajpoots—divided into the Tamboli and Kâyasta clans.
5. Sikhs (*a*).

The two last divisions,—namely, Rajpoots and Sikhs,—need further explanation. Mr. Lewis conjectures that the Rajpoots are immigrants from Northern India. If this conjecture be true, the Tambolis and Kâyastas, to whom Mr. Lewis refers, are not Rajpoots at all. The Tambolis are pawn-sellers, and the Kâyastas are of the writer-caste.

III.—The Vaisya Castes.

These constitute the chief portion of the trading community in Mysore as in other parts of India.

1. *Komati.*

This is the highest in rank among the Vaisyas, and is divided into four clans, namely:—

1. Yaramanta.	3. Kannada Komati.
2. Tuppada Komati.	4. Myâda (*b*).

(*a*) Gazetteer of Mysore and Coorg, Vol. I, p. 325.
(*b*) *Ibid*, 328.

The Komatis practise the pernicious custom of cousins intermarrying, which is the established rule of the caste. The four clans eat together, and intermarry.

2. *Gujerâti.*

Traders in jewels and cloths; they are also money-lenders. The caste originally came from Gujerât.

3. *Marwâri.*

Traders from Marwâr, who deal in silks and cloths of many kinds, in embroidered stuffs, and in pearls. Many are of the Jain religion.

4. *Agarwâla.*

Traders from Northern India.

5. *Multâni.*

Traders from Mooltân, in the Punjab.

6. *Nagarta.*

These are partly traders and partly agriculturists. Brahmans and Komatis refuse to allow them the rank of Vaisya. The caste is divided into two clans, namely:—

1. Nâmâdhâri.	2. Sivâchâr.

These clans hold no social intercourse with each other. The Nâmadhâris are worshippers of Vishnu; and the Sivâchârs, of Siva. The latter have a sub-clan, called Bheri, inhabiting the district of Bangalore, and holding no communion with other members of the caste.

7. *Lâdar.*

Mahratta traders. They wear the sacred thread, and lay claim to the rank of Kshatriyas; but their claim is not generally acknowledged.

IV.—THE SUDRA CASTES.

The Sudra castes are twenty-two in number, each of which is commonly subdivided into several clans:—

1. *Vokkaligara, or Kunbi.*

These are the most numerous of all the Sudras, and number one million, one hundred and ninety thousand persons, who are scattered over the entire province. They are, for the most part, cultivators, yet many are engaged in a great variety of avocations, and all have a reputation for honesty and fidelity. Some of the castes eat animal food, while others abstain from it. The Dâsaris, or mendicants, who worship Vishnu, and wear a peculiar dress, will not eat such food. Generally, however, the Vokkaligaras will eat fish and mutton; and some of the lowest in rank will even eat pigs. They worship a great many deities, and are ignorant and superstitious, though mild and simple. Their widows are permitted to remarry, 'the children of their late husbands inheriting their property' (*a*).

The Vokkaligaras have the following subdivisions:—

The Vokkaligara Clans.

1. Gangadikâra.	19. Nâduvar.	37. Gampala Kammeru.
2. Kove.	20. Banderu.	38. Gosangi.
3. Uppina Koliga.	21. Kusali.	39. Musuku Wakliga.
4. Swalpa.	22. Râjapuri.	40. Kambavalli.
5. Hema Reddi.	23. Hanama.	41. Morasu Wakliga.
6. Motáti.	24. Singadavaru.	42. Sankara Jâti.
7. Jotradava.	25. Yelumaneyavaru.	43. Sanna Kodu.
8. Arvediga.	26. Yelanâti.	44. Gangi Wakliga.
9. Ajamâra.	27. Kodati.	45. Hallikâra.
10. Malava.	28. Pâkinâti Reddi.	46. Hale Wakkalu.
11. Maniga.	29. Yettina Kunchitiga.	47. Kâma Wakkalu.
12. Nâmadhâri.	30. Tanda Gauda.	48. Kunchitiga.
13. Tuluva.	31. Maddera.	49. Lâlagunda.
14. Angalika.	32. Megada.	50. Devan Maklu.
15. Kûli Bedaga.	33. Holakalavaru.	51. Nonaba.
16. Pandâru.	34. Dasavantige.	52. Reddi.
17. Boggaru.	35. Roddagâru.	53. Samudra Kula.
18. Male Gauda.	36. Alamatti.	54. Kammevâr (*b*).

These clans only intermarry among their own people, yet eat and drink together without distinction. "The Gangadikâras and Nonaba Wakligas are, doubtless, the representatives of indigenous tribes who formed the subjects of the Gangavâdi and Nonambavâdi provinces, which occupied the greater part of Mysore up to the twelfth century. The Gangadikâras are found principally in the Ashtagram Division, in which quarter Gangavâdi was situated. Nonambavâdi was the north and west of the Chittledroog district. Gubbi in Tûm-

(*a*) Descriptive Sketch of the various Tribes and Castes of Mysore, by Mr. S. B. Krishnaswamy Iyengar.
(*b*) Gazetteer of Mysore and Coorg, Vol. I, p. 338.

kûr district claims to have been founded by the hereditary chief of the Nonaba Wakligas. The Morasu Wakliga are most numerous in the Nundydroog Division" (*a*). A singular custom prevails among one branch of this tribe, of amputating the two smallest fingers of the right hand of a girl before her betrothal.

2. *Kuruba.*

These are shepherds, and in number come next to the Vokkaligaras, having a population of three hundred and seventy-one thousand persons. The Kurubas are divided into two great branches:—

Principal Branches.

1. Hande Kuruba.	2. Kurubas Proper.

These branches are split up into the following clans:—

Kuruba Clans.

1. Heggade.	5. Sangama Kula.	10. Dhanaga.
2. Aidu-Varahâda-Sûla.	6. Beddala Kula.	11. Kambali Kuruba.
3. Nâgara Kula.	7. Attikankana.	12. Kaukaiyana Jâti.
4. Sâvanti Kula.	8. Hâlu Kuruba.	13. Bandâ Nûliru.
	9. Hande Kuruba.	

The caste worships Junjappa, a box supposed to contain the garments worn by Krishna (*b*).

3. *Agasa, or Asaga.*

Washermen. The caste has an hereditary right to bear a torch before images and great officers in public processions. The Agasas have two divisions. The first has two branches, according to nationality, namely:—

1. Kannada Agasa.	2. Telugu Agasa.

The second division is three-fold, thus:—

1. Madivâli.	2. Mailiga.	3. Mâchiya.

These washermen chiefly worship Ubbe, or the steam issuing from the boiling water in which the clothes are steeped. It is said that animals are sacrificed to Ubbe, in order to preserve the clothes from burning (*c*).

4. *Besta, Kabbara, Gange Makkalu, Toriya, Ambiga, or Parivâra.*

Fishermen and palankeen-bearers. They are called differently according

(*a*) Gazetteer of Mysore and Coorg, Vol. I, p. 338.

(*b*) *Ibid*, pp. 333, 334.

(*c*) *Ibid*, p. 330.

to the districts they inhabit, and correspond in many respects to the Kahârs of Northern India. Many leave the special pursuit of the caste and engage in other avocations, such as weaving, cotton-spinning, lime-burning, and agriculture, while some are employed in the lower grades of the Government service.

The clans of the tribe are the following :—

Besta Clans.

1. Ray Râvuta.	5. Bojoru.	9. Pârigitta.
2. Chammadi.	6. Maleboi.	10. Channavarasiga.
3. Kolavar.	7. Toriya.	11. Ambiga.
4. Kabbar, or Gange Makkalu.	8. Parivâra.	12. Kâru.

These clans can eat and drink together, but intermarriage is only practised between families in friendly alliance with one another (*a*).

5. *Bedar, Nayak, Kirâtaka, Bârika, or Kannaiya.*

These are properly hunters, but many are agriculturists, village police, and Government servants. They are dark in colour, tall in stature, and warlike in disposition. Their dress is a kind of close-fitting trousers and leathern cap. Formerly, many were employed as soldiers. In this capacity they were employed by Hyder Ali in his invasion of the Carnatic, and in the subjugation of the Poligars. It is said that the Poligars of Mysore consist largely of Bedars (*b*).

The Bedars are partly Karnâtas and partly Telingas, which two races abstain from all social intercourse with each other. The clans of the caste are as follows :—

Bedar Clans.

1. Kirataka.	5. Muchala-mire.	9. Settiyâla.
2. Yanamaloru.	6. Sabara.	10. Anchâla.
3. Râyapâlya.	7. Gujjâra.	11. Paluvyâdha.
4. Kannaiyana Jâti.	8. Bârika.	12. Myâsa Bedar.

6. *Golla, or Yâkula.*

Cowherds and herdsmen. These are a numerous community, corresponding to the Gwâlas and Ahîrs of Northern India. They are separated into two great branches, which do not intermarry. These are—

1. The Gollas.	The Uru Gollas.

(*a*) Gazetteer of Mysore and Coorg, Vol. I, p. 330.

(*b*) Sketch of the Tribes and Castes of Mysore, by Mr. S. B. Kristnasawmy Iyengar.

The clans are much less numerous than in the north, and are apparently much in mutual intercourse. They are the following :—

Golla Clans.

1. Yâkula, or Yâdavakula.
2. Kilâri.
3. Kâvadiga.
4. Kadu Golla.
5. Kuri Golla.
6. Gopâla.
7. Nanda Vamsika.

The Gollas are chiefly found in the Nundydroog Division and Chittledroog District. In Chittledroog and Kolar they bear the name of Yâkula. This caste was once 'largely employed in transporting money, both public and private, from one part of the country to another ;' and was famous for its great integrity in doing so (*a*).

7. *Banajiga.*

These are traders, merchants, agriculturists, bricklayers, carpenters, manufacturers of glass bangles, lime-burners, musicians, and dancers. Most of the clans eat meat and drink spirits, but one of them, variously styled Balegara, Devâdiga, and Bannagar, abstains from both. Many dancing-girls of the temples are of this caste. Its clans are numerous, and are the following:—

Banajiga Clans.

1. Nâmadhâri Malura.
2. Aravattu-wokala-setti.
3. Râjabanna.
4. Bidâra.
5. Pasaluvâte.
6. Telugu Banajiga.
7. Gauri Kulam.
8. Vaduga.
9. Mutta Râju.
10. Devâdiga.
11. Chiravalu.
12. Râjabandar.
13. Yale Banajiga.
14. Dâsa Banajiga.
15. Naidu.
16. Kavare.
17. Gopatiga.

The most important of these clans are the Dâsa, Yale, and Gopatiga. Many of the women of the Naidu and Kavare clans have received some education, and are able to read and write (*b*).

8. *Darji.*

These belong to the same caste as the Dirzis of Northern India. They are tailors ; some, however, are calico printers. Their clans are as follows:—

Darji Clans.

1. Ashtaghar.
2. Simpi, or Chippiga.
3. Nâmadev.
4. Rangâre (*c*).

(*a*) Gazetteer of Mysore and Coorg, Vol. I, p. 332.
(*b*) *Ibid*, p. 331.
(*c*) *Ibid*, p. 332.

9. *Goniga.*

Sack-weavers and makers of gunny-bags. Some of the caste are agriculturists and labourers. The caste is chiefly found in the Nundydroog Division. They are divided into three clans, namely:—

1. Janaba.	2. Sanapa.	3. Sâdu Vamsasta (*a*).

10. *Ganiga and Jotipan.*

These are oil-expressers and general traders in oil, and are divided into various clans according to the precise occupation they follow :—

Ganiga Clans.

1. Heggâniga, who yoke two oxen to their stone oilmill, and wear the sacred cord after marriage.
2. Kirgâniga, who express oil in wooden mills.
3. Ontiyettu Gâniga, who yoke only animal to their mill.
4. Yeune Telugaru, who clarify oil.

The Gânigas worship Shaivite and Vishnuvite deities, but pay especial homage to their oilmills (*b*). Some of the castes are employed as cultivators.

11. *Gudikâra.*

These are turners and carvers, and have acquired considerable reputation for their beautiful workmanship in sandal-wood. They are Mahrattas, and are chiefly found in the Sorab subdivision of the Shimoga District (*c*).

12. *Idiga and Halepaika.*

Toddy-makers. They are numerous all over the province, except in Kolar and Bangalore. "They worship all the Hindu deities, also Saktis, or evil spirits; and especially adore pots containing toddy. The hereditary occupation of the caste is to extract the juice of palm-trees, and to distil spirits from it. They are also agriculturists, particularly in the Shimoga District. In the Nagar Division, they are known as Halepaika; and were formerly employed as soldiers under the Pâlegârs. They eat animal food, but are prohibited from drinking toddy or spirits even of their own manufacture—a prohibition which,

(*a*) Gazetteer of Mysore and Coorg, Vol. I, p. 332.
(*b*) *Ibid.*
(*c*) *Ibid.*

it is needless to say, is seldom regarded. The following are the subdivisions of the caste :—

Idiga Clans.

1. Sânâr.	5. Mombal.	8. Pangadavaru.
2. Badderu.	6. Hâlperî.	9. Bella Reddi.
3. Sâsimore.	7. Hombâliga.	10. Halepaika or Halepaiki (*a*).
4. Dîvar.		

13. *Kumbâra.*

Potters and indigo-dyers. The caste is the same as the Kumbârs of Northern India, with this difference, that in Mysore the potters and indigo-dyers belong to one caste, whereas in the north they form two distinct castes. They are of two races however in Mysore—Telugus and Karnâtas—who do not intermarry. The Kumbâras pay especial religious homage to the kiln (*b*).

14. *Neyiga.*

Weavers. Most of the caste pursue this avocation in some form. A few are cultivators and labourers. The entire caste is devoted to the worship of Vishnu ; and their *gurus*, or religious teachers, 'are hereditary chiefs of Sri Vaishnava Brahmans of the Tâtâchâr and Bhattrâchâr families.' Their clans are fourteen in number.

Neyiga Clans.

1. Sakunsâle. This clan and the next are Telingas ; but, as they belong to two distinct religious sects, they do not intermarry. 'The Sakunsâles worship Siva, and wear his symbol, the *linga*. Their sacred book is the Sâlesvâra Purâna, and contains the doctrines peculiar to the sect. This book all the Sakunsâles may read.

2. Padmasâle. These are now worshippers of Vishnu, but are said to have been originally Shaivites.

3. Iâda.

4. Kuruvina.

5. Settigâra.

6. Bilimagga. These assert that they are properly Banajigas, and style themselves Kuruvina Banajigaru. They are a Carnatic tribe, and are divided into *gotras*, with the same customs regarding affinity of marriages as Brahmans.'

(*a*) Gazetteer of Mysore and Coorg, Vol. I., p. 333.
(*b*) *Ibid.*

7. Devânga. Weavers, some of whom, the Karnataka Devângas, wear the *linga* of Siva; the others, or the Telugu Devângas, abstain from this decoration.

8. Seniga. These speak Canarese, and originally came from the Lower Carnatic. They are a wealthy class.

9. Togata. Telinga weavers, who manufacture very coarse cloth, such as is worn by the humbler castes.

10. Revanakara.

11. Kaikal.

12. Patvegâr. Silk weavers, speaking a dialect of Mahratti. "They worship all the Hindu deities, especially Saktis, or evil spirits, to whom they offer a goat as sacrifice on the night of the Dasara festival, a Mahomedan officiating as slaughterer, for which he receives certain fees. After the sacrifice, the family of the Patvegâra partake of the flesh. The caste have the reputation of being filthy in their habits" (*a*).

13. Katri. Silk weavers. Their habits and manners correspond to those of the Patvegârs. The two clans eat together, but do not intermarry. The Katris pretend to be of Kshatriya origin. They are chiefly found in the Bangalore and Chittledroog Districts.

14. Jamakhânavâlâ, or Patnûbâlâ. These are immigrants from the Madras Presidency, where they are known by the latter designation. They manufacture woollen carpets of excellent fabric. Some are cotton and silk weavers (*b*).

15. *Mochi.*

Workers in leather, tanners, shoemakers, harnessmakers, and so forth. Great numbers of this caste are scattered about Northern India, where they are generally called Châmârs, and are divided into seven sub-castes (*c*). In Mysore, as elsewhere, they eat animal food, drink spirits, and are commonly regarded as a low-caste race. Probably they are a mixture of aboriginal and outcast Hindu tribes. In Mysore they worship the goddess Durga (*d*).

16. *Nâyinda, or Hajâma.*

Barbers and musicians. They speak both Canarese and Telugu. Some

(*a*) Gazetteer of Mysore and Coorg, Vol. I, p. 335.

(*b*) *Ibid*, pp. 334—336.

(*c*) The Author's "Hindu Tribes and Castes," Vol. I, pp. 391—395.

(*d*) Sketch of the Tribes and Castes of Mysore, by Mr. S. B. Kristnasawmy Iyengar.

of them are Lingayats. They have Brahmans for their priests. The caste has the following clans :—

Nâyinda Clans.

1. Kelasi.	3. Mann Karnâtaka.
2. Nâvûn.	4. Konda Mangala (*a*).

17. *Natva.*

Dancers. These Natvas are probably the same as the Nats of Northern India. Mr. Rice says, that they can scarcely be called a distinct caste, as many persons from various castes join the fraternity. The females of the caste lead an immodest life. Those attached to temples are known as Devadâsis and Basavis. The caste has the following subdivisions:—

Natva Clans.

1. Kaikola.	3. Kunda Golaka.	5. Natvânga.
2. Basavi.	4. Naikasâni.	6. Devadâsi (*b*).

18. *Sâdar.*

These are Dhârwar Sudras, and consist of Nâmadhâris, Sivâchârs, and Jains. They are chiefly engaged in agriculture.

19. *Uppâra, Uppâliga, and Melusakkare.*

The chief occupation of the caste is the production of salt, nevertheless some of its members are employed as bricklayers, builders, agriculturists, and labourers. It is divided into two sections, the Karnâtaka and Telugu Uppâras.

20. *Waddar.*

Stonemasons, tankdiggers, wellsinkers, and so forth. They are a hard-working people, but have a bad reputation for rendering assistance to highwaymen and robbers. The Waddars are prone to take several wives. "The marriage ceremony is not a tedious one : it consists of the bride and bridegroom walking three times round a stake placed for the purpose in the ground. Re-marriage of widows and divorced women is permitted. The men and women of the caste eat together" (*c*). The Waddars are divided into two branches :

1. Kallu, or Stone Waddas.	2. Mannu, or Earth Waddas.

(*a*) Gazetteer of Mysore and Coorg, Vol. I, p. 334.
(*b*) *Ibid*, p. 336.
(*c*) *Ibid*, p. 337.

The clans of the caste are as follows :—

Waddar Clans.

1. Boja.	3. Kallu Wadda.	5. Bailu Wadda (*a*)
2. Yattinavaru.	4. Mannu Wadda.	

21. *Tigala, or Palli.*

These include the Vanne-kula and Nâmadhâri Halepaika, and are divided into the Ulli Palli and Vanne Palli sects, which hold no social intercourse with each other. They are market-gardeners, and are found, for the most part, in the Nundydroog Division (*b*).

22. *Modali and Pille.*

These are traders, contractors, and the like. Many of them are well educated, and are in the employment of the Government. Not a few of the women of the caste are able to read and write. The caste has a subdivision called Agamudi (*c*).

V.—Marka, Hale Kannadiga, or Hale Karnataka Caste.

This caste lays claim to the rank and dignity of Brahmans, but the claim is disallowed by the Brahmanical community. They do not worship the sun. Their chief object of adoration is the Hindu triad. Most of the fraternity, however, are Vishnavites. The designation of Marka is regarded by the caste as one of reproach. It is probable that the Markas are an outcast race of Brahmans. They are addicted to agriculture, yet many of them are village accountants and Government servants (*d*).

VI.—The Lingayat Tribe.

The term Lingayat designates a large class of people of certain religious tenets, who are found not merely in Mysore, but also in Dharwar, Canara, and in many other districts of Southern India. In Mysore they are very numerous, and have numerous subdivisions, which do not intermarry, and keep altogether separate one from another. They are devotedly attached to the worship of Shiva; and wear his emblem, in gold or silver, or other metal, or perhaps in stone, enclosed in a casket, or wrapped up in cloth, or naked, tied to the neck. They are an industrious people, and trade in grain, spices, and other productions.

(*a*) Gazetteer of Mysore and Coorg, Vol. I, p. 337.
(*b*) *Ibid.*
(*c*) *Ibid.*
(*d*) *Ibid*, pp. 341, 342.

The Lingayats resemble devotees in several important respects. In addition to the peculiarity respecting the wearing of the *lingam* just alluded to, they exhibit another, which is only practised among Hindus by persons of strong religious pretensions,—namely, that of burying their dead, instead of burning them. At the burial, all the friends and kindred of the deceased assemble around the body, and partake of food together previously to its interment. When one of their *gurûs*, or priest, dies, he is buried in a temple, and his tomb henceforth becomes an object of worship. These people drink no spirits, and eat no animal food. Their women have a reputation for great beauty.

The tribe is divided into the following branches:—

Subdivisions of the Lingayats.

1. Janagonda.	8. Pâvaliyoru.	15 Arâdya (*a*).
2. Basale.	9. Wâra Bande.	16. Virabhande.
3. Bâvani.	10. Sajjana.	17. Kambe.
4. Gâvaniga.	11. Silavanta.	18. Hiri Hasube.
5. Naradi.	12. Tamadi.	19. Linga Banajiga.
6. Nâgalika.	13. Koriyavaru.	20. Gauda Lingayat.
7. Aidugadayadavaru.	14. Panchamsâle.	21. Gurikâra.

The Linga Banajigas are the most important of these subdivisions.

VII.—The Panchala, or Artisan Castes.

These castes are five in number, as the word *panchala* indicates. They are as follows:—

1. Agasâla, or goldsmiths, who are at the head of the Panchalas.
2. Bogâra, or Kanchugara—Brass and copper-smiths.
3. Kammar, or Lohâr—Ironsmiths.
4. Badagi—Carpenters.
5. Kallu Kutaka—Stoneworkers.

The following are the subdivisions of the Panchalas:—

Panchala Subdivisions.

1. Oja.	6. Fattari.	12. Jatagâra.
2. Badagi.	7. Sonâr or Sonagâra.	13. Silpi, or Kallukutâka.
3. Gejjegâra.	8. Tavaradoru.	14. Visvakarma.
4. Lohar.	9. Hanatâru.	15. Agasâle.
5. Maya.	10. Gampala Kâmmâra.	16. Anekammâra.
	11. Bogâra, or Kanchugâra.	

(*a*) Gazetteer of Mysore and Coorg, Vol. I, p. 341.

The Panchalas wear a sacred triple thread, and, it is said, imagine themselves to be on an equality with Brahmans (*a*).

VIII.—Sects of Devotees and Religious Mendicants.

Many of the sects of devotees and religious mendicants found in Mysore and other parts of Southern India have their representatives in Northern India, of which an account of forty-eight is given in the former volume of "Hindu Tribes and Castes (*b*). There are sects in the south, however, not met with at all in the north. The Mysore Gazetteer contains a list of thirty-seven sects in Mysore, which are as follows:—

1. Kanjâla.
2. Kâdri (a class of Sâtânîs).
3. Pâdasi.
4. Handigada.
5. Renuka Jangam.
6. Renâdu Jangam.
7. Samagi, or Samerâya (a class of Sâtânîs).
8. Suragi (a class of Sâtânîs).
9. Handiclûkaru.
10. Demangala.
11. Pândâs, or Panasumakkalu or Hale-makkalu.
12. Kutuma.
13. Kulasekhara (a class of Sâtânîs).
14. Aneganti Battela.
15. Gogangi
16. Jogi.
17. Kasavarâjulu.
18. Maçlâri
19. Solâre.
20. Budabudike.
21. Bairâgi.
22. Dâsari.
23. Domba.
24. Gûradiga.
25. Gondaliga.
26. Gosâyi.
27. Helava, or Pichukunte.
28. Pâkinâti Jogi.
29. Wader, or Charanti.
30. Sillekyâta.
31. Sudugâdu.
32. Sidda.
33. Sâtâni.
34. Virakta (Lingayat).
35. Jangaliga.
36. Battaru.
37. Gorava (*c*).

IX.—The Inferior Castes.

The Mysore Gazetteer gives a list of forty-four of these castes, which are designated 'outcasts.' The chief of these are the Holaya, the lowest of the right-hand castes, and the Mâdiga, the lowest of the left-hand castes.

X.—Wandering Tribes.

These are as follows :—

1. Bandikâra.
2. Medar or Gauriga.
3. Lambâni.
4. Brinjâri.
5. Sukâliga.
6. Tambûri.
7. Sabbâvat.
8. Dâdi.
9. Khetâvat.
10. Bhûtya.
11. Râmâvatpâda.
12. Dhûmâvatpâda (*d*).
13. Kyataiyanajâti.
14. Koraga.
15. Korama.
16. Koracha.

(*a*) Gazetteer of Mysore and Coorg, Vol. I, pp. 342, 343.
(*b*) Hindu Tribes and Castes, pp. 255—270.
(*c*) Gazetteer of Mysore and Coorg, Vol. I, p. 343.
(*d*) *Ibid*, p. 348.

The Lambânis are a migratory race living in the forests of Mysore. "When there were few or no roads," says Mr. S. B. Kristnaswamy Iyengar, "they carried grain and salt from place to place on oxen, as also bamboos and firewood on their own heads. They are numerous in the western districts of Mysore. They were formerly considered as suppliers of grain to armies; and their value in this respect is often mentioned in the Mysore despatches of the late Duke of Wellington. But they are, properly speaking, a predatory tribe. The formation of good, grand, and cross roads all over India impeded their trade to the greatest imaginable extent; and now they act as coolies, and sometimes resort to plunder. Their women are peculiarly clad and decorated. The hand and finger rings, bangles and bracelets, worn by them, and the rows of flowers and balls which are suspended from their hair, are made of a kind of white bone resembling ivory. Their dirty dress is chiefly composed of thick aprons, interwoven with black and red coarse cotton thread and rude needlework, suspended from the waist downwards, and also a boddice made of the same material. The men wear tight breeches, coming a little below the knees; and cover their heads with coarse turbans. They are considered by other castes as churlish in their disposition. They eat both vegetable and animal food, such as rice, beans, mutton, and fowls, and in fine all that can be got in the shape of animal food in the jungles. They are generally upwards of five feet and-a-half in height, and speak a peculiar dialect of their own" (*a*).

The Korachars carry salt and grain from one market to another. They are said to be thieves and robbers from childhood.

XI.—Tribes inhabiting the jungles.

These probably are, for the most part, descendants of aboriginal tribes. Little seems to be known respecting them. According to the last census the population of seven tribes amounted to between sixteen and seventeen thousand persons. The tribes are twelve in number—

1. Iraliga. These are the most numerous, and form a community of more than six thousand persons. They resemble the Jenu Kurubas.

2. Betta or Hill Kuruba, or Kâdu or Jungle Kuruba. A diminutive race, five feet two inches in height, but very active, and capable of enduring great fatigue, living in the forests on the south-west of Mysore, and among the hills at the foot of the Neilgherries.

(*a*) Descriptive Sketch of the Tribes and Castes of Mysore, by Mr. S. B. Kristnaswamy Iyengar.

3. Jenu Kuruba. They are darker than the Bettas, and lower in civilization, and hold with them no social intercourse. These people collect honey and beeswax.

4. Soliga. These speak old Canarese, and inhabit the Biligirirangan hills on the south-east of Mysore. "They live in small communities of six or seven huts in the dense parts of the forests, and cultivate with the hoe small patches of ground. They avoid strangers as much as possible ; and seldom visit the low country except when they have occasion to procure supplies, when one of their number is sent off to the nearest village to purchase whatever is required for the whole community. Owing to their keenness of sight, and skill in tracking animals, they are invaluable aids to any sportsman who visits the hills in search of game" (*a*).

5. Hasular. This tribe resembles the preceding. 'They are a short thick-set race, very dark in colour, and with curled hair.' The Hasulars are fellers of timber, and inhabit the ghauts on the north-west of Mysore.

6. Yerava. These have African features, thick lips, and compressed noses.

7. Bilva. They inhabit Vastara, and live by collecting forest produce, and by extracting toddy from the palm.

8. Paniyar. A small community in the Mysore District.

9. Malasa.

10. Arikâra

11. Malâru.

12. Masâlar (*b*).

XII.—The Mahomedan Tribes.

These are Arabs, Persians, Afghans, Dakhani Mussalmans, Labbe, Mâpile, and Pindâris or Kâkars, and number two hundred and eight thousand persons in all, of whom two hundred and two thousand are Dakhani Mussalmans (*c*).

(*a*) Gazetteer of Mysore and Coorg, Vol. I, p. 351.

(*b*) *Ibid*, p. 350.

(*c*) *Ibid*, p. 352.

CHAPTER VII.

TRIBES OF THE NEILGHERRY HILLS.

Sec. I.—The Toda or Todawar Tribe. Sec. II—The Kota Tribe. Sec. III.—The Burgher, Badaga, or Vadaga Tribe. Sec. IV.—The Irula Tribe.

Section I.—The Toda or Todawar Tribe.

The Neilgherries have a superficies of about six or seven hundred square miles; and their extreme central altitude is eight thousand, seven hundred and sixty feet. All persons who have carefully investigated the question are agreed that the Todas are the earliest known inhabitants of these hills. It is certain that they have resided on them for many ages; and that all other tribes now found there have migrated to the hills subsequently to their possession by the Todas. Indeed, this tribe claims proprietorship over them by right of prior occupancy; and endeavours to enforce the payment of tribute from the other tribes for permission to dwell in its neighbourhood.

Although the Todas may be regarded in one sense as aborigines of the Neilgherries, yet signs of an earlier race are abundant. Numerous cairns are scattered about the summits of the hills, of which the Todas know nothing. "They are sometimes single," says Captain Ochterlony, who in 1847 made a minute examination of some of them, "but more frequently in groups or rows of from three to six. They are singular in form, raised with large unhewn blocks of stone, four feet or more above the level of the ground, and varying in diameter from twelve or fifteen feet to twenty-five or thirty. The interior is hollowed out to some depth below the original surface, usually until the solid rock is reached; and the space thus cleared filled with earthen pots, with the covers strongly luted on, pieces of bone, charcoal, and fragments of pottery, all tightly packed in a soil so black and finely pulverized, as to give cause to suppose it to be decomposed animal matter. On breaking these pots or urns, which many of them are in the form of, they are found to contain ashes, charcoal, and pieces of half calcined bones, with sometimes a small quantity of a pure scentless fluid, which in two instances I found to be pure water slightly impregnated with lime. Images of tigers, elks, bisons, leopards, and some domestic animals, pieces of half-decomposed bronze resembling spearheads, tripods, &c., are also found occasionally mixed with the other remains. But it is a singular fact that, on breaking up the strong pavement of slabs of stone with which the cairns are covered in, and mining down until a second pavement is come upon, which from its tightness and weight has, to all appearance, never been disturbed since it was first laid, we find, on removing it, that the contents of the vault below, instead of being laid in the order befitting the repose of consecrated ashes, are generally smashed, and broken up, and mixed with the soil, leaving barely one or two pots of bones and ashes entire, just as though the pickaxe of the destroying explorer had been already there" (*a*). The Todas permit these cairns to be opened and destroyed without any interference on their part; which they certainly would not do were they conscious of any historical connexion with them.

While there are important points of resemblance between the Todas and the builders of the cairns, there are also important points of difference between them. Both are alike in the respect they pay to the buffalo, in the sacred reverence with which they regard the bell it wears, and in their funeral obsequies. But they differ considerably in their civilization. The Todas are far behind their predecessors in their knowledge of agriculture, and are inferior also in the skill exhibited in their stone erections in memory of the dead (*b*).

Lieutenant-Colonel Marshall, in his amusing volume, 'A Phrenologist among the Todas,' has some interesting and discriminating remarks on the characteristics of this singular people. "The Toda talking voice," he observes, "is peculiar, particularly that of the women. Whilst on the part of the men it is strikingly grave and sedate, spoken almost *sotto voce*, the women's voice, on the contrary, is rather high, appearing to come altogether from the region at the back of the ear, the 'mastoid process.' In both sexes, but particularly with the female, the sound of the voice is somewhat musical and refined, though fatiguing to listen to from its monotonous tone. Indeed, it is somewhat astonishing that some harsh syllables of their language should come so softly from such mouths. The refinement arises, doubtless, from the gentleness of their dispositions, void of asperity, and friendliness, accompanied by desire to please—not from any innate sense of tune, for they have no more ear for music than so

(*a*) Geographical and Statistical Memoir of a Survey of the Neilgherry Mountains, by Captain J. Ochterlony. Madras Journal of Literature and Science. Vol. XV, pp. 79, 80.

(*b*) A Phrenologist among the Todas, by Lieutenant-Colonel W. E. Marshall, Bengal Staff Corps, p. 9.

many crows" (*a*). Again, "the general type of the Toda character is most unvarying; singularly frank, affable, and self-possessed, cheerful, yet staid: respectful, seemingly from a sense of conscious inferiority rather than from an active principle: fearless, from small cause for fear more than from the stimulus of a latent power of oppositeness: communicative, yet watchful and shy, as if their natures impelled them to divulge what their natures also prompted them to maintain quiet: willing to take money, yet accepting what is proffered with callousness, allowing it to lie on the ground, or their children to play with it" (*b*). "They are intelligent within limits. Although they take contracted views of things, yet they work and act within the circumscribed limits of their mental vision with great steadiness, intelligence, and some sense" (*c*).

The Todas are a fine, well proportioned powerful people, with large and sometimes aquiline nose and receding forehead; and in physique are much superior to all the other hill tribes. Although so manly in appearance, they are nevertheless indolent and useless, being disinclined to work of every description. Their sole labour is of a pastoral character, and consists in watching their herds of cattle, milking the kine, and manufacturing ghee, or clarified butter. They are capable of much endurance, and possessing a splendid physique and great natural strength, might, if properly educated and trained, become a noble race. As it is, however, they are the most useless of human beings. Their bodies are enwrapped in one long garment: their heads are uncovered; their hair, both of head and beard, is uncut: they are copper-coloured in complexion; their women being somewhat fairer than the men, and often tall and handsome. Many Todas have a Jewish expression of countenance; but in carriage and dignity they are more like to ancient Romans. The women decorate themselves with massive and very beautiful gold and silver necklaces, and wear their hair flowing over their shoulders. Sometimes it is curled up with short sticks. They are accustomed to tatoo with black dye their necks, hands, and legs in the imitation of jewellery. Their marriage rites are simple, consisting of reciprocal offices and the bestowal of presents by the intended husband.

The Rev. Dr. Caldwell, in the Appendix to his work on the Dravidian languages, has shown that the language of the Todas is essentially Dravidian, and is more nearly allied to Tamil than to any other dialect. He also considers

(*a*) A Phrenologist among the Todas, by Lieutenant-Colonel W. E. Marshall, Bengal Staff Corps, p. 41.

(*b*) *Ibid*, p. 45.

(*c*) *Ibid*, p. 46.

that notwithstanding the peculiar physical types which the race presents, it is, like its language, of Dravidian origin.

The Todas live in villages situated in the western division of the hills, in a tract called Todanaad, as here the larger portion of the Todas reside. "The sites chosen are in general most picturesque; always adjacent to a wood, and usually on an open space of grass almost completely embosomed in it; and extending in gentle slopes covered with the richest turf, which the grazing of their cattle, and the consequent manuring, maintains in the finest order. Their huts are low-arched buildings, resembling a haycock, but admirably contrived to keep out rain and cold, the roof and side walls forming one continuous curve of split bamboos, rattan, and thatch; having an end-wall strongly built, and a front wall with one small opening or door in it, so small indeed that the inhabitants have to crawl on their hands and knees to enter by it" (*a*).

Although the Todas have their villages (which consist only of a few huts), yet they are not content to remain permanently in them, but shift from one to another according to inclination. The tribe only numbers a few hundred persons; and there is great fear of its soon becoming extinct. They have a language said to be peculiar to themselves; but in reality it is a dialect of Canarese. They live in apparent comfort, their means of subsistence being abundant. A small tax is levied on them by the Government for every female buffalo in their possession, the males being free; and also for the grazing land on which their cattle feed.

The Todas are a peaceable and unwarlike people; and it is highly improbable that they took possession of the country in which they are found by forcible means. They carry no weapons of offence or defence whatever, and wander among the hills infested by wild animals in perfect fearlessness, and in absolute contempt of danger. They shun violent exercise, and neither fight, dance nor box. They do not hunt, either for food or pleasure. They have no implements of agriculture, and consequently do not till the soil. The grain eaten by them is received from the Burghers and other vassal tribes. "Their moral fearlessness of character," says Lieut.-Colonel Ross King, who has studied these hill tribes with great care, "with its accompanying consciousness of power, is felt and acknowledged by all the other tribes, who voluntarily bow to an influence they can neither cope with nor emulate" (*b*). The Todas are

(*a*) Geographical and Statistical Memoir of a Survey of the Neilgherry Mountains, by Captain J. Ochterlony. Madras Journal of Literature and Science, Vol. XV, p. 48.

(*b*) The Aboriginal Tribes of the Neilgherry Hills, by Lieut.-Colonel W. Ross King, p. 16, 17.

greatly attached to their buffaloes, which they never kill, but keep solely for their milk. On returning from the fields in the evening these animals are saluted with much respect by their masters. Some buffaloes are held as sacred, and are never milked, but roam about with their calves at pleasure. The Todas have a repugnance to the dog, which is never seen in their huts or *munds*, that is, their small villages.

The tribe is divided into five very distinct clans, or even six, but about the last there are some doubts. These clans are as follows :—

The Toda Clans.

1. Peiki.	4. Kenna.
2. Pekkan.	5. Todi.
3. Kuttan.	6. Taral (?)

The Peikies are regarded as highest in rank. These clans are socially quite distinct, and do not intermarry. They all practise polyandry, one woman being the wife of all the brothers of a family, with each of whom she lives a month at a time. The children are distributed among her husbands according to seniority, 'the eldest of the brothers being considered the father of the first child, and so on.' A family, however, seldom consists of more than two or three children. Formerly, when the tribe was not under British supervision, only one female child was allowed to survive in each household; the rest, when born, were destroyed (*a*). The marriage ceremony is of striking simplicity. The bridegrooms in succession place first their right feet, and then their left, on the head of the bride, and then order her to fetch water for cooking, which having done, the ceremony is at an end.

Respecting their religious sentiments, "the Todas believe in the existence of an invisible and supreme spirit and in a future state ; though this they seem to regard as one of a somewhat mundane character, inasmuch as buffaloes and abundance of milk are to be the portion of the faithful. They also pay reverence to inferior objects, such as hills, and forests, and the rising sun, precisely as did the ancient Celts. In connexion with the adoration of light, they also make an obeisance to their evening lamps on lighting them." (*b*).

The tribe has seven small sacred buildings, which are the abode of their principal priests, called Pulâl or milkman, and Kavilâl or herdsman, and are at a distance from their villages, having a temple attached to each. Three of

(*a*) The Tribes inhabiting the Neilgherry Hills, by the Rev. F. Metz, pp. 15, 16.

(*b*) Aboriginal Tribes of the Neilgherry Hills, by Lieut.-Col. W. Ross King, p. 21.

them have been entirely deserted, and a fourth is rarely visited. A herd of sacred buffaloes is kept at the other three for the use of the priests, who are regarded as very holy personages. In addition, every *mund* or village has its own priest. A hearse is also used in some of the larger villages for religious purposes. Rangaswâmi is held in great veneration by all these hill-tribes. He is worshipped on the Rangaswâmi peak. "The only emblems of the deity on it are a few rude stones and iron tridents, fixed in the ground, and surrounded by a low circular wall of loose stone, with a couple of large iron-pans in it. The peak is also celebrated for a cavern on the north declivity containing holy earth, in request by Brahmans and other castes. Much of it is carried away by pilgrims to different parts, who come here during the annual festivals" (*a*). The Todas worship the sacred Buffalo-bell, a bell generally of great antiquity, which they imagine to be representative of Hiriadeva, or 'chief god.' "Before this Bell libations of milk are poured, and prayers offered, by the priests, by whom alone it is seen or touched. They make a distinction, however, between this deity and the God of the Christian." They likewise worship a hunting god supposed to reside at Nambili Kotay, who is supposed to give them success in killing tigers (*b*). The Todas leave all their religious duties to be performed by the priests. "The only sign of adoration," says Mr. Metz, "I have ever seen them perform, is lifting the right-hand to the forehead and covering the nose with the thumb when entering the sacred dairy; and the words, 'may all be well!' are all that I have ever heard them utter in the form of a prayer" (*c*). The duties of the village priests are simply to milk the buffaloes and perform the labours of the dairy, the holiest duties which, in the opinion of the Todas, a man can perform. "The Toda religion," says Lieut.-Colonel Marshall, "has not the slightest sympathy with idolatry; nor does it pay attention to natural objects, as trees or rivers, to birds, beasts, or reptiles, or the elements. No offerings to a god, whether of flesh, human or animal, or fruit of the soil, are made; no human victims, and no self-torture" (*d*).

The funeral ceremonies of the Todas are singular. The body is burned, and a great feast of slain buffaloes is given. This is termed the 'green funeral.' A twelve-month later a much more important ceremony is held, when a larger

(*a*) Descriptive and Geographical Account of the Neilgherry Hills, by Messrs. Fox and Turnbull. Transactions of the Bombay Geographical Society, Vol. IV.

(*b*) The Tribes inhabiting the Neilgherry Hills, pp. 17, 18.

(*c*) *Ibid*, pp. 29, 30.

(*d*) *Ibid*, p. 188.

number of buffaloes are killed, and friends from the Badaga, Kota, and Kurumba tribes are invited to the feast. This is called the 'dry funeral.'

None of these hill tribes engage in any manufactures, with the exception of the Kotas, who make baskets, rough pottery, and some kinds of agricultural implements and personal ornaments.

Section II.—The Kota Tribes.

The Kotas formerly inhabited the Kollimale, a mountain in Mysore. They now occupy seven considerable villages called in the aggregate Kotagiri, on the Neilgherries. There is little difference between their dialect and that spoken by the Todas. The latter have a deep guttural pronunciation, while the former have a peculiar dental pronunciation.

It is commonly believed that the Kotas are the most ancient inhabitants of the Neilgherries, next to the Todas; but they rank much lower in native opinion, and are nowhere regarded like them as a superior race. They rank indeed with the low caste Pariahs of Southern India; and are unclean and despicable. The two tribes are about equal in number. The Burghers will not drink the water of the streams flowing by their villages

The Kotas differ exceedingly in their habits from the Todas. They wear occasionally a similar dress, yet commonly are seen with 'only a dirty cloth round the loins, and the uncomely women the wrapper of the country.' The Kotas are of very dark, indeed black, complexion, and of thin, spare bodies. "The bare heads of both sexes are shaggy, with matted locks of dusty hair, sometimes tied in a knot behind, and invariably uncombed from the day of their birth. Dirty in their dwellings and persons, they are also unclean feeders, devouring dead cattle, putrid flesh, birds of prey, or vermin, with as much apparent relish as fresh buffalo meat" (*a*). They till the ground, and are very industrious and energetic. The land around their villages is carefully cultivated, and a portion of the grain produced—which should be one-sixth part—is paid to the idle Todas as the lords of the soil. They are also excellent smiths and carpenters. They likewise make baskets, and their wives manufacture earthen pots. In addition, they cure and prepare hides for commerce, in which occupation they are remarkably expert. As these people are a small community, and engage in so many avocations, their lands, which are extensive, are not properly attended to; and consequently a large portion lies waste. Kotas will never, if possible, labour for Europeans, or on the public works.

(*a*) The Aboriginal Tribes of the Neilgherry Hills, by Lieut.-Colonel W. Ross King, p. 34.

Although the members of this tribe set such a meritorious example of industry to the other hill tribes, yet by reason of their filthy and abominable habits and customs they are held by some of them in great contempt. In regard to marriage, the men content themselves with one wife each, and the women with one husband, and thereby set an example which many of the more civilized tribes and castes of India would do well to imitate.

The Kota villages are disordered and dirty; but as the houses, which are chiefly of mud and thatch, are well made, and are somewhat closely compacted together, the villages appear thriving and prosperous. They worship Shiva as a deity called Kamataraga deposited in small shrines covered with thatch, and have separate temples for men and women; but have no separate sacred class. like the Todas, yet each village has a family which performs by hereditary succession the duties of the priesthood. They are great opium-eaters.

Section III.—The Burgher, Badaga, or Vadaga Tribes.

This is the most numerous, enterprising, and intelligent of all the native tribes on the Neilgherries, and is spread over a large portion of that region. Captain Ochterlony computed the entire population of the tribe to amount to between six and seven thousand persons. The Madras Census Report of 1871 gives their number as upwards of nineteen thousand. The word Badaga means 'people of the north,' and hence it is supposed that they came originally from the north, probably the northern part of Mysore and Canara, about four hundred years ago. The people of Talemale, low hills to the north-east of the Neilgherries, regard them as of their own race, and will eat food with them.

The Badagas pay a small tribute to the Todas in acknowledgment of the feudal relations they sustain to this primitive race; and moreover, always treat them with great deference and respect. They devote themselves chiefly to agriculture; but some are employed as labourers and coolies. These people are not noted for industrious habits like the Kotas. The women, however, are laborious, and are more modest than Toda women. Not a few of the Badagas are in prosperous circumstances, and are consequently slothful and indolent. They profess the Shaivite form of the Hindu religion, and are exceedingly ignorant and superstitious. Their principal deity is Rangaswâmi. Their temples are of a simple structure, being made of sun-dried mud, covered with thatch. They worship professedly three hundred and thirty-eight deities. There are traditions abroad that about a century before Hyder Ali held sway in Mysore, the Burghers, Kotas, and other hill tribes were governed by three chiefs, one residing in Todanaad in a fort called Malaycotta, the remains of which are still visible, east of the village of Shûlûrû, and west of Mûtenad and the Seepur Pass; a second in the fort in Meikenaad, the ruins of which, situated on a high ridge above the Coonoor Pass, are called Hûlikal Drûg; and a third in a fort in Parangenaad, of which nothing now is seen. These chiefs, it is reported, fix the boundaries of the Bargher and Kother villages, which continue unchanged to the present time.

The Burgher villages, says Captain Ochterlony, "are in general very neat and clean; the houses, which are few in number, averaging ten or twelve—being built in a row on the summit of a low smooth hill, and having a wide level terrace running along the front, for the purpose of spreading out the grain to dry after damp weather, and also to pick and husk it on. They have usually two substantial cattle-pens, or more, according to the size of the village, with high, rough, dry stone-walls and barricated entrances, to secure their cows and bullocks against cheetahs and tigers; which, though not common on these hills, occasionally find their way up from the forests below, and traverse the district, doing much mischief as they pass. The houses are built of mud, or mud and stone, and covered with a good roof of thatch, grass for which is abundant in all parts of the hills. There are altogether two hundred and twenty-seven Burgher villages on the Neilgherries" (*a*).

The Burghers are a thin, smooth-skinned, beardless race, of lighter complexion than Hindus generally, and the other hill tribes, and may at once be distinguished from the latter by the turbans they wear. The women perform a kind of modified *suttee* on the death of their husbands. They make a rush towards the burning pile, with the pretence of casting themselves upon it, when they are caught by their friends, and their garments are thrown on instead.

The Badagas are separated into eighteen clans, which belong to two great divisions. The first contains seven clans, which are higher in rank than the remaining eleven.

Superior Clans.

1. Wodearu.
2. Kongaru.
3. Adikâri.
   1. Lingadikari—who wear the *lingam.*
   2. Adikâri—who have been deprived of the *lingam.*
   3. Meatadikari—who intermarry with the lowest Badagas.

(*a*) Survey of the Neilgherry Mountains, by Captain Ochterlony. Madras Journal of Literature, Vol. XV, pp. 48, 49.

4. Kanakaru—Accountants.
5. Chittre.
6. Belli—An offshoot of the Wodearu clan.
7. Haruvaru—Degenerate Brahmans.

Inferior Clans.

1.	Hattara, or Marriage.	7.	Dumah.
2.	Anearu.	8.	Gonaja.
3.	Mari.	9.	Manika.
4.	Kastury.	10.	Torea.
5. 6.	Two classes of Vellalars.	11.	Kumbararu—Potters.

The Wodearu are highest in position, and are a proud, self-conceited people, inhabiting five villages. "They will scarcely notice an European, when they meet one; and will not sit at meals with the common Badagas, regarding themselves as their *gurûs* or priests. When a Badaga gives a feast, which he generally does when he shaves the head of one of his children, he invites a Wodearu to bless the food. At a funeral, the Badagas in general take off their turbans, but the Wodearu keep theirs on. Every native, not excepting the petty hill chiefs, must bow down before them, and pay them adoration (*a*).

The Kongaru came originally from Sargoor, and inhabit the hills in the neighbourhood of the Rangaswâmi peak. Like the Wodearu, they wear the *lingam*, but have much less pride. They are remarkable for their excessive loquacity.

The Adikâris are divided into three classes, as noticed above.

The Kanakaru are the only Badagas who have preserved the art of reading and writing. They are said to have emigrated from the Tamil country. By reason of their superior knowledge they act the part of exorcists and physicians to all the Badagas.

The Chittres came to the hills originally in company with the Wodearu, in the train of the Rajah of Malekote (*b*).

The Bellis assert that they once belonged to the Wodearu, but were separated from them through some misfortune. They are a very cunning people, of low and disreputable character.

The Haruvaru are an unclean race, and although proud and wearing the sacred cord, are regarded by the other clans with something like contempt (*c*).

(*a*) The Tribes inhabiting the Neilgherry Hills, by the Revd. F. Metz, pp. 48, 49.

(*b*) *Ibid*, p. 53.

(*c*) *Ibid*, pp. 55, 56.

The Hattaras are descended from seven brothers, 'each of whom is said to have erected a house for himself and his family in a different part of the hills,' where villages were eventually constructed.

The Anearu are only found in the Todannad. They are notorious for their mendacity.

The Maris are also settled in the Todanaad, but came originally from the neighbourhood of Nanjanagoody. The headmen of the Anearu and the Maris are the richest, and, consequently, the most influential of all the Badagas.

The Kaity people and also the Koonde Badagas belong to the Kastury clan. The former are also styled Gangalaru.

The Dumahs have villages in three separate villages, and are so designated from their common ancestor of this name (*a*).

The Gonajas inhabit the country on the borders of Mekunad, near the Koonde river.

The Manikas dwell near Kotagherry.

The Toreas are socially of the lowest rank among the Badaga clans, and are not permitted to eat food with the rest of the tribe. They are said to have been watchmen and menial servants to the other Badagas, before the migration of the tribe to the hills.

The Kumbararu occupy two villages near Kalhutty. Although they resemble the other Badagas, and have similar customs, yet they do not intermarry with them (*b*).

Section IV.—The Trula Tribe.

A small tribe, a little more numerous than the Todas and Kotas, speaking Tamil, found on the lower slopes of the hills, beyond the imaginary jurisdiction of the Todas, and therefore not paying tribute to them. They are an unsettled, vagrant race, not confining themselves to one spot, but delighting in wandering from place to place. They profess to cultivate the soil, yet do so in a wasteful, unsatisfactory manner, consequently they are poor and dishonoured. They raise crops of various kinds of grain, but to no great extent, "being very improvident in their arrangements, and eating up all their produce at once, without laying any by for the rainy season, when they subsist chiefly on plantains, jack, and other fruits, which they cultivate in patches near their villages, and which thrive in consequence of the lower level on which the Trulas are

(*a*) The Tribes inhabiting the Neilgherry Hills, by the Revd. F. Metz, p. 59.
(*b*) *Ibid*, p. 60.

mostly settled. They also work occasionally as coolies on plantations, preferring employment in the jungle to working in the field, and being expert fellers of trees, hewers of planks, rafters, and so forth" (*a*). They are courageous hunters, and pursue the most ferocious animals with singular fearlessness. They are scantily clothed, of diminutive stature, and of a strange misshapen appearance. Their marriages do not take place until several children have been born. Colonel King states, that they have no notion of marriage and live promiscuously. In appearance they are something like the Pariah on the one hand, and the Kûrumba on the other. Their dress resembles that of the former tribe. Their religious rites are few. Sometimes they sacrifice a cock to propitiate evil spirits. The funeral rites of this tribe are peculiar. A very deep hole is dug outside a village, into which the dead bodies of the village are thrown without ceremony.

Like other hill tribes, the Trulas are of dirty habits. They are low in social rank, owing chiefly to their poverty, improvidence, and restlessness. Nevertheless, at the great annual festival of the god Rangaswâmi, held on the peak of that name, at which many thousands of Hindu pilgrims are present from the plains, several of their number officiate as priests in the ceremonies of the temple. The small patches of land cultivated by this people are to the eastward, near the Rangaswâmi peak and the Kotergherry Pass. They pay a small tax for their land, so long as they cultivate it.

Several appellations are given to this tribe, which has two hereditary distinct branches. On the eastern ridges, in the direction of Danaikencota, they are always called Trulas; on the ridges of the Bhawâni valley to the south they are termed Mûdûmars; and towards Davaroypatam in the north they are known as Kûssûwars. In customs and occupations these clans are alike. They bury their dead in houses set apart for the purpose, leaving the door always open to the east, the males being buried on one side, the females on the other (*b*).

Section V.—Kûrumba, or Mullukûrumba Tribe.

It is conjectured that as the physical differences between the Trulas and Kûrumbas is but slight, they were originally the same race. The chief food of the latter tribe is "wild roots or berries, or grain soaked in water, with occasional porcupines or pole-cats. Their dwellings are nothing more than a few

(*a*) Survey of the Neilgherries, by Captain Ochterlony. Madras Journal, Vol. XV, p. 61.

(*b*) Descriptive and Geographical Account of the Neilgherry Hills, by Messrs Fox and Turnbull. Transactions of the Bombay Geographical Society, Vol. IV.

branches piled together like heaps of dead brushwood in a plantation, often simply holes or clefts among the rocks. Their clothing is, with the males, a small dirty cloth round their loins; and with the females a rag thrown on any way that its condition and size render most available" (a).

The Kûrumbas inhabit the lowest slopes of the Neilgherries and the plains below, so that they can hardly be regarded as a tribe peculiar to the hills. Moreover, they have the vagrant habits of the Trulas, and spend their lives in migrating from place to place in the dense forest. They are supposed to have come from Malayalim. The tribe raises scanty crops of grain on the small patches of land which it cultivates; but depends for its supplies, says Captain Ochterlony, "chiefly on the fees in kind which it receives from the Burghers for the offices performed by it in consecrating their crops and seed." It prepares the soil for the reception of the seed by the use of the hand-hoe.

In stature, and in general external appearance, these people present a sharp contrast to the Todas of the uppermost ridges of the Neilgherries. Short and ugly, with matted hair, large mouth, and bleared eyes, and altogether of a strange figure, given to necromancy and dark secrets, no wonder that they are regarded as a forbidding weird-like race, to be shunned and feared, rather than honoured and courted. By the other hill tribes they are believed to be in possession of supernatural powers of blessing and cursing, and to have control over life and death, disease, prosperity, and adversity. The Burghers especially are in perpetual terror of the Kûrumbas, and will carefully avoid meeting them. Should they meet any one of their number suddenly, they consider the event as ominous of evil and disaster, and sometimes die of sheer terror. Nevertheless, such is their confidence in their mysterious powers, that they will undertake no enterprise without first obtaining their benison. A Kûrumba drives the first plough into the soil—sows the first few seeds—reaps the first ears of corn—blesses the cattle and the produce—blesses the home, the parents, and the children—and thus acts the part of priest, physician, astrologer, demon, and deity combined. He is priest and musician to the Todas as well as the Badagas.

A tradition prevails among the tribes, that the Kûrumbas have resided on the lower hills from a very remote period, and that in reality their occupation of them is as old as that of the Todas, and consequently that they possess an equal right with them as original proprietors of the soil. They speak a dialect

(a) Aboriginal Tribes of the Neilgherry Hills, by Lieut.-Colonel King, p. 42.

peculiar to themselves, which circumstance favours this supposition of their great antiquity. The dialect, however, is said to be a corrupt jargon of tongues rather than a distinct language. "No such ceremony as marriage exists among these people, who live together like the brute creation. Their dead are sometimes burned, sometimes buried; in either case, with as little form or trouble as possible. They are, in short, among the most debased types of mankind" (*a*).

The tribe has three divisions, as follows :—

1. The Mulla Kûrumbas.
2. The Naya Kûrumbas.
3. The Panias (*b*).

The Panias are not sorcerers like the other two clans, and are chiefly employed by the Badagas as labourers in the Wynaad. The Kûrumba villages consist only of a few huts, commonly spoken of by the term Motta. The Kûrumbas are stolidly ignorant, and have no traditions. They worship a deity called Kuribattaraya, lord or possessor of sheep.

(*a*) Aboriginal Tribes of the Neilgherry Hills, by Lieut.-Colonel King, p. 44.
(*b*) The Tribes inhabiting the Neilgherry Hills, by the Rev. F. Metz, p. 116.

CHAPTER VIII.

TRIBES AND CASTES OF TRAVANCORE AND TINNEVELLY.

SECTION I.—TRIBES OF TRAVANCORE.

I.—THE BRAHMANICAL TRIBES: PAGODAS. II.—THE AMBALAVASIS, OF THE MUTHATHU WARRIOR CASTE. III.—THE KSHATRI TRIBE. IV.—THE NAIR TRIBES. V.—THE SHANAR AND TLAVAR TRIBES. VI.—THE PULAYAN, OR PULAYAR TRIBE. VII.—THE PALLAR TRIBE. VIII.—THE PARIAH TRIBES. IX.—THE COWDER TRIBE. X.—THE VAISHWAN TRIBE. XI.—THE MADAVENMAR TRIBE. XII.—THE ARIAMAR, OR VAILAMAR TRIBE. XIII.—THE URALAI TRIBE. XIV.—THE VAITAWAN, OR KONAKEN TRIBE. XV.—THE VAIDAN TRIBE. XVI.—THE ULANDAR TRIBE. XVII.—THE NAIADI TRIBE.

SECTION II.—TRIBES OF TINNEVELLY.

I.—THE REDDY TRIBE. II.—THE NAICKER TRIBE.

SECTION I.—TRIBES AND CASTES OF TRAVANCORE.

The Province of Travancore has an area of six thousand six hundred and fifty-three square miles, a revenue of forty-two lacs and eighty-five thousand rupees, and a population of one million, two hundred and sixty-two thousand six hundred and forty-seven persons (*a*). These are divided into numerous tribes and clans.

I.—The Brahmanical Tribes.

In the year 1854 there were, according to the census then taken, about thirty-nine thousand Brahmans in Travancore, of whom upwards of ten thousand were Nambûri, or professedly indigenous Brahmans, and the rest were immigrants from other States. The Brahmans of this province exert a superior influence over all other castes and tribes of the Province, as they do elsewhere throughout India.

1. *The Nambûri Tribe.*

The recognized head of the Nambûri Brahmans is Alwanchairi, who possesses, however, no real authority over them. "Their head-quarters," says the Rev. S. Mateer, "are at Arâncheri, in the Cochin State, where the chief Nambûri

(*a*) The Native States of India, by Colonel Malleson, p. 323.

resides. The highest class of Nambûris, with rare exceptions, refuse to reside under the sway of the Sudra Rajah of Travancore; and any of the females going south of Quilon are said to lose caste. Hence the Nambûris, resident within the limits of Travancore, are not recognized as belonging to the purest class" (*a*). The members of this tribe in Malabar are said to be a 'tall, fair, and handsome race.' They may each marry seven wives. The principal clan is the Adhinmar, which is reputed to be descended from former rulers of Kerala. They lead a quiet, retired, contemplative life, taking little part in public affairs. Some are wealthy, and live in spacious mansions. Their marriages are only between members of their own caste, and not with Potîs, or other Brahmans. They seldom practise polygamy. The eldest son only marries into the tribe, younger sons forming temporary alliances elsewhere. This immoral custom arises from the desire to prevent a rapid increase of the caste. The women live in close seclusion; and if compelled at any time to leave the house, take the utmost care to protect their faces from public gaze. The Nambûris recognize several inferior divisions of their own caste, separated from themselves by reason of some ceremonial offence, and forming distinct sub-castes, with which the purer Nambûris do not intermarry :—

Inferior Sub-castes of Nambûri Brahmans.

1. Nambadi.	4. Oval.
2. Mûtûda.	5. Iliadû.
3. Aghapâd.	

2. *Non-indigenous Brahmanical Tribes.*

These are of various nationalities. Some of the most numerous are :—

1. The Patras—from Tinnevelly, Tanjore, and Coimbatore..
2. The Imbrantris—from Tûlanâd, in Canara.

Most of these latter Brahmans are engaged in commerce, and trade in cloth and grain. They differ in character from the Nambûri Brahmans; and while eschewing the luxurious indolence and arrogance for which the latter are distinguished, are far from copying their excellences. Some of the Canara Brahmans remain in Travancore only for a time, keeping up an intercourse with their families in their own country.

Travancore has two thousand, seven hundred and eighty-four pagodas, of which thirteen hundred and eighty-two are under the management or support of the native government, and fourteen hundred and two are the property of

(*a*) The Land of Charity. A Descriptive Account of Travancore and its People, by the Revd. Samuel Mateer, F. L. S., p. 29.

village communities, and are free from official control. Each pagoda has a manager, called Annavaul, Sheeaureyem, or Samñdanyem, according to the custom of the district in which the pagoda is situated. A moiety of the expenses of the pagodas is invariably defrayed in money, and the other moiety in rice. These institutions are liberally provided for, and are well looked after; those belonging to villagers being perhaps more carefully directed than those in the hands of the Government. In the southern districts, from Kulcolum southwards, dancing-girls and musicians—Pandy Vathiars—attend the pagodas five times every day. To the north of Velavancode, no dancing-girls or musicians practise their arts in the pagodas, with the exception of those at Vurkalay, Areepaud, Ambalapuley, Vyekam, and Yetmanoor. The offerings made by worshippers at the Government pagodas, consisting of silk, money, gold, and silver images of snakes and jewels, are not appropriated by the priests, but are carried to the credit of the Government, and a correct account of them is furnished to the District Courts of Law monthly. "In some large pagodas there are Vunjis, or treasure coffers, which are not opened, and cannot be opened, until they are filled to the brim. They are placed in front of the pagodas, between it and the *mundapom* or porch; and the person bringing any offering, should himself put it into the coffer" (*a*).

In addition to the support rendered by the Government of Travancore to the pagodas within the limits of that province, it also maintains temples within the territories of the British Government of India, situated at the following places, namely:—

Benares.
Madura.
Ramaswarom.
Vulloor.
Thiroocanjoody.
Nanjanarey.
Trichendoor.
Tinnevelly.
Alvarcoorchy.
Shenkarananaircoil.
Thircoolalum.
Thirroomanaparrah.

Coodungaloor, or Cranganoor.
Chathamungalum.
Chittore.
Suranulloor.
Torchekarapooram.
Theroponathoor.
Shothanekarray.
Thiroovenjacolum.
Ernacolum.
Theroomalayoor.
Chethumbrum (*b*).

(*a*) Description of the Administrative System of Travancore, pp. 5—7. By V. Kristna Row, late Dewan of Travancore. Edited by Major Drury, at the request of F. N. Maltby, Esq., Resident at the Courts of Travancore and Cochin.

(*b*) *Ibid*, p. 18.

There are in Travancore forty-two Uttûperrahs, or houses in which Brahmans are fed at the expense of the Government. Servants are appointed to see that they are well fed; but the same recipients are not allowed to partake of more than three meals in succession, unless prevented from leaving the place by sickness or other unavoidable cause. There is a feeding-house for Brahmans at every stage throughout the province of Travancore.

II.—The Ambalavâsis—of the Mûthathû Warrior Caste.

This caste is below the Brahmanical in dignity, and yet ranks much above the Sudras. It is hard to say to which of the four great Hindu castes it belongs. Without knowing more about its history and characteristics, it would be premature to relegate it to the Vaisya, or third great Hindu caste. Many of its members wear the sacred thread, and are either agriculturists or temple servants. The caste has several divisions, as:—

1. Shakaiar. Dancers in the Kûtha Ambalams of the pagoda.
2. Pûshagam. Collect flowers for decorating the idols.
3. Pûsharanda. Attendants on inferior deities.
4. Variar.
5. Nangiar.
6. Maurayan.

} Principal musicians of the pagodas; blowers of the temple shells; astrologers.

The Maurayans are lowest in rank, and perform certain menial services for the dead.

Such of the Ambalavâsîs as are sweepêrs of the interior of pagodas, and are otherwise engaged in temple duties, have an hereditary title to the offices which they hold.

III.—The Kshatri Tribe.

This tribe must not be confounded with the high-born, pure-blooded, royal Rajpoot tribes of Northern India, as, whatever their origin, they are, in many respects, a much inferior race. Some of their social habits would be regarded with detestation by the Kshatris of the North, as for instance, that their women should be appropriated by the Nambûri Brahmans, and that they themselves should be contented with alliances formed with women of Nair families. Like Brahmans they refrain from eating animal food, and imitate them also in their religious observances and in many other things. These are some of their divisions:—

1. Tambemar. These are highest in rank, and are termed Râj Kumâr.

2. Tavûmapâd. Second in rank.
3. Saumandar. In rank much below the two preceding.

IV.—The Nair Tribes.

The term Nair is applied to a large number of castes and clans representing a very important and influential portion of the native community. They are all Sudras, and, as such, occupy, in public estimation, a position of honour and respectability which members of the same great Hindu caste in Northern India do not enjoy. They are divided into numerous classes. Some of them are as follows:—

1. Valaima. First in rank; inhabit the northern parts of the province.
2. Kirtathi. In the northern districts.
3. Ilakara.
4. Shrûbakara.
5. Paudamangalam.
6. Tamilpaudam.

(3–6) Found throughout the province. The two last are under the authority of certain temples.

7. Palicham. Bearers or servants to the Nambûri Brahmans.
8. Shakaular, or Velakaudû. Dealers in oil.
9. Pûlikai, or Andam Nairs. Potters.
10. Velathadam, or Erinkulai. Washermen for Brahmans and Nairs.
11. Pariari, or Velakathara. Barbers for Brahmans and Nairs.
12. Agatacharnavar. Menial servants to Brahmans and Nairs.
13. Yedachairai, or Yarma. Cowherds.
14. Kulatu, or Velûr. Empirics.
15. Yahbari. Merchants.
16. Udatû. Boatmen.
17. Atikurchi, or Sidiar. Perform the obsequies for the dead.
18. Silversmiths and goldsmiths.
19. Braziers.
20. Blacksmiths.
21. Carpenters.

(18–21) Lowest in social rank.

Each of these classes boasts of several subdivisions. Besides those classes given above there are many others. These sub-castes hold themselves distinct from one another, and some of them refuse to eat with others, or to intermarry with them. The Nairs are in character much like the Sudras in Northern India, intelligent and energetic; they are also cunning and deceitful. The Government offices are filled with them; yet, in point of ability, they can hardly be compared with the Kaisths of Bengal and the North-Western Provinces, who throng the courts of law. The Nairs generally burn their dead; but in cases of poverty they bury the bodies in the gardens attached to their houses in a southern position.

The features of the Nair are said to be very regular, and of the Grecian type, with an oval head; but they are deficient in muscular power. The women are of small stature; "and their features are more to be praised than their figures, which are generally wanting in grace from the squareness of their shoulders." Their hair is drawn up in a knot on the top or one side of the head. Both men and women are of cleanly habits, and bathe and change their dress frequently (*a*).

The Nairs are a very powerful community. This arises not merely from the circumstance that the ruling family belongs to the tribe, but also from their *members* and the wealth they possess. About half a million of persons, or a full third of the population, are Nairs, the larger portion being Malayalin Sudras. "The greater portion of the land is in their hands, and until recently they were also the principal owners of slaves. They are the dominant and ruling class. They form the magistracy and holders of the Government offices, the military and police, the wealthy farmers, the merchants and skilled artizans of the country" (*b*).

The marriage tie is very loose among the Nairs, and is easily broken at the pleasure of either party. The children of a Nair woman inherit the property not of their father, but of their maternal uncle. This rule is observed also in the succession to the throne. "The sister of the late Rajah," says Mr Mateer, "left two sons, the elder of whom is now reigning. He will be succeeded by his younger brother, the heir apparent. Next in succession come the two sons of their late sister, who are entitled respectively to be the *second* and *third* princes of Travancore. Their mother had no daughters, so that it became necessary, for the continuation of the succession by the female line, to adopt some one into the family. Two daughters of the petty Rajah of Mâvelikkara were accordingly adopted, who, by Hindoo law and custom, are regarded as the sisters of the second and third princes, and are called respectively the senior and junior Ranees of Travancore. The senior Ranee is without issue; but the junior Ranee has three sons, the *fourth*, *fifth*, and *sixth* princes, who follow next in the succession" (*c*). Polyandry is practised by several of the lower Nair tribes.

(*a*) Pharoah's Gazetteer of Southern India, p. 511.

(*b*) The Land of Charity, by the Rev. S. Mateer, p. 35.

(*c*) *Ibid*, p. 37.

Some of the Nairs of Malabar occupy a high social position, and were formerly more or less independent. Among them may be reckoned the Colongode Nambiddy, the Kudravattatha Nair, the Kangad Nair, the Maugara Nair, and the Kanampra Nair.

V.—The Shânâr and Tlavar Tribes.

These tribes bear two appellations. In the north they are known by the term Tîan and Ilavar, and in the south by that of Shânâr; but there is so little distinction in the habits and characteristics of the two classes, that they are evidently one and the same race. They are below the Sudras; and yet far above the menial tribes. Their occupation is almost exclusively agricultural. They are, for the most part, poor; and very few rise to affluence. Many largely subsist on the products of the palmyra tree. Those who live on the coast employ themselves in fishing. By the last census there were three hundred and twenty-one thousand persons belonging to the two tribes. The Shânârs are much more intelligent than the downtrodden menial tribes of Travancore. A considerable number have embraced the Christian religion. Some, perhaps many, of these rise to a far higher civilization than that of other members of the tribe. Their morality and social habits, likewise, are of a nobler type. When properly educated, the Shânârs as a race are destined to make a much more important and conspicuous figure in Travancore than they have ever yet done. Each of the Tlavar villages has a kind of hereditary chief or headman, called Tanolan, who exercises considerable authority, especially over the lower castes. He is the arbiter of the caste difficulties, and presides at village gatherings. The Panikan, or village priest, takes spiritual cognizance of the people, and also teaches the young.

The natives have a tradition that these tribes came originally from Ceylon. The word 'Ilavar' derived, it is said, from 'Ilam,' or Ceylon, lends some support to this tradition. These people are also designated, in some parts, by the term Choganmâr, or serfs: and in other places are called Teeyars and Billavers.

The peculiar marriage customs of the Nairs, together with their singular rules of inheritance, are practised by many Ilavars, and by a few Shânârs. Husband and wife easily separate, and contract other alliances. All inherited property descends to maternal nephews; while other kinds of property are shared equally by nephews and sons.

Socially these tribes are degraded, and are treated with great ignominy by the Government. Their women were, until recently, not permitted to wear clothing above the waist. "They were not allowed to carry umbrellas, to wear shoes or golden ornaments, to carry pots of water on the hip, to build houses above one-story in height, to milk cows, or even to use the ordinary language of the country." And even now their position is one of great humiliation.

Protestant Missions have been very successful among the Shânârs. Under native rule, says the last Census Report of Madras, they were "a downtrodden race; under Christian teaching and enlightenment their social position is vastly improved, and many of them, by their Christian training, have become educated, and now hold positions of influence and respectability" (*a*).

The Kanians are a division of the Tlavar tribe, and are professed exorcists and necromancers. They are an agricultural people, though many of them are engaged in the manufacture of umbrellas.

The Panians also are a division of the Tlavar tribe, and, like the Kanians, are devoted to agriculture. They are distinguished, however, as musicians, strolling players, doctors, astrologers, and alchymists.

The religion of the Shânârs is demonolatry, and although they make use of the name of God, yet "practically they are destitute of the belief in God's existence" (*b*). Even Rama, the Hindu deity so celebrated in Northern India, is converted by the Shânârs into a demon, and as such worshipped. Ravana's Prime Minister, Mahodara, is believed to have been a Shânâr.

The Revd. Dr. Caldwell, in his essay on 'The Tinnevelly Shânârs,' gives the following interesting account of their origin, occupation, and social position:— "There is reason to suppose," he remarks, "that the Shânârs are immigrants from the northern coast of Ceylon, where the same or a similar caste still exists, bearing a grammatical and intelligible form of the same name, 'Shândrâr' of which 'Shânâr' is etymologically a corruption. It is also tolerably certain that the Ilavars and Teers (*i.e.*, Singhalese and Islanders), who cultivate the cocoanut palm in Travancore, are descendants of Shândrâr colonists from Ceylon. There are traces of a common origin among them all; 'Shânâr,' for instance, being a title of honour among the Travancore Ilavars. It is traditionally reported that the Shânârs who inhabit Tinnevelly came from the neighbourhood of Jaffna, in Ceylon; that one portion of them, the class now called Nâdâns (lords of the soil), entered Tinnevelly by way of Ramnad, bringing with them the seed nuts of the Jaffna palmyra, the best in the east, and appropriating, or obtaining from, the ancient Pundya princes, as the most suitable region for the cultivation of the palmyra, the sandy waste lands of Mânâd

(*a*) Madras Census Report, Vol. I, p. 315.

(*b*) The Tinnevelly Shânârs, by Dr. Caldwell, p. 15.

in the south-east of Tinnevelly, over which, to the present day, they claim rights of seignorage; and that the other portion of the immigrants, esteemed a lower division of the caste, came by the sea to the south of Travancore, where vast numbers of them are still found, and whence, having but little land of their own, they have gradually spread themselves over Tinnevelly, on the invitation of the Nâdâns and other proprietors of land, who, without the help of their poorer neighbours as climbers, could derive but little profit from their immense forests of palmyra. Some of these immigrations have probably taken place since the Christian era; and it is asserted by the Syrian Christians of Travancore, that one portion of the tribe, the Ilavars, were brought over from Ceylon by *their* ancestors, for the cultivation of the cocoanut palm. The Shânârs, though probably immigrants from Ceylon, are Hindus, not of the Brahmanical, but of the Tamil or aboriginal race; the inhabitants of the northern coast of Ceylon being themselves Tamilians, the descendants either of early Tamil colonists, or of the marauding bands of Cholas, who are said repeatedly to have made irruptions into Ceylon both before and after the Christian era. The Shânârs of Ceylon, who are considered as forming the parent stock, now occupy a more respectable position in the social scale than any of the offshoots of the castes. But it is probable, that they have risen in civilization through the example and influence of the higher castes among whom they live; and that the Shânârs of Tinnevelly, forming the bulk of the population in their various settlements, and having few dealings with any other class, may be considered as retaining their original condition, and as still representing the religious and social state of the entire family prior to its separation and dispersion.

"The caste of Shânârs occupies a middle position between the Vellalars and their Pariah slaves. Their hereditary occupation is that of cultivating and climbing the palmyra palm, the juice of which they boil into a coarse sugar. This is one of those occupations which are restricted by Hindu usage to members of a particular caste, whilst agriculture and trade are open to all. The majority of the Shânârs confine themselves to the hard and weary labour appointed to their race; but a considerable number have become cultivators of the soil, as landowners, or farmers, or are engaged in trade. They may in general be described as belonging to the highest division of the lower classes, or the lowest of the middle classes; poor, but not paupers; rude and unlettered, but by many degrees removed from a savage state" (*a*).

(*a*) The Tinnevelly Shânârs, by Dr. Caldwell, pp. 4—7.

VI.—The Pulayan, or Pulayar Tribe.

The most numerous of the slave tribes of Travancore. It is exceedingly degraded, and is consequently much abhorred by pure Hindus. It has three divisions, as follows:—

1. Valava.	2. Kanaka.	3. Muuri Pulayan.

These three clans differ in comparative debasement in the order in which they are given; the vilest, in popular estimation, being the last. The tribe numbers nearly one hundred thousand persons.

"The Pulayars," says Mr. Mateer, who has resided for many years in Travancore, and has had excellent opportunities for studying the native tribes and their characteristics, "dwell in miserable huts on mounds in the centre of the rice swamps, or on the raised embankments in their vicinity. They are engaged in agriculture as the servants of the Sudra and other landowners. Wages are usually paid to them in kind, and at the lowest possible rates. To eke out their miserable allowances, therefore, they are accustomed to enter the grounds of their neighbours at night, to steal róots, cocoanuts, and other produce; and they are but too ready to commit assault and other crimes. These poor people are steeped in the densest ignorance and stupidity. Drunkenness, lying, and evil passions prevail among them, except where, of late years, the Gospel has been the means of their reclamation from vice and of their social elevation. They differ from the Pariahs, however, in abstaining from the flesh of all dead animals" (*a*). Although legally emancipated from bondage, the social abjectness of this and the other slave tribes has undergone little change.

The Pulayan wears a coarse cloth around his loins, and another small piece he wraps round his beard. He must not wear shoes or use an umbrella; and his wife must only decorate herself with brass ornaments and beads. In speaking he must not say 'I,' but 'your slave;' must not call his own rice by its proper name, but as dirty gruel; must not talk of his children by this appellation, but as 'monkeys' and 'calves;' must live in a small hut without furniture, and built in a certain miserable situation far from the habitations of the upper castes; and in speaking must place the hand over the mouth, lest the breath should go forth and pollute the person whom he is addressing. He is "not allowed to use the public road when a Brahman or Sudra walks on it. The poor slave must utter a warning cry, and hasten off the road, lest the high

(*a*) Land of Charity, pp. 42-43.

caste man should be polluted by his near approach, or by his shadow. The law is, that a Pulayan must never approach a Brahman nearer than sixty-six paces, and must remain at about half this distance from a Sudra. He could not, until lately, enter a court of justice, but was obliged to shout from the appointed distance, and took his chance of being heard and receiving attention. A policeman is sometimes stationed halfway between the Pulayan witness or prisoner and the high caste magistrate, to transmit the questions and answers, the distance being too great for convenient hearing. As he cannot enter a town or village, no employment is open to him except that of working in rice fields and such kind of labour. He cannot even act as a porter, for he defiles all that he touches. He cannot work as a domestic servant, for the house would be polluted by his entrance; much less can he (even were he by some means to succeed in obtaining education or capital) become a clerk, schoolmaster, or merchant. Caste affects even his purchases and sales. The Pulayars manufacture umbrellas and other small articles, place them on the highway, and retire to the appointed distance, shouting to the passers by with reference to the sales. If the Pulayan wishes to make a purchase, he places his money on a stone, and retires to the appointed distance. Then the merchant or seller comes, takes up the money, and lays down whatever quantity of goods he chooses to give for the sum received—a most profitable mode of doing business for the merchant!" (a) Such is the position of the Pulayar and of the other slave tribes —a scandal to the semi-civilized Government of Travancore, and by no means honorable to the British Government of India, by which it is controlled.

VII.—The Pallar Tribe.

A small slave tribe, numbering barely four thousand persons. Its characteristics are somewhat similar to those of the Pulayars.

VIII.—The Pariah Tribes.

A large community among the slave races, numbering upwards of forty thousand persons. They speak Tamil, and inhabit the same part of the country as the Shânârs,—namely, the southern districts of Shencotta, east of the Ghauts. The Perûm Pariahs and Mannai Pariahs, in the interior, are considered more impure, if possible, than the Pariahs inhabiting the coast. They eat carrion, and indulge in the vilest habits. They are, however, a laborious people. Some of them are skilful in wicker-work. They are fond of necromancy and

(a) Land of Charity, pp. 45—47.

magic. In rank and habits the Pariahs are considered to be a shade lower than the Pulayars.

For a detailed account of the Pariah tribes, see the chapters on the tribes and castes of the Madras Presidency.

IX.—The Cowder Tribe.

Found in the Kodagiri hills, in the northern districts of Cochin. They are dark, well-made, flat-nosed, and occasionally of curly hair. They file their teeth sharp like a saw; and altogether are in some respects like negroes of Africa, although their cast of countenance is of a mild rather than of a repulsive character. These people collect and sell the products of the forest which they inhabit.

Most of the hill tribes are migratory in their habits, remaining in one spot only for a year or two, which they clear, cultivate, and reap, and then pass on to other tracts. They are, observes Mr. Mateer, "exceedingly wretched, uncivilized, and degraded. The men go almost naked. They are short in stature, but strongly built. The women wear bracelets of iron or brass, numerous necklaces of corals or beads, and leaden rings in the ear. They are unable to read or write, or to count above a dozen. Fibres of various climbing plants are knotted in a particular way to express their wants" (*a*).

X.—The Vaishwan Tribe.

A debased, low-statured race, scattered about the Idiara and Muliator hills. They were formerly much addicted to the use of opium, and were consequently lifeless and dull. They support themselves by cutting down the wood of the forest and selling it.

XI.—The Mudavenmar Tribe.

This tribe leads a sequestered life among the Chenganad and Nireamangalum hills, and holds no intercourse with the towns and villages of the plains. Its women are treated with respect and honour. Among hill tribes it occupies a position of some distinction. It is reputed to have been originally connected with the Vellandar tribe.

XII.—The Ariamar, or Vailamar Tribe.

The former appellation is applied to those families spread over the northern ranges of hills, and the latter to those found among the southern ranges; but

(*a*) Land of Charity, p. 49.

the tribe is one and the same. They are more settled in their habits than most hill tribes, and are not disinclined to intercourse with other races. They are an indolent people, not fond of work, and only resorting to it to supply their immediate wants; and yet they cultivate the soil, though in a rude fashion, for themselves, and cut down the jungle for their neighbours in the plains. They are also employed in the capture of wild elephants.

XIII.—The Uralai Tribe.

A rude, unfriendly tribe of the Thodhawalai hills, few in number, and accustomed to migrate from place to place. They are expert in the chase, to which they train their dogs; and are clever in shooting with the bow and arrow. They abhor above all things the buffalo, which they avoid in every possible manner. Their aversion to this animal is so strong that they pride themselves upon it as an indication of the greater purity of their caste as compared with other hill tribes. In their family relations great deference is paid by children to both father and mother, whose authority is unimpeachable. They are shy and inoffensive; and are by no means fond of intercourse with strangers.

XIV.—The Vaitawan, or Konaken Tribe.

A low caste people attached to the soil, and formerly kept in a kind of bondage. They are employed in various ways. Some make excellent boatmen; others manufacture salt. They are, for the most part, gentle and faithful; and occupy a superior position among the outcast races of Travancore.

XV.—The Vaidan Tribe.

A wild, dark-skinned people, with long, dishevelled hair, timid and shunning human society. They cut down forest timber, and act the part of watchmen over growing crops; but are too rude, or too timid, to cultivate the soil. They lead a precarious existence of various degrees of misery, and are among the most degraded of the outcast races. Their necks are encinctured with shells, and their loins with leaves, the completion of their toilet.

XVI.—The Ulandar Tribe.

A tribe of similar characteristics to the Vaidans, but somewhat inferior in social position.

XVII.—The Naiadi Tribe.

One of the most degraded and wretched of all the debased tribes of this part of India. Almost naked, shunned by all classes, subsisting on roots or food purchased from the alms received from benevolent travellers. They live far away from villages in small huts erected in solitary places. No one permits them to approach near, nor do they venture to do so; and even the alms, whether of food or of anything else, intended for them, is deposited on a certain spot by the giver, who then retires in order that the unclean, miserable Naiadi may, on his departure, come and take it away. The tribe is found in the northern tracts of Cochin.

Section II.—Tribes of Tinnevelly.

Northern Tinnevelly is chiefly inhabited by two tribes, the Naicker or Naick, and the Reddy or Retta. Although they have been in that country a long period, yet they are not aborigines. This is manifest from the fact that, while speaking Tamil, the language of Tinnevelly, in trade and in all public matters, they make use of the more familiar Telugue in their social and domestic concerns.

I.—The Reddy Tribe.

A tradition prevails among this tribe, that they originally came from Oudh, at the other extremity of India, and that their ancestors formed part of the army of Râm, the ancient king of Ajoodhiya, the modern Oudh, when he went on his famous expedition from that country to Ceylon, and fought with, and overcame, Rawana, the king of the island. We know that, in very early times, people from Ajoodhiya settled in Kalinga, inhabited by Telugus; and it is not unlikely that some of the Reddy tribe, abounding in Kalinga, migrated to the south, and finally took up their quarters in the northern tracts of Tinnevelly, where they are now found.

Probably other migrations of this tribe took place from various causes. "At one period," says the Revd. J. F. Kearns, who has written upon these tribes, "the Reddys, under the chieftainship of one of their tribe, rose to considerable eminence, and their power eventually became so great, that they carried their arms against the kingdom of the Pandion; and where their arms found an entrance, we may rest assured they were not slow to avail themselves of its advantages. On the fall of their principality of Kondaver, with which their power declined, many of them appear to have fled southwards in search of peace and of new homes; and as the southern parts were at that time overrun with jungle and but little inhabited, there were no difficulties to their settling in them" (*a*).

(*a*) Tribes of South India, by the Revd. J. F. Kearns, Missionary of the Propagation Society, Tinnevelly, p. 10.

This tribe has twenty-four subdivisions, which, as they do not intermarry, are practically distinct tribes. It is exceedingly remarkable that these separate clans, though all bearing the same generic designation, and doubtless proceeding from the same common stock, should nevertheless keep themselves so rigidly distinct one from another.

The Reddys are worshippers of Vishnu, and are attached to the Râmanuj sect of Vaishnavas. They have no idols in their temples, which contain simply a lighted lamp and occasionally a garland of flowers suspended in front of it. Only the priest and his wife enter the temple. Other worshippers are not permitted on any consideration to enter, but perform their religious ceremonies outside, at the entrance. The priest presents their offerings in the temple, and pronounces *mantras* in their behalf, at which time the worshippers observe profound silence. At the conclusion of the ceremony, they cook their food, presenting a portion to the priest, and drink arrack. This meal is accounted sacred, as forming a component part of the religious service. The Reddys are very superstitious, and practise all the rites of demonolatry like the low caste Shânârs, and besmear their bodies with ashes. They eat meat, which strict Vaishnavas in other places will not do. Four of the Reddy clans pay especial honour to Vishnu as 'Senna Rayer Perumal,' or the Bâlbhadra incarnation of that deity.

The custom observed at marriages in this tribe is singular and unnatural. The rule is, that, in all cases in which it is possible, a man should marry his sister's daughter,—that is, his niece on the mother's side. They will not marry at all into the families of their father's brothers or mother's sisters, on the ground of consanguinity! The law of entail, as interpreted in the civil courts, is connected with this rule of marriage; for the hereditary property of the father must descend to the issue of his son and grand-daughter. The marriage ceremonies of the Reddys are performed in the house, while those of the Naickers are performed abroad in the open air.

The Reddy is dull and heavy as contrasted with the Naicker, and evidently lacks the quickness and energy which the other tribe exhibits. He is entirely devoted to agriculture, in the pursuit of which he displays considerable industry. Both races are tall, muscular, and well-proportioned. They make excellent soldiers. As they are frugal in their habits, eat good and wholesome food, are but slightly given to strong drunkenness, and are accustomed to hard labour, the consequence is, that they are healthy and little affected by disease The women are even finer than the men. They are tall, presenting an average height of five feet nine inches. "Though so tall, they are well formed: their carriage—indeed, that of all Hindu women—is very graceful, and would bear comparison with that of the most perfect *modiste* in Europe. No European moves with so much grace and elegance. Their faces are extremely intelligent; the nose is prominent, well-formed, and angular; the eyebrows well and gracefully arched; and the forehead rising gracefully, rounds off over the temples, giving them quite an aristocratic look" (*a*).

II.—The Naicker Tribe.

Many of the characteristics of this tribe are the same as those of the Reddys, just described. Yet they are a different race, and of different origin. They are separated into eight clans, sprung from a common ancestor. There is also a ninth, the Chuckler, which, for some act of impropriety, has been excommunicated, but yet, though unrecognized, belongs to the family stock. All these clans bear the generic designation of Kombelathar. The offence of the Chuckler's ancestor was, that, in the primitive family, his ancestor fed his father and eight brothers on a calf which he had killed, for which offence the curses of the entire family were hurled upon the head of himself and his descendants. The Chuckler, however, in spite of social excommunication, has certain perquisites, and enjoys certain privileges. The perquisites are the disordered and diseased cattle belonging to the other eight clans. The privileges are more agreeable. One is, that he has a legal right to a portion of the money of a Naicker dying without a direct heir. Another is, that at important councils held by the Naickers he is present and takes part in their consultations.

The Naickers have already been described as a robust and powerful people, and of greater versatility than the Reddys. They are not merely excellent agriculturists, but devote themselves to other occupations. They are shopkeepers, merchants, brokers, writers, and the like. Some of them wander all over the country hawking their wares. In short, they are an enterprising race, of capacity and perseverance.

Little is known respecting their early history. The Naicker soldiers fought in the army of the Rayer; when this personage "obliged the declining Pandion race to hold their crown at his hands, the Naickers dwelt in the south in considerable numbers." "An event, characteristic of those times, occurred, which opened the way to their immigration to an extent much greater than at

(*a*) Tribes of South India, by the Revd. J. F. Kearns, Missionary of the Propagation Society, Tinnevelly, p. 62.

any preceding period. The Pandion kingdom was too much for the cupidity of the Tanjore Rajah to resist seizing upon. Easily discovering a pretext for war, he marched his forces against the Pandion capital, and obliged its unfortunate prince to seek safety in flight. He hastened to Vijaynagar, and throwing himself at the feet of his sovereign, related his disasters, the loss of his kingdom, and his consequent distresses. The Rayer ordered a large army to be equipped." This was placed in charge of Nackama Naicker, who fought with the Tanjore Rajah, and obtained possession of Madura. Instead, however, of restoring it to the Rayer, the Naicker general took charge of the government, and proclaimed himself Rajah. To consolidate his rule, he divided the country into seventy-two dependencies, and entrusted them to the same number of Naicker chiefs or Polygars, each of whom was attended by a company of Naicker warriors. In course of time the Rayer sent another army against the new Naicker Rajah, commanded by the Naicker's son. The two opposing armies of father and son fought a severe and bloody battle, which ended in the defeat and capture of the father. The Pandion Rajah was then restored to his throne. As he had no children, he adopted Viswanath Naicker, the young general who had restored him, as the successor. "With a Naicker upon the throne of the Pandion," says Mr. Kearns, "we may conclude that the immigration of the tribe was at that period numerous. The Naicker dynasty reached its meridian in the time of Tirumali Naicker, after whose death we notice a gradual decline. The Tinnevelly country eventually became the inheritance of a competitor for the crown; the true but imbecile offered no objections to an arrangement which despoiled him of a splendid province. From that period the Tinnevelly Polygars gradually increased their demands, and at length became no better than bold turbulent barons. The Naicker dynasty would have perished beneath the hand of the notorious Chunda Sahib, had not the Rajah of Hyderabad, for political motives, lent the expiring power a little aid which prolonged its existence, until it eventually passed into the hands of the Nawab of the Carnatic" (*a*).

In their marriage and religious customs and ceremonies, the Naickers resemble the Reddys. Like them they are Vaishnavas. The Naicker emblem of Vishnu is an octagonal pillar seven feet high without inscription or device. As before remarked, the Naicker's marriages are celebrated in the field, while the Reddy's marriages are performed in the house. The morality of both

(*a*) Tribes of South India, pp. 13—16.

tribes is low. This arises to a large extent from the peculiar regulations respecting consanguinity and affinity prevailing among them.

For an account of the Vellâlars, Maravers, and other tribes and castes of Travancore and Tinnevelly, not described in this chapter, see the chapters on the tribes and castes of the Madras Presidency, where they have found a place.

CHAPTER IX.

SEC. I.—THE SUDRA AND INFERIOR TRIBES OF THE VIZAGAPATAM DISTRICT. SEC. II.—THE HILL TRIBES OF JEYPORE:—1, ABORIGINAL TRIBES; 2, PRE-ARYAN COLONISTS, IMMIGRANTS FROM THE EAST AND NORTH, IMMIGRANTS FROM THE WEST; 3, THE GAUDU, OR HERDSMEN AND SHEPHERD TRIBES. SEC. III.—THE HILL TRIBES OF GANJAM. SEC. IV.—THE KORAGAR TRIBE OF KANARA. SEC. V.—OTHER HILL AND JUNGLE TRIBES OF SOUTH CANARA.

SECTION I.—THE SUDRA AND INFERIOR TRIBES OF THE VIZAGAPATAM DISTRICT.

1. *The Baliji Tribe.*

Some of the principal subdivisions of the tribe are the following:—

1. Gâzula Baliji ... Manufacturers of glass *bangles* or armlets.
2. Vâda Baliji ... Sailors.
3. Pagadala Baliji ... Dealers in corals and pearls.
4. Linga Baliji ... Traders.
5. Dûdi Baliji ... Traders.
6. Periki Baliji ... Traders and agriculturists.

2. *Soldiers, belonging to the undermentioned Tribes:—*

1. Bhaktâlu.
2. Telagâlu.
3. Nagarâlu.
4. Majjulu.
5. Vantarlu.
6. Aiyarakâlu.
7. Berilu.

3. *The Karnam, or Writer Castes.*

These are eleven in number in Jeypore; but in Vizagapatam there is only one Karnam caste,—namely, Sristi Karnalu, a tribe of great influence. In many respects, the customs of the Karnams resemble those of Brahmans; but they do not wear the sacred thread.

4. *Agricultural Tribes.*

1. Kapula.
2. Koppula Velamalu.
3. Tottadi Velamalu.
4. Gavarulu.
5. Yanadulu.
6. Reddikilu.
7. Kaligulu.
8. Nagavasulu.
9. Kurâkulavâllu.
10. Muttirajulu.
11. Gollalu. Also shepherds, and sellers of milk and ghee.
12. Gaudu Gollalu. } These tribes are also cowherds and keepers of buffaloes.
13. Erra Gollalu. }

In Jeypore there are eleven Agricultural Tribes; and the Gour, or Shepherd Tribes, are nine in number.

5. *Traders travelling from one province to another.*

1. Banjâri.
2. Kudiyalu.

These tribes convey grain, chalk, salt, and other articles, between Nagpore, Ganjam, and other provinces.

6. *Weaver Castes.*

1. Devangula.
2. Salilu.
3. Pattu Salilu.
4. Kaikalavallu.
5. Dasarivallu.
6. Goni Periklu.

7. *Dyers.*

1. Rangirijulu.
2. Vudupulavallu.

8. *Barbers.*

Mangali.

9. *Diggers.*

1. Vupparlu.
2. Vaddarlu.

10. *Shampooers.*

Jetti.

11. *Toddy-drawers.*

Most of these tribes are also palanquin-bearers.

1. Yatavallu.
2. Idigavallu.
3. Segidilu.
4. Gamallavallu.
5. Bestalu.

12. *Washermen.*

1. Kapa Cakali.
2. Vaddi Cakali.

13. *Manufacturers of boxes, sieves, &c.*

1. Medarlu.
2. Gudalavallu.

14. *Drug-sellers.*

Mandulavallu.

15. *The Kamsâli Castes, i. e., Smiths, Masons, and Carpenters.*

These are five in number, namely:—

1. Goldsmiths.
2. Braziers.
3. Ironsmiths.
4. Carpenters.
5. Stone-cutters.

16. *Painters.*

Muchchi.

17. *Oilmen.*

1. Deva Telukali.
2. Kapa Telukali.

18. *Cotton-beaters.*

Dudekulavallu.

19. *Slipper-makers.*

1. Godarivallu.
2. Madigavallu.

20. *Meat (mutton) Sellers.*

Katikilu.

21. *Repairers of Hand-mills.*

Tiragati Gantlavallu. They also hunt the antelope.

22. *Dancers, Prostitutes, &c.*

1. Bhogamvallu.
2. Sanivallu.
3. Kurmapuvallu.
4. Nagavasula.

23. *Actors, Wrestlers, Jugglers, Conjurers, Rope-dancers, Snake-charmers, Musicians, &c.*

1. Itevallu.
2. Bhagavatulu.
3. Bommalatavallu.
4. Chitta Jalluvallu.
5. Neravidyavallu.
6. Pailamanlu.
7. Garidivallu.
8. Pamulavallu.
9. Vipravinodulu.
10. Ranjaluvallu.
11. Bhatrajulu.
12. Gangiredlavallu.

24. *Gardeners.*

1. Rellivallu. | 2. Chaccadivallu.

25. *Fishermen.*

1. Jalarlu. | 2. Pallilu.

26.—*Servants, Watchmen, Cultivators.*

1. Malalu (Pariahs). | 2. Paidimalalu. | 3. Boyalu.

27.—*Religious and other Mendicants*

1. Gosangulu.
2. Panasavallu.
3. Podapotulavallu.
4. Varugubhatlu.
5. Addapusingulu (*a*).
6. Viramustivallu.
7. Sataulu.
8. Dasarlu.
9. Jangalu.

28. *The Sauras.*

A wild tribe inhabiting the hilly country behind Palconda, and to the east of Gunapur; and also the neighbourhood of Bhadrachalam, on the Godavery. They are said to be the same, though with what truth I know not, as the people known as the Chensuvandlus of the Kistna and Nellore districts.

29. *The Gadabas.*

A wild tribe scattered among the hills of Vizagapatam, where they are employed as palankeen bearers. Their women wear a peculiar dress, manufacture from the fibre of the *Asclepias gigantea*, and other shrubs, and dyed in various colours. "Immence rings of brass adorn the ears; and they carry great 'bustles' made of some jungle twigs" (*b*).

30. *The Koyis.*

A wild tribe of Malkagiri, in Jeypore, in the direction of the Godavery. They resemble both the Khonds and the Gonds.

31. *The Nangas.*

A wild tribe inhabiting about fifty villages of Vizagapatam. Both sexes are almost entirely naked. They keep their heads shaved, under the superistitious dread of being destroyed by tigers, should the custom not be observed (*c*).

(*a*) Manual of the District of Vizagapatam, by D. F. Carmichael, Esq., Magistrate, and Agent to the Governor of Fort Saint George, Madras, pp. 63—68.

(*b*) *Ibid*, p. 86.

(*c*) *Ibid*, p. 87.

These four aboriginal tribes bury their dead, and ten days after the ceremony, feast themselves on a cow or buffalo.

SECTION II.—THE HILL TRIBES OF JEYPORE.

An elaborate and carefully prepared list of these tribes has been drawn up by Mr. H. G. Turner, Assistant Agent in Jeypore, in which he classifies the purely aboriginal tribes, and also the pre-Aryan colonists, separating the latter from the former. Those regarded as primitive races, he arranges under two heads, Kolarian and Dravidian, according to the system adopted by Sir George Campbell, in his Essay on the aboriginal tribes of the Central Provinces. They are as follows:—

1. *Aboriginal Tribes.*

Kolarian.

1. Gadabâs.
2. Kerang Kâpus.
3. Bhûmiyas.
4. Bhûnjiyas.

Dravidian.

1. Parjâs.
2. Dhûrwa Gonds, including the Raj Gonds.
3. Batrâs.
4. Kois.
5. Matiyâs.
6. Konda Kâpus.
7. Konda Dorâs.
8. Khonds.
9. Kottiyâs.
10. Pentiyâs.
11. Muryâs (*a*).

The word 'Parjâ,' as suggested by Mr. Carmichael, formerly Magistrate of Vizagapatam, is the same as the Sanskrit *praja*, a subject, in contradistinction to râjâh, a king. The Parjâs are allied to the Khonds of the Ganjam Maliahs. "They are," says Mr. Taylor, "thrifty, hard-working cultivators, undisturbed by the intestine broils which their cousins in the north engage in; and bear in their breasts an inalienable reverence for their soil, the value of which they are rapidly becoming acquainted with" (*b*). When disputes arise concerning land in their neighbourhood, it is customary to appeal to the Parjâs, in order that they may point out the boundaries.

They are a patriarchal and energetic people, passionately fond of the lands which they cultivate. There is a tradition prevalent in the country that all the territory now called Jeypore formerly belonged to the Parjâs, who made a voluntary surrender of it to the Raja. In the uplands they occupy a high

(*a*) Report of Mr. H. G. Turner on the Hill Tribes of Jeypore. Madras Census Report, Vol. I, p. 224.
(*b*) *Ibid.*

social position; but in the tract known as 'the middle level' they are, for the most part, mere husbandmen.

The Parjâs of the 'lower level,' or the Malangiri country, are divided into two tribes.

1. The Dudai Parjâs.	2. The Bonda Parjâs.

These tribes have the tradition that they originally came from the east.

The Gadabas are a race inferior to the Parjâs. They have peculiar customs, and adopt a peculiar dress. Having been in Jeypore for many ages, they are regarded as an indigenous people. They differ greatly from the Parjâs.

The Konda Kâpus, the Konda Dorâs, and the Ojâs (pre-Aryan colonists), inhabit the elevated land of the eastern Ghauts. The dialects spoken by them are substantially those of the Parjâs and Khonds. Nevertheless, they "seem to have entirely lost all those rights to the soil which are now characteristic of the more northern tribes; and are completely at the mercy of later immigrants, so much so, that though they call themselves Konda Dorâs, they are called by the Bhaktâs, their immediate superiors, Konda Kâpus. If they are found in a village with no Telugu superior, they are known as Dorâs. If, on the other hand, such a man is at the head of the village affairs, they are to him as *adstricti glebae*, and are denominated Kâpus or ryots" (*a*). Mr. Taylor contends, that "the comparatively degraded position that this particular soil-folk holds, is due to the influence of Telugu colonists; and that the reason why they have been subjected to a greater extent than the cognate tribes further inland, is possibly that the Telugu colonization is of more ancient date than the Uriya. It may further be surmised," he holds, "that from the comparative proximity of the Telugu districts, the occupation of the crests of these Ghauts partook rather of the character of a conquest than that of mere settlings in the land" (*b*).

The Batrâs were classified by the Ethnological Committee of the Central Provinces, in the year 1868, as members of the great Gond family, though, as a fact, they speak a corrupt Uriya. They are not found in those provinces beyond Bustar. Most of the aboriginal tribes of this region have forgotten their primitive language by reason of dwelling amidst Uriya-speaking colonists; and only retain certain words and phrases of their ancient tongue.

The Bhûmiyas chiefly inhabit the Subdivisions of Râmgiri and Bâkdiri. Many are still addicted to wandering habits without settled habitation. Both

(*a*) Report of Mr. H. G. Turner on the Hill Tribes of Jeypore. Madras Census Report, Vol. I, p. 225.
(*b*) *Ibid.*

these and the Bhûnjiyas, and some other aboriginal tribes of Jeypore and the Central Provinces, are reputed to have languages of their own.

There are two tribes of Gonds in Jeypore: the Râj Gonds, who occupy a superior position; and the Dhûrwa Gonds, who are more numerous than the former. The Râj Gonds speak Uriya, or a dialect known as Chattisgahrî; while the other Gonds retain the use of their original language. They are higher in the social scale in Jeypore than their brethren of the same tribe in the Central Provinces.

The Kois inhabit the country to the south of the town of Malangiri, as far as the Godavery, and to Kummumpet, in the Nizam's territory, beyond that river. Their language seems to be akin to that spoken by the Gonds. "They are a listless, drunken race, bad cultivators, unthrifty and debased" (*a*).

The Matiyâs are as a people superior to both the Kois and the Parjâs. They speak Uriya, are good cultivators, and affect Brahmanical habits by wearing the sacred string. "They say, they spring from the soil; and go so far as to point to a hole, out of which, they affirm, their ancestor came.".

The Kerang Kâpus of the Kolarian family are much like the Gadabâs. "They will not admit any connexion with them; but, as their language is almost identical, such gainsaying cannot be permitted them. They are called Kerang Kâpu, from the circumstance of their women wearing cloths, which they weave from the bark of a jungle shrub called 'Kerang' (*Asclepias gigantea*). This is practised by the Gadabâs, the Dudoi Parjâs, and the Bonda Parjâs. A most extraordinary method they have of proposing marriage. The headman is sent to the bride's father with a stick, which he, after compliments, leaves behind, as if by accident. This the bride's father throws out of the house. Whereupon, the headman goes again, and makes, as it were, a casual visit, when the stick is once more left behind. Should the stick, on the third occasion, be thrown out, the suit is taken to be finally rejected; otherwise, the suitor may make the matter subject of conversation, and fix arrangements for the feast" (*b*).

2. *Pre-Aryan Colonists.*

These are divisible into two great branches, representing immigrants from the east and north, and immigrants from the west, who, at various periods, have settled down in the country as farmers and cultivators. They consist of several

(*a*) Report of Mr. H. G. Turner on the Hill Tribes of Jeypore. Madras Census Report, Vol. I, p. 227.

(*b*) *Ibid.*

tribes, most of which speak the Uriyalanguage, though some speak Telugu. The tribes are as follows:—

Immigrants from the East and North.

1. The Ronâ Tribe ...	...	... Speaking	Uriya.
2. The Mâli Tribe ...	...	... ditto	Uriya and Telugu.
3. The Amanâtiya Tribe	...	... ditto	Uriya.
4. The Bhaktâ Tribe	...	... ditto	Telugu.
5. The Dûleya Tribe	...	... ditto	Uriya.
6. The Dhâkûdo Tribe	...	... ditto	do.
7. The Ojâ Tribe (?)	...	... ditto	do. (*a*).

The Ronâs have their lands among those of the Parjâs, from whom they have been, by the adoption of various methods, acquired. Socially, they are a superior race, with more refined habits than the Parjâs. Compared with these, however, their entrance into the country is of recent date.

The Mâlis are gardeners who have been long in the country. "The only evidence to show that their possessions were formerly Parjâ lands, is perhaps a row of upright stones erected by the older race to the memory of their village chiefs."

The Bhaktâs are scattered about Hill Mâdugulu. They have imposed their yoke on the Kâpus. "In the low country, they consider themselves to take the rank of soldiery, and rather disdain the occupation of ryots. Here, however, necessity has divested them of such prejudices, and they are compelled to delve for their daily bread. They, nevertheless, generally manage to get the Kâpus to work for them, for they make poor farmers, and are unskilled in husbandry" (*b*).

The Amanâtiyas came from the east coast.

The Dûleyas are said to be cultivating paiks.

The Dhâkûdo Tribe are illegitimate descendants of Brahmans, and are consequently Aryans, and not pre-Aryans. They are engaged in agriculture.

Immigrants from the West.

1. The Saourâ Tribe	...	... Speaking	Uriya.
2. The Halabâ Tribe	...	... ditto	do.
3. The Tagarâ Tribe	...	... ditto	Telugu.
4. The Boukâ Tribe	...	... ditto	Uriya.

The Saourâs came from the Central Provinces many generations ago.

(*a*) Report of Mr. H. G. Turner on the Hill Tribes of Jeypore. Madras Census Report, Vol. I, p. 224.
(*b*) *Ibid*, p. 225.

They are much more civilized than most of the other tribes. They wear the sacred string, burn their dead, and marry their children at the age of maturity (*a*).

The Halabâs not only inhabit parts of Jeypore, but also some of the neighbouring districts of the Central Provinces.

Respecting the condition of some of the tribes described above, Mr. Taylor has made the following concise and weighty remarks:—"The Kois," he observes, "cultivate this year the fields they cultivated last year, unmanured, unweeded, and uncared for. If they are the people who built the mud embankments, and dug the tanks, that are found in Malakangiri (and there is no reason to suppose that they did not), it is evident that they have degenerated to a melancholy extent. Turning now to the Parjâs, it is certain that, within the memory of man, they have advanced from the knowledge of hoe tillage to that of the use of the plough. The Matyâs have recently begun to weed their lands. The women of the Parjâs and Ronâs are now employed in preparing their fields for the plough by dressing them with manure; and amongst these people, where they are found in the open uplands of Nandupore, they have adopted a system of corporation. Follow the Parjâ into the recesses of the hills, and you will find him still hacking down a forest to grow a couple of crops of coarse grain as his more skilled brother in the open used to do before civilization came upon him" (*b*).

3. *The Gaudu, or Herdsmen and Shepherd Tribes of Jeypore.*

These have entered the province in association with other colonists. The aboriginal tribes not only in Jeypore, but also in other parts of India, not being subject to caste regulations which cause the Hindu race to be split up into a multitude of subdivisions, which, for the most part, pursue hereditary occupations of a distinctive character, do not disjoin the cultivation of the soil from the duties of herdsmen and shepherds. The Gaudus are Hindus, and are divided into four tribes. These are not so prejudiced as similar tribes in Northern India, which make a great distinction between these offices. The Gaudus, however, unite them together. The separate tribes are as follows:—

1. Solokondia.
2. Bastaria.
3. Mogodho.
4. Dongaito.

The Solokondias came from the seaboard of Orissa, and are the highest in social position. The Bastarias originally came from Bâstar. The two tribes last mentioned have no trustworthy traditions respecting themselves.

(*a*) Report of Mr. H. G. Turner on the Hill Tribes of Jeypore. Madras Census Report, Vol. I, p. 237.
(*b*) *Ibid*, p. 228.

The Gandus are largely employed as village servants. Many possess considerable wealth in cattle (*a*).

Section III.—The Hill Tribes of Ganjam.

These form a community of two hundred and eighty-five thousand persons, distributed as follows:—

1. *The Uriya Tribes.* (25,958 persons.)

These are the wealthiest and most important of all the hill tribes. "They inhabit the valleys, engross the cultivable land, and monopolise the trade of the country" (*b*).

2. *The Khond Tribes.* (88,082 persons.)

The Khonds are divided into three classes:

1. Khonds. | 2. Bado Khonds. | 3. Sono Khonds.

The Khonds are landowners, cultivators, and hunters. "The men are of medium height, stout, strong, and not uncomely, with aquiline noses, high cheek bones, and receding foreheads." The women are diminutive in stature, coarse in feature, and of unclean habits. Their bosoms are left bare; and they wear a scanty cloth round their loins, extending halfway down the thigh. The dress of the men is still scantier. The women wear a peculiar head-dress; while both sexes decorate themselves profusely with brass and glass ornaments. Boys are married at the age of ten or twelve to girls three or four years older.

The system of government of these tribes is patriarchal.

3. *The Sawrah Tribes.* (77,105 persons.)

Of these there are five divisions:

1. Sowrahs.
2. Jara Sowrahs.
3. Sudda Sowrahs.
4. Arisa Sowrahs.
5. Tekkally Sowrahs.

4. *The Sond Tribe.* (1,332 persons)

An Uriya tribe of arrack-sellers.

5. *The Pano Tribe.* (34,670 persons.)

A degraded race of Uriya origin.

(*a*) Report of Mr. H. G. Turner on the Hill Tribes of Jeypore. Madras Census Report, Vol. I, p. 229.
(*b*) The Madras Census Report, Vol. I, p. 209.

6. *The Erikula (Vánlu) Tribe.* (2,379 persons.)

7. *The Jannaloo Tribe.* (2,164 persons.)

8. *The Pittala (Vánlu) Tribe.* (2,439 persons.)

9. *The Gartula Tribe.* (6,375 persons.)

10. *The Yanadi (Vânlu) Tribe.* (9,839 persons.)

11. *The Jatafee (Vânlu) Tribe.* (16,029 persons.)

12. *The Golla (Vánlu) Tribe.* (3,528 persons.)

13. *The Agurtu Tribe.* (5,256 persons.)

14. *The Gadabalu Tribe.* (4,664 persons.)

15. *The Konda Kajulu Tribe.* (282 persons.)

16. *The Loddi Rajulu Tribe.* (4,614 persons.)

17. *The Telega Tribe.* (128 persons.)

18. *The Gonda Tribe.* (92 persons.)

19. *The Pydelu Tribe.* (79 persons.)

Section IV.—The Koragar Tribe of Canara.

Respecting this strange people inhabiting the Canara jungles, ignorant and superstitious, yet remarkable for the rigid practice of some of the most prominent virtues, an intelligent native gentleman, Mr. N. Ragavendra Row, gives the following comprehensive account, which, although lengthy, is so pertinent, and so full of interesting and important facts, that it must find insertion in this work with little curtailment:—

"With a black face, forehead of moderate size, and strong body, all bespeaking contentment, the Koragar is separated from the rest of mankind, alien in dress, in manners, customs, and dialect. Uneducated and illiterate as he is, in his circle virtue thrives as in her proper soil. He may not know whether India is governed by the English or the Mahomedans; he may think that a clock turns not on its wheels, but is the result of some divine miracle; railways and telegraphs may be to him wonders as yet to know; but he is as nature made him, 'frank as a dove, and mild as a lamb.' He has a god, and him he knows to love—him he knows to pray to, however incoherent his language be. Lying, stealing, adultery, and other social evils, he knows not. He has never appeared in a Court of justice as a defendant in a suit. He does drink toddy, it is true; and the practice, I believe, he must have acquired from intercourse with the higher class of Sudras. He does eat flesh. On what else should he live, while we have denied him every means of subsistence? While every nation, every society, nay every individual is striving for honours and improvement, the Koragar, born as a slave, is richly content with his ignorance, with his *koppu*, and with his squalid poverty. Ambition finds in him no place. He eats but the rotten flesh of the dead cattle. He clothes himself but with rags, which are to him what the most costly raiment is to us. Persuade him to change his clothing—lecture him on his nakedness—and he will run away, or say, 'I am well off with my poverty.'

"It is a common belief that the Koragars have a peculiar dialect generally spoken by them at their *koppus*. But the omnipotent mammon himself, as the Brahmans would have it, cannot tempt a Koragar to tell anything on this important subject. He may be induced to give an account of his feasts, his god, and his family; but a word about his dialect will frighten him out of his wits. At that moment alone, he will become impolite and unmannerly. He thinks his dialect is a shield in his hand, and cannot be parted with ; and therefore keeps it as a sacred secret. But good words and kind treatment can do something. A few words that have been gathered with great difficulty resemble those of the Keikadi and Naikunde Gondi tribes of Nagpore.

"The dress of the Koragar does not greatly differ from that which the lower classes, such as the Billawars, make use of during their daily labour. The only point of difference is, that the poverty of the Koragar does not allow him to replace the narrow piece of threadbare cloth, little better than a rag, by a more recent suit of clothes on festive occasions; while the other classes invariably reserve some sort of finery for gala days. The dress of the females, however, is very peculiar. While the males gird a piece of cloth around their loins, the females cover their waist with the leaves of the forest interwoven together. The custom of their nudity is attributed to different reasons; and a tradition, which has been handed down to posterity among the upper classes, who boast of the glory of the past, is hardly worthy of belief. Whatever the merit of the story may be, it is sufficient to show us the extent of despotism of the upper class at the time. One of these 'black-legged' (the usual expression by which they are referred to during the night) demanded a girl of high birth in marriage. Being enraged at this, the upper class withheld, after the overthrow of the Koraga empire, every kind of dress from the Koraga women, who, to protect themselves from disgrace, have since had recourse to the leaves of the forest, conceiving, in the meantime, that God has decreed them this kind of covering. It is no wonder that this is the dress of the Koragars, for we see that the other oboriginal tribes, as savage as the Koragars, are content with a similar dress. On the east of Chunda district, the men wear no covering for their head, or for the upper part of their bodies, and constantly go about with a battleaxe in their hands. The women deck themselves with thirty or forty strings of beads, to which some add a necklace of pendant bells. Bangles of zinc adorn their wrists; and a chain of the same metal is suspended from the hair and attached to a large boss stuck in the ear. But the greatest peculiarity connected with their costume, is the practice which prevails in the remote districts, of the women wearing no clothes at all; instead of which they fasten with a string passing round their waists a bunch of leafy twigs to cover them before and behind. They are known by the name of Madians, and are perfectly savage. In Bustar, they are called Jhorias. This custom was observed by Mr. Samuells to exist also in Orissa. A similar custom is said to obtain among the Chenchawas, who inhabit the jungles between the Madians and Masulipatam.

"A Koragar generally selects a woman younger than himself as his wife. Sunday is held an auspicious day for marriages. The ceremony is performed at the bridegroom's house; and he bears the expenses. An elderly man usually presides on this occasion. The bridegroom and the bride take a cold water bath; and on a mat spread by the president, both are seated with a handful of rice placed before them. The blessing of the sun are invoked; and the president of the ceremony takes in his hand a few grains, and sprinkles them over the head of the bridal couple. This process is followed by the others present; first by the men, and then by the women. When it is gone through, the bridegroom is required to make wedding presents to the bride, which consist of two silver pieces. Six dinners are to be given by the bridegroom, when every Koragar rivals his neighbour in eating and drinking.

"The mania of caste supremacy is not confined to a few, but prevails among all classes of Hindus; and the Koragar is not exempt from it. Within his own circle he has three divisions.

1. *The Ande Koragars.*

"These are described as having had a pot suspended from their neck. This class, which is the lowest, has been rarely seen since the establishment of British rule in Canara. They were considered so unholy, that they were not allowed to spit on the public way; and, consequently, the pot was worn for this purpose.

2. *The Vastra Koragars.*

"This appellation has reference to their wearing clothes such as were used to shroud a dead body, and were given to them in the shape of charity, the use of a new cloth being prohibited.

3. *The Sappu Koragars.*

"These Koragars are such as we now generally see, wearing leaves for clothes.

"These three divisions are named simply after their different kinds of dress.

"They have no separate temple for their god; but a place called *kata*, beneath a Kasaccana tree, is consecrated for the worship of their deity, and is exclusively their own. Worship in honour of this deity is usually performed in the months of May, July, or October. Two plantain leaves are placed on the spot, with a heap of boiled rice mixed with turmeric. As usual in every ceremony observed by a Koragar, the senior in age takes the lead, and prays to the deity to accept the offerings, and be satisfied. But now, by following the example of Bants and Sudras, they have changed their original object of worship for Bhutas.

"It is an undecided question as to the law which governs them,—that is, for it is either the Aliya Santanam Law, or the Makkala Santanam Law. But it may be rightly surmised, that the majority of them are governed by the Aliya Santanam Law, whereby the higher grades of Sudras are ruled. The Koragars have no fixed feasts exclusively their own; but for a long time they have generally been observing those of the Hindus. Of them, two are important: one is called Gokalastome, in honour of the birthday of Krishna; the other bears the name of Chowte.

"No proof is wanting to show how slavery prevailed before the British Government took possession of Hindustan, and convinced every heart to abhor and shun it. Now, while liberty shines throughout the world under this Christian Government, slavery still lurks in those darkest corners where the rays of education have yet to penetrate. The Koragars and Holeyas are victims to this vestige of past despotism. The ceremony of buying a slave needs a little explanation. The destined slave is washed and anointed with oil, and new clothes are given him. The master takes a *batlu*, or plate, pours some water in it, and drops in a piece of gold. The slave drinks up the water, and taking some earth from his future master's estate, throws it on the spot which he has chosen for his use, which is thereupon given to him with the trees thereon. Although these slaves are in a degraded state, they by no means appear to be dejected or unhappy. The greater number of slaves belong to the Aliya Santanam castes, and among these people a male slave is sold for three Bhaudry pagodas, and a female slave for five pagodas; whereas the few slaves who follow the Makkala Santanam custom, fetch five pagodas for the man, and only three for the woman. This is because the children of the latter go to the husband's master, while those of the Aliya Santanam slaves go to the mother's master, who also has the benefit of the husband's services. He has, however, to pay the expenses of their marriage, which amount to a pagoda and-a-half; and, in like manner, the master of the Makkala Santanam slave pays two pagodas for his marriage, and gets possession of the female slave and her children. The master has the power of hiring out his slaves, or mortgaging them" (*a*).

SECTION V.—OTHER HILL AND JUNGLE TRIBES OF SOUTH CANARA.

These tribes reside partly on the hills, partly in the jungles, and partly in secluded localities in the plains. They are as follows:—

1. The Kunalie Tribe.
2. The Mali Kunalie Tribe.
3. The Nad Kunalie Tribe.
4. The Kari Kunalie Tribe.
5. The Male Kudi Tribe.
6. Kumri Mahrathi Tribe (*b*).

(*a*) Extract from Mr. N. Ragavendra Row's Pamphlet on the Koragars. Madras Census Report, Vol. I, pp. 343—345.

(*b*) Report of Mr. Thomas, Collector of South Canara. Madras Census Report, Vol. I, p. 61.

CHAPTER X.

SEC. I.—THE WHITE AND BLACK JEWS OF COCHIN. SEC. II.—THE MAHOMEDAN TRIBES.

Section I.—The White and Black Jews of Cochin.

The following interesting and concise account of these Jewish colonies is given by a writer in Pharoah's Gazetteer of Southern India:—"The Cochin Raja," he remarks, "has an extensive, though unsightly, *cotarum*, or palace, at Muttuncherry; and immediately adjoining it is the synagogue of the Jerusalem or White Jews, at the commencement of what is termed Jews' Town, the streets of which run south half a mile, the upper part being occupied by the White, and the lower by the Black or Ancient Jews. The Jews' houses, unlike any others in India, are all of one shade, with extraordinary pent-roofs. They form a separate community, have synagogues of their own, and are in dress, manners, and customs entirely distinct from both Europeans and natives. There are, however, hardly any of the present inhabitants of this place of pure unmixed European blood, being mostly descended from the original emigrants supposed to have fled from Jerusalem when it fell into the hands of the Romans. A great number of Black Jews inhabit the interior of the Province: their principal towns are Trittoor, Paroor, Chenotta, and Maleb. The Black Jews have a grant or license from the sovereign of Malabar, engraven on copper, bearing a date corresponding to A. D. 388 of the Christian era. They have no record of their pilgrimage; and how they contrived to reach a place so distant, or in what numbers they arrived, is left entirely to conjecture. The synagogue of the Black Jews is very plain, with a small belfry at one end, in which a rude clock, two hundred years old, regulates their time. The floor is all paved with china, very neatly inlaid; and at one end is a recess carved and gilded, with a rich curtain before it, in which, within folding doors, are deposited, in silver cases, five copies of the Pentateuch, written on vellum, in Hebrew characters, and so extremely well executed as to resemble the finest copperplate. Each case is covered with a rich brocade, the gift of Colonel Macaulay, when Resident there.

This synagogue differs little from places of Christian worship, except in having the women in a gallery apart from the men, with railings and net-work to conceal them from public view. The wives even of the most respectable are dressed like the natives of India, and chew betel; and, save as to skin and features, are very little superior to ordinary Malabar women" (*a*).

A writer in the *South of India Observer*, of May 9th 1872, says,—that the White Jews profess to have settled in Cochin eighteen hundred years ago, and that they hold grants dating back to the fourth century of the Christian era. He states, moreover, that the White Jews are a "handsome and singularly fair race, compared even with European Jews."

Section II.—The Mahomedan Tribes.

These tribes are, for the most part, the following:—

1. The Labbays.
2. The Mapilahs.
3. The Arabs.
4. The Sheiks.
5. The Sayid.
6. The Pathans.
7. The Moguls (*b*).
8. The Wahabis.

The Labbays are three hundred and twelve thousand in number. There are many along the seacoast, where they are 'fishermen, boatmen, sailors, and traders.' Their habits are very similar to those of the aborigines, from whom it is not unlikely they have sprung. They belong chiefly to the Suni sect.

The Mapilahs or Moplahs are a mixed Mahomedan race, settled in Malabar, and partly of Arab and partly of aboriginal extraction. They receive frequent additions from the slave tribes. The Mapilahs are fanatical Mahomedans attached almost exclusively to the Shagaite branch of the Suni sect; and are as superstitious and ignorant as many of the outcast races. Their language is Malayalim, written in 'a modified form of the Arabic alphabet.' This character is used by the Mahomedans in the Tamil country, and indeed throughout Southern India. The Mapilah mosques are of peculiar form, and often have several stories, the sides of the buildings having a slope inwards at the bottom. The Mapilahs are energtic, enterprising, and industrious, and while of independent spirit, are, neverthless, peaceable in character.

The Arabs are a small community, amounting to two thousand, one hundred and twenty-one persons, scattered about the provinces of Tinnevelly and Trichinopoly (*c*).

(*a*) Pharoah's Gazetter of Southern India, pp. 592, 593.

(*b*) The Madras Census Report, Vol. I, p. 171.

(*c*) *Ibid*, p. 174.

There are more than half-a-million of Sheikhs, and less than one hundred thousand of Sayids, in the Madras Presidency. The former predominate in the northern and ceded districts. The Pathans number seventy thousand; and the Moguls, twelve.

The Wahabis are few in number. There are one hundred and ninety-two in the Vizagapatam, nineteen in the Godavery, and one or two here and there in the Kistna districts, two hundred and forty-one in Nellore, fifty-three in Bellary, nineteen in Kurnool, eleven in Chingleput, one hundred and thirty in North and South Arcot, a few in Tanjore, Coimbatore, Madura, Tinnevelly and Salem, eigthy-nine in Trichinopoly, twenty-eight in South Canara, and two thousand seven hundred and ninety-four in the city of Madras.

PART III.

THREE DISSERTATIONS ON THE FOLLOWING SUBJECTS:—

THE NATURAL HISTORY OF HINDU CASTE;
THE UNITY OF THE HINDU RACE; AND
THE PROSPECTS OF INDIAN CASTE.

DISSERTATION THE FIRST.

THE NATURAL HISTORY OF HINDU CASTE.

To any one who has seriously reflected on the multiplicity of castes and tribes in India, with their almost endless ramifications, the questions will naturally arise—What cause or causes have brought them into existence? And what, if any, are their mutual relations? No such system of national dismemberment, and of tribal strictness and autonomy, has ever prevailed in any other country. The Egyptians in ancient times practised caste to some extent, and there was a separation between the priests and the warriors, the merchants, the agriculturists, the mariners, the artisans, and the shepherds. Thus they were divided into various great classes. But this was all. It does not appear that there were any subdivisions, so that in a large population little inconvenience could have been practically felt. There was much less intermingling among the Highland clans of Scotland in feudal times than among the inhabitants of Lower, Middle, and Upper Egypt.

The Jews of Palestine, also, throughout the whole of their career, were no doubt under the bondage of a modified caste. They could not intermarry with the surrounding nations, and although they could intermarry with themselves, yet the tribes were placed under certain restrictions in doing so. Jewish caste, however, differed widely and essentially from that which has been in existence in India for the last thirty centuries.

The caste of India is indissolubly blended with the social life of the Hindu, and is as much a necessity to him as food to eat, as raiment to wear, and as a house to live in. Indeed, he can often dispense with raiment, and during most of the year prefers the court outside his house to the hot rooms within; but he can never free himself from caste—can never escape from its influence. By day and night,—at home or abroad,—in waking, sleeping, eating, and drinking, and in all the customs of the society in which he moves, and the events governing his entire life, he is always under its pervasive and over-mastering influence. Professedly, there are four great branches of Indian caste, representing Brahmans, Kshatriyas, Vaisyas, or merchants and traders, and Sudras; but in reality the divisions among Hindus, involving complete separation in respect of marriage and social intercourse, number not hundreds, but thousands. In other words, the Hindu brotherhood is split up into innumerable clans, holding not the smallest connexion with one another, acknowledging no common bond save that of idolatry, which in truth no more unites them together than does the word sand applied to the hard grains on the seashore cause them mutually to cohere.

Caste dissolves the social compacts found in other countries, infuses the poison of deadly strife into the small village communities scattered in tens of thousands over the land, produces enmity between neighbours on the most trivial grounds, carries out its own childish rules and laws with Draconian severity, exercises the strongest power of disintegration the human race has ever been subjected to, and only displays a spirit of binding and uniting, in relation to those selfish creatures who belong to one and the same caste, and who thereby are kept apart from all the rest of mankind by an unnatural divorce.

This extraordinary domestic institution has yielded strange ethnological results. In Europe, the Hindu race is spoken of as an integer, which, although separable into parts, is nevertheless a whole containing all the parts; or it is a circle which may be cut up into innumerable portions, every one of which, however, is necessary to the integrity of the circle. But it would be much more correct to regard the numerous Indian tribes and castes as so many distinct integers, complete in themselves, independent and unassociated. It is quite true that most of them once belonged to the same family, and stood in intimate relation with each other. But we have to search for this happy relationship into the remote ages of antiquity. In India at the present day, we find an infinite variety of physiognomy, colour, and physique among its inhabitants, such as is exhibited among different nationalities in other parts of the world. The fair-faced, keen-eyed aquiline-nosed, and intellectual Brahman, the stalwart and commanding Rajpoot, the supple Bunniah, the conceited yet able Kayasth or writer, the clever barhai, or carpenter, the heavy-browed lohâr or blacksmith, the wiry and laborious Kumbhi or agriculturist, the short and handsome Chamâr, the dark Pâsi, the darker Dom, the wild and semi-barbarous aborigines, and hundreds of other tribes and castes, are in reality so many distinct types of the human family, with their own special characteristics and marked idiosyncracies. The wonder is, that such a diversity could have been produced among the inhabitants of one country.

In Great Britain not a few ethnological differences are manifest. Suffice it to mention the peculiarities of the Highlander as distinguished from the man of Kent, from an Essex peasant, from a Somersetshire farmer, from a Cornishman, from a Yorkshireman, or from a Welshman. All these differ from one another in a very decided manner, not in speech merely, but also physically and mentally; and yet it would not be difficult to classify all the people of Great Britain according to the ethnological and provincial distinctions which they now present.

But what shall we say of the two hundred and fifty millions inhabiting India, who have chosen to separate themselves from one another for a multitude of reasons, which in England would be deemed preposterous as a ground of separation,—reasons arising from difference of occupation, from religious feeling, from social interests, from a love of superiority, from selfishness, from caprice, from arrogance, from a spirit of exclusiveness, from eating certain things and not eating others, from adopting certain usages and not adopting others ? In England no social distinction really exists between the families of different counties throughout the country, and unions frequently take place between people of the North and people of the South. But the boundary lines dividing the vast Hindu race into multitudinous clans, which are literally beyond computation, are impassable barriers which it is absolutely impossible either to break down or to leap over. The divisions never reunite, never amalgamate, never associate together, have no mutual sympathy, or interest, or confidence, or love.

There was a time when castes were comparatively few, and although the rules which governed them were stringent, yet a considerable blending together was permitted among the castes themselves. From the Code of Manu we learn a good deal respecting the thraldom to which Hindus were subjected on account of the punctilious details and the extreme rigidity of caste regulations. At the same time, we are plainly informed of the comparative laxity and easiness of caste itself. Under certain restrictions even a Brahman could legally marry a Sudra, and intermarriages between the high castes and low castes were freely allowed. Such freedom, however, has long since passed away. Illicit intercourse is still practised to a degree that is a scandal and disgrace to men of the upper castes, but the honourable condition of marriage between separate castes, and to a large extent between branches of the same caste, is absolutely prohibited.

As every effect has a cause, we may assume that the extensive disintegration of the Hindu family which we now behold may be sufficiently accounted for. This wonderful phenomenon is not a fortuitous event, an ethnological caprice, a monstrous oriental production, the fruit of a tree which grew up spontaneously, from neither seed nor root. Nevertheless caste as developed in India is one of the most difficult problems concerning the races of men. Many theories have been started to account for its origin, and its earliest history is clouded in uncertainty and conjecture. Yet, in my judgment, the intricacies, inconsistencies, and singularities of its progress and elaboration in India, until its arrival at its present wild grotesqueness, are much more perplexing and exciting.

It is quite certain that caste as now existing was totally unknown to the Hindu race on first entering into India. The most ancient books they have are silent about it, and although referring to differences in social position among various classes, yet those differences are much more in accordance with distinctions in rank which have prevailed in civilized countries in all ages, than with the exclusiveness of the Indian caste-system of post-vedic times. In a review of Dr. Muir's Sanscrit Texts, Professor Max Müller asks the question: "Does caste, as we find it in Manu and at the present day, form part of the religious teaching of the Vedas? We answer with a decided 'No.' There is no authority whatever in the Veda for the complicated systems of castes—no authority for the offensive privileges claimed by the Brahmans—no authority for the degraded position of the Sudras. There is no law to prohibit the different classes of the people from living together—no law to prohibit the marriage of people belonging to different castes—no law to brand the offspring of such marriages with an indelible stigma. All that is found in the Veda, at least in the most ancient portion of it—the Hymns—is a verse, in which it is said that the four castes—the priest, the warrior, the husbandman, and the serf—sprung all alike from Brahmá. Europeans are able to show, that even this verse is of later origin than the great mass of the Hymns." This is an important opinion from one who has made the Vedas his life-study. Respecting the last statement, Max Müller, in his "History of Sanscrit Literature," further remarks, that there can be little doubt that the verse or passage alluded to "is modern both in its character and in its diction" (*a*).

This testimony especially refers to the Rig Veda, or most ancient portion of the Vedas.

Social distinctions are doubtless noticed in the Vedas, especially in those of later origin; but they never, in any sense, amount to what now bears the specific and technical designation of caste. The Black Yajur Veda notices social distinctions as prevailing among the people, and in sacrificial rites Brahmans evidently occupy the most prominent and influential position. The Kshatriyas too are powerful, and worthy of great honour. In the White Yajur Veda the

(*a*) Max Müller's History of Sanskrit Literature, p. 572.

Brahman is specially pointed out as a student and man of knowledge, and the chief divisions of native society are referred to as connected with their occupations, much in the same manner as they would be in other countries. The nobles and warriors represent power, and so are Kshatriyas. The Vaisyas till the soil. The Sudras are a servile, aboriginal, or separate race. These distinctions evidently exist in the later Vedas — yet there is no caste. These classes blend together more or less, greater respect is paid to one than to another, one is higher socially than another, but there is some amount of reunion between them nevertheless. In the Atharvan, or latest of the Vedas, a change is somewhat apparent. The Brahman is not merely domineering priest, but exercises authority over princes and other persons.

In the ages succeeding those of the Vedas, the distinctions, of which the bare outlines only were visible previously, gradually became more and more marked. The self-asserting Brahman assumes the position of the spiritual head and guide of the rest of the community. This is noticeable in the Brahmanas, the Aranyakas, and the Upanishads. The Brahman comes to be an associate with the gods, and in a certain sense divine. He claims a personal purity not allowed to others; but, it should be borne in mind, that this is only in connection with his ceremonial and sacrificial duties, and not in regard to his social position in relation to other classes of people.

That the Brahmans did not gain their ultimate ascendancy till after long and violent conflicts with the Kshatriyas and others in association with them, is abundantly proved by the allusions to, and records of, such struggles in some of the early Sanskrit writings. The great epic of the Râmâyana, although devoted to the exploits of Râma and his wife Sita, glorifies the Brahmans, and represent their power as much superior to that of the Kshatriyas, referring expressly to the destruction of the latter in a previous age by Parusrâma, the son of Jamadagni, because of their opposition to the former. Indeed one object which Valmiki, the celebrated author of this fine poem, had in view, seems to have been to show that the four chief castes were in existence, if not really established, in the days of Râma, the king of Ajudhiya. The other famous epic, the Mahâbhârata, exhihits clearly some features of the struggle between the two principal castes, and of the fierce enmity subsisting between them. In one place a long dialogue between two worthies, Bhisma and Judhisthir, is recorded, the purport simply being that the Brahman is super-eminent, and the Kshatriya is subordinate to him, and should rule by his counsel.

It is thus manifest that caste was of gradual growth, and that, at the outset, when the Aryan settlers crossed the Himalayas, and descended on the plains of India, no such distinction whatever existed among them. Some differences, religiously and socially, they no doubt exhibited, which is as much as to say, that they were not in rank on a dead level. He who officiated at sacrifices may have been regarded with more respect than other persons, yet it should be remembered that the performance of such rites was not restricted to one class. On arriving in India the Brahman does not seem to have claimed any special privileges in virtue of his position. In fact, he was surpassed and more highly honoured occasionally by others. Those who received the highest meed of praise were the Rishis, or sacred bards, who might be Brahmans, or Kshatriyas, or Vaisyas, or even Dasyas, that is, aborigines, people of the country.

It was not long, however, that this state of perfect concord lasted. Nevertheless, although social distinctions began to wax strong, and certain classes were treated with some dishonour, while others were greatly exalted, intermarriages under prescribed rules were permitted down to the time of Manu, and later. "As the influence of the Brahmans extended," says Max Müller, "they became more and more jealous of their privileges, and, while fixing their own privileges, they endeavoured, at the same time, to circumscribe the duties of the warriors (Kshatriyas), and the householders (Vaisyas). Those of the Aryas who would not submit to the laws of the three estates, were treated as outcasts; and they are chiefly known by the name of Vrâtyas or tribes. They spoke the same language as the three Aryan castes, but they did not submit to Brahmanic discipline, and they had to perform certain penances, if they wished to be readmitted into the Aryan society. The aboriginal inhabitants, again, who conformed to the Brahmanic law, received certain privileges, and were constituted as a fourth caste, under the name of Sudras, whereas all the rest who kept aloof were called Dasyas, whatever their language might be."

Now, although caste had by the time of Manu assumed many of the functions and prerogatives which it displays at the present day, yet it was not so stringent as it afterwards became. Nevertheless, it is abundantly plain from his Code that the life of the Hindu had already become a burden, by reason of the numberless caste rules by which his life was regulated. Every event pertaining to himself and his family, in their mutual relations, in their intercourse with the members of their own caste, and in relation to other castes, was controlled with extraordinary punctiliousness, so that they became abject slaves to a thousand ceremonial formalities intrinsically trivial and puerile. This was especially true of the Brahmans, who were, however, reconciled to the burden by the enormous power which this system of caste conferred upon them. To all other Hindus caste was intolerable. Yet for a time they submitted to it, because of its wonderful fascination and authority.

Eventually came the great revolt against caste, under the guidance of Sakya Muni, or Buddha, and his disciples, a revolt which became very largely successful over a considerable portion of India. Throughout the whole of the Buddhist period in India, of a thousand years and upwards, strong opposition was cherished by the Buddhists against caste. During the dominancy of their religion, which lasted perhaps six or seven hundred years, caste was necessarily in a very depressed state, and the people generally enjoyed a condition of social freedom, which they had not enjoyed since the earliest ages of Hinduism, and of which they have known nothing whatever in the long centuries subsequent to the downfall of the Buddhist religion. It is, moreover, manifest that the Brahmans, during the dark night of their own religion, strove to the utmost to keep alive the flame of Hinduism and the customs of caste in some parts of the country, in spite of the gigantic difficulties which at one time they had to face. This was especially the case in the tract of country lying between Mathura and the Punjab, which apparently was never subdued by Buddhism, and always retained a preponderance of allegiance to the Hindu faith with its concomitant institutions and practices. But this region, though extensive in itself, was small in comparison with the rest of India. And even here, judging from existing Buddhist relics, the Brahmans must have found it a hard task to hold their own. A less persevering, subtle, and able foe would have succumbed. But the Brahmans are, and have ever been, among the most persevering, most subtle, and most intellectually keen and forcible men that have trodden this earth. And so, thwarted, baffled, resisted, overwhelmed, they never despaired. Consequently, as their enemies became weak, they became strong, and were at last victorious, because they determined to be. Yet this thousand years' conflict affords a lesson to the world of what may be achieved by the few against the many, by a small band of resolute men who prefer their convictions to their lives, against a tame-spirited and multitudinous host, whose strength lies in their numbers, and who, through irresolution and bad leadership, are unable to make proper use of any power which they may happen to possess.

Thus it came to pass that, with the revival of Hinduism, caste re-asserted itself, and stealthily spread over the land as in former times. But its tone, like that of Hinduism, was altered. It has been more arrogant, more tyrannical, more persuasive in its influence, and has held the people with a stronger and more savage grip, than in pre-Buddhist ages. Hindus now cannot marry out of their caste on any pretence whatever. They are tied hand and foot, and are willing slaves to the most intolerant and exacting taskmaster that ever placed a yoke on the neck of man.

But this historical development of caste, and with it the subdivision of Hindus into a multitude of tribes, of which a slight sketch has thus been given, has two aspects. It is an effect produced by certain causes. The effect is manifest. I shall endeavour now to trace out its causes.

It is not sufficient to state that caste is the custom of India, and that Hindus have been born and bred to its observance. This is a truism of no meaning, for it explains nothing. Nor is it of much more interest to be informed, that, very soon after the Aryan race entered India, in distant ages of the past, the germs of caste began to be seen. If there had not been favouring circumstances in the race, or in the country, or in both combined, we may take it for granted that the phenomenon would never have appeared. I will discuss these two subjects separately.

In the first place, are there any peculiarities or special conditions among Hindus, sufficient in any degree, either in part or in whole, to account for the institution of caste with its numberless tribal ramifications, as handed down from generation to generation, with occasionally important increments added to it to increase its intensity and force? This is the proposition we have now to consider, with all the patience, calmness, and candour which the subject demands.

One striking feature of character is distinctly traceable throughout the whole of the Hindu's career, and is that to which our attention is forcibly directed in the very earliest records of his race. This is his religiousness. He is a religious being of wonderful earnestness and persistency. His love of worship is a passion, is a frenzy, is a consuming fire. It absorbs his thoughts, it influences and sways his mind on every subject. He thinks of everything in connexion with it. It gives a hue to every event of his life, to his occupations, his habits, his social duties, his conversation, his pleasures, his festivities, his sorrows, his sicknesses, his hopes, his fears, and to every circumstance, material, intellectual, and moral, related to him. He is not merely diligent in the daily observance of prescribed ceremonies, but his religiousness abides with him constantly, and is indissolubly blended with his nature.

It is not my purpose to show the inconsistency and grossness of many of his religious sentiments, or to point out the perfunctoriness with which he, for the most part, performs his religious duties. Nor is this at all necessary. The objects of his adoration, judged by the light of Christianity, may be, and no doubt are very largely, unworthy of human respect and veneration. But the feeling I speak of is subjective. It dwells in the heart of the Hindu. It is not indeed independent of an object, for that would involve a paradox and an impossibility. On the contrary, it is modified by his conception of that object, and so is conformable thereto. It thus harmonises with his beliefs. So that in fact the religious feeling of the Hindu and his creed are in union ; and the errors of the latter give a tone to the former. The feeling may not be of a high cast, may, on the other hand, be low, coarse, even sometimes base and impure, inspired by fear, or sensuality, or mysterious undefined awe.

Yet, whatever the intrinsic character of this religiousness, there it is. I speak of its existence, not of its nature ; of its reality, not of its goodness or badness ; of its quantity and intensity, not at all of its quality. It is amply sufficient for my purpose to point out, that the Hindu, from the outset of his national life down to the year 1880, has been engrossed by his religion, which has been at once a magnet to draw him, and a pole-star to direct him.

Nor is the question at all affected by the varied phases which his religion has assumed, with the exception of the great, though temporary, religious revolt of Buddhism. Throughout his entire history,—whether worshipping only the elements and the heavenly bodies, or deified heroes, or plants and animals, or Brahmans and other sacred personages, or shapes and figures of strange invention, or simple stones of varied shapes, or rivers and pools, or numberless imps and goblins infesting mountain, forest, and stream, or imaginary beings of immense power supposed to possess the highest attributes both of good and evil, or demons and devils, incarnations of wickedness, or sacred cities, sacred books, and other sacred objects,—he has shown always and everywhere the strength of his religious convictions and the dominancy of his religious nature.

At the same time, it is of considerable moment in this inquiry to endeavour to ascertain the general influence of his religiousness on the social habits and conduct of the Hindu. This influence is primarily mental, for actions are the results of thoughts. The chief practical effect produced on the Hindu mind has been that of servility. It has been first subdued, then debased, and finally enslaved. Thus it has become ready to offer willing and prompt obedience to the voice of acknowledged authority. If led by a master hand, it will follow, no matter where. Having lost its freedom, it has also lost its vision, perceiving nothing either before or behind. No incongruity, no absurdity, no error or delusion however gigantic or monstrous, awakens the common sense of the Hindu. He is wildly eager to believe in the truth of the most baseless fictions that cunning ingenuity, in its most frolicsome moods, could invent. The very air is filled with illusion, and he is totally unconscious of the circumstance. To him illusion is the same as truth—truth the same as illusion. All is illusion, unreality. He believes whatever he is told to believe, asking no questions, and troubled by no conclusions. A voluntary slave is the most abject of all slaves. The Hindu, in surrendering reason, judgment, moral sense, common sense, in short his intellectual manhood, is enchained with stronger fetters than were ever applied to the neck of the unemancipated Negro of the Southern States of America.

This credulous and servile condition of the Hindu mind has afforded a golden opportunity to the wily Brahman, thirsting for rule and for the exercise of his superior gifts. Though himself a Hindu, addicted to all the vagaries into which he has step by step led his fellow-countrymen, he has been far too self-opinionated, and has had far too much self-respect, to associate on an equality with the common herd of Hindus. His mind revolted from such communism. He saw that they followed his directions as sheep follow a shepherd. And he gradually came to despise, to abhor, and to loathe them. He shrunk from his own flesh and blood, as affected by some horrible taint. He could not, and would not, associate with the rest of his nation. Eventually many of them he kept at a distance, for the very contamination of their touch distressed him intolerably. This is surely in the highest degree extraordinary, unnatural, and cruel, and is altogether unprecedented in the annals of the world. And yet, if examined into, how closely does it harmonize with the laws of the human mind when untamed and unscrupulous, subtle and masterly!

I can imagine the curling of the Brahman's lip and the elevation of his fine expressive eyebrows as he contemplated with supreme disdain the reception of one of his fictitious manuscripts, dashed with a flavour of truth, by the masses of the people. Having finished a Purana, for example, containing here and there a few historical allusions, intermingled with elaborate dissertations on the habits and ways, and the domestic lives, of gods and goddesses, in writing which his inventive brain was taxed to its utmost in devising the most grotesque, and occasionally the most shamelessly immoral, situations for his favourite divinities, then with imperturbable *sangfroid* producing it to the open-mouthed multitude, as a revelation, a divine thesis, and watching the pleasure with which they received it, and the absence of all incredulity and distrust on their countenances, what wonder that he intensely despised a people of such gross blindness, and so miserably feeble in intellectual discernment! Yet he was withal exquisitely conscious that they had been trained by him, that he had been their *guru* or religious teacher, that he had fascinated them by the charm of his manner and by his oracular and authoritative words, and that they stood to him in the relation of a bird spellbound by the eye of a serpent. It is only in this way that we can possibly account for the universal and absolute belief of the abominable stories of Brahmá, Vishnu, Shiva, Krishna, and other deities, found in the Puranas and elsewhere, which the Brahman has palmed upon the victims of his mental tyranny and despotism.

Doubtless this peculiar influence was not gained all at once. There were marked stages in its development. Yet we can trace it with singular clearness from the first allusion to the Brahman in the earliest Sanskrit records on through the subsequent ages down to modern times. He is ever the clever and talented dogmatist, laying down the law on every subject for the guidance of his benighted fellow-countrymen. He tells them what to worship, and when to worship, and how to worship. He points out the nature of sacrifices and ceremonies. He regulates home life. He interferes in politics and state-craft. Moreover, he is very mysterious in everything, and surrounds himself with an impenetrable religious sanctity. He is at once philosopher, poet, and priest, and to his credit it must be confessed, performs each part with matchless ability and wonderful success. He can talk and write on abstruse metaphysics, he can compose odes replete with sublime thoughts addressed to the elemental deities, love-songs for women, epics and ballads for men; he can produce historical romances, full of the deeds of heroes and gods, all creations of his overwrought brain. Indeed, it is hard to say what, in the judgment of all other Hindus, he cannot do? From the first his claims have been very high, and he has come to believe himself to be what he has compelled the rest to acknowledge that he is,—namely a divinity.

We can now understand not merely the nature of that superiority which the Brahman has exercised over his brother Aryans in India, which has always been a potent fact in the history of the country, but also the effect which it has produced on his own mind and habits. Conscious of his high intellectual gifts, he has cultivated them with immense diligence, and has devoted a large amount of his time to meditation and discussion, and to reading the books which the genius of his order has produced. Having separated himself at an early period from other Hindus, the separation has continually widened. He has become more estranged from them, and more unlike them, from year to year, until the difference between them has become the greatest possible. Moreover, it is worthy of very special note, that the author of this estrangement and separation is the Brahman himself. It was he who made the difference between himself and his brethren.

This feud among the Hindu race, which has split it up into a thousand clans, is the most unnatural of all feuds ever known; and is none the less so because for many ages it has been accepted by them as a social necessity, having lost in their estimation its offensiveness, and having come to be regarded as a happy condition instead of a bright social calamity. Its monstrous unnaturalness and its consummate violation of the principles of humanity, will be more vividly seen by an analysis of some of the moral characteristics of the Brahman, to which it has given birth.

One of these characteristics is arrogance and pride. It may be said that all men of every nation who are raised above their fellows, are proud. And there is truth in the statement. Wealth, knowledge, rank, and many other causes foster pride in the human heart, not merely in India, but in all other countries likewise. But the pride of the Brahman is *sui generis*, is a quality, thank Heaven, peculiar to him, and not to be found except in his family. Being so purely idiosyncratic, it is difficult to describe; and needs to be seen in order to be rightly known. Strange to say, the Brahman is so accustomed to it as to be, for the most part, unconscious of its existence and of its habitual display in his life and conduct. With him it is a second nature. He has received it from his forefathers. He will transmit it to his posterity. It is the air he breathes. It is a part of himself from which he can now no more be dissociated than he can from his own intelligence. Possessed with a sense of unlikeness to, and exaltation above, other people, he disdains their companionship. Were the question put to him, why he did this, he would be unable to reply further than by asserting that this habit had been transmitted to him by his remote ancestors, who cherished the same repugnance to castes beneath him, which he does. He feels that his tastes, his sympathies, and his very nature, raise him above all other persons. He is a being the like of whom is not to be found on this great globe. He was born to greatness and nobility,—nay, he is a divine being, and how can he then associate on common terms with mere human clods destitute of the divine ray?

A second characteristic is intense selfishness. Of this too he seems to be unconscious. He lives for himself, and for himself alone. Perhaps the same may be said of most people. Nevertheless, it certainly may be said of the Brahman in a special and emphatic manner. 'Everything, everybody, was made for me, for my behoof and enjoyment,' is his first and last thought every day of his life. He should have the best of nature's products. He should receive peculiar honour and respect. Consideration not shown to others should be shown to him. He is properly above law, yet, if at any time amenable to it, he should not by any means be governed by laws regulating other people, but favourable laws should be made for him, a favoured and distinguished personage. The common people must not swear against his life, though he may swear against theirs. His life is too precious to be sacrificed even for the commission of the highest crimes. He not only enjoys liberty, or rather liberties, but is entitled to special privileges. His smile must be propitiated by other Hindus on occasion of every event of a social or domestic character affecting them. He expects the costliest presents, the most luxurious dinners, the finest muslins and silks. At births, at marriages, in times of sickness and death, in seasons of great trouble and adversity, at all festivities, his presence and blessing are sought, and paid for. He takes what he gets, partly as a sacrificial and family priest, and partly as the superior creature styled Brahman. That he is an incarnation, as he imagines himself to be, is no doubt correct, but it is an incarnation of selfishness.

A third characteristic of the Brahman is the tyrannical spirit which he cherishes and exercises. He has ever been the fountain of authority and law. His word is law, from which there is no appeal. In former times, until in fact the Brahman had attained the supreme and sovereign position he now occupies, he had to encounter the fierce opposition of other Hindus, especially of the Rajpoots, who were at first little inclined to surrender their independence, and moreover as warriors and princes thought themselves as good as the subtle, self-seeking Brahman. They resisted therefore most strenuously the claims and assumptions of what they doubtless regarded as the upstart Brahmans, and fought for the freedom which was dear to them. But they reckoned ignorantly; I say ignorantly, for they knew not the mental resources of their oppressors, whose fertility and strength of intellect gave them immense advantages, and ultimately complete victory. In the world's history all great struggles have eventually been decided in favour of the side which has possessed the most powerful understanding. And in India no non-Brahmanical tribe has ever been a match for the clear, penetrating mind of the Brahman. At first the physical contest went on hand-in-hand with the moral and intellectual; and the latter, we may suppose, continued long after the former had ceased. All resistance, however, has for many ages been abandoned, and at length Hindus of every grade have willingly and cheerfully succumbed to the Brahman. 'What does the Brahman say?' is the question of questions among a people of prostrate intellect, with no opinion of their own, and with an entire and abject confidence in the superior gifts of their national leaders. His curse is considered to be the most appalling calamity, his blessing the highest possible good. Hindus are a nation of slaves, who obey his will in all things, humble themselves in the dust before him, live on his smiles, and die beneath his frowns.

A fourth characteristic of the Brahman, which has been already presupposed, is his intractability. He yields to no one, has never done so. He never swerves from his own sentiments, from the codes which his predecessors have laid down as laws and principles of Hindu life and action. He is a conservative of the purest water. In his estimation, it is sufficient that the minutest rules for the government of his order and of other great castes, are given in detail in the Laws of Manu, a book on caste and other matters dating much prior to the Christian era. He is determined to adhere rigidly to them, and not to deviate from them by a hair's breadth. No one has been a greater enemy of progress and development than the Brahman, and India is advancing in civilization in spite of him. Indeed he too is yielding himself to the exciting and transforming influences around him, and is changing. But I am speaking of him in relation to his own principles, and to their natural consequences, principles which, as we shall presently see, have moulded the tribes of India into the forms they have assumed for thousands of years. Had the Brahman been other than he is,—had he possessed the smallest flexibility and leniency in his nature,—had he been in any degree less pertinacious in the maintenance of his own ideas,—had he at any time throughout his career been willing to accept a compromise with other castes,—had he been less rigid, less dogmatic,—had he ever been inclined to listen to other people, and to regard their interests as equal in importance to his own,—had he, in short, behaved more like a neighbour and a brother, and been more genial and less exacting, India would have assumed a different character, and the growth of caste would have been checked.

Perhaps I ought to add a fifth characteristic, that of ambition, which in truth has been the hidden secret in the breast of the Brahman, prompting and regulating all his movements. His ambition has been, not only to be the first and foremost of Indian tribes, but to stamp his will on the institutions of his country, so that they should all appear, directly or indirectly, to have sprung from him. This ambition, therefore, has not been one of vile and sordid conquest, like that of the soldier, who seeks to subdue his enemies by their destruction; or of the mere party politician who gains glory as much by thwarting his adversaries as by the propagation of his own ideas. But the Brahman's ambition has been to subjugate the intellects of all other Hindus, to dominate them by his will, to bring them to look to him as their example to follow, and to be passive in his hands, as the inspirer of their thoughts and the guide of their actions. He has cared little for wealth or for what the world calls honour. He has been, for the most part, poor, certainly much poorer than many Hindus of a lower grade. He has rarely arrived at political rule and kingly government. He has been content to see Rajpoot and even Sudra potentates exercising sway, from generation to generation, over great provinces. His own thoughts have been from the first in a different direction. His ambition has been of another order, of a more refined and elevated character. He has sought to govern human intellect, and to regulate the social relations of men on a prodigious scale. This has been the sublime object of his ambition ;—and he has succeeded, wonderfully succeeded. The triumph of reason, will, genius, was never more complete. The Brahman's achievement in directing the thoughts of the vast population of India throughout a period of not less than three thousand years, of first inventing, and then controlling, its intricate social machinery, of being the motor power whence have sprung the thousand-fold ramifications of the inner life of this great social fabric, is the most gigantic and astounding feat of ambition recorded in the history of mankind.

Caste, therefore, owes its origin to the Brahman. It is his invention. It is a necessary condition incident to his assumptions and to the extraordinary success of his projects. The subject, however, has its gradations and divisions. The first aspect of it is that which applies to the Brahman himself. A second has relation to the castes below him. As to the former,—namely, its origin, so far as the Brahman is concerned,—the only sufficient explanation of his motives and objects, is caste. In the exercise of those peculiar characteristics of which I have now been speaking, and in withdrawing himself from association with other Hindus, it was impossible for him to stop short of caste. These same qualities have been found in certain shades in other nations, but never to the extent in which they have combined together in the Brahman. Yet it is singular to observe, that to the degree in which any nation has exhibited them, to that degree has it found it necessary to ordain and recognize a kind of caste distinction among its inhabitants.

As the Brahman is an ethnological phenomenon and paradox, so is caste. The two are inseparable. The Brahman could not now exist, and could not have existed at all, bearing the distinctive characteristics which he has exhibited during the time in which he has displayed them, without having caste as the objective form in which his ideas were realized. Caste was not handed down to him. It was begotten by him, was a necessity of the situation to which he had brought himself, was conceived in his own fruitful brain, was as much a result of his imaginings as Brahmanism itself. He did not become a complete Brahman all at once, nor did he give, so to speak, bodily shape to caste by an instantaneous volition. There were, doubtless, historical gradations in the development of Brahmanism and caste; but, nevertheless, the growth of both was comparatively rapid, and they attained maturity together.

Let us now endeavour to ascertain in what manner all other Hindus have been affected by the unnatural and selfish course pursued by the Brahman. We know, historically, that at first this course was resisted very strenuously, though impotently. The rest of the Hindu tribes, though doubtless much more numerous than the Brahmans, being worsted in the conflict, and being repudiated, scorned and despised by their proud victors, were not long in following in their footsteps. They were bound to acknowledge the superiority and immense ability of the Brahmans, and it is nothing wonderful that they soon became animated with their spirit. The Brahmans had been successful in the national struggle, the Brahmans were men of genius, the Brahmans had inaugurated a system of social life, which flattered pride and excited powerfully some of the commanding passions of the human breast. In such circumstances the example set to them was of ommipotent force. And thus it came to pass, that the commencement of caste among the Brahmans and among the remaining Hindu tribes was, as nearly as possible, contemporaneous.

Feeling the necessity of their position, and yet unwilling to make sweeping changes among themselves, these tribes were for a time contented with changes, which, compared with those which were subsequently made, and are now in force, were of a very limited character. Only two more castes seem originally to have been established. One was that of the warriors or fighting men, who, by virtue of their warlike qualities and habits, assumed the position of rulers, and so formed themselves into a distinct tribe. The other was appropriated by the agriculturists, who were also traders. The former were styled Rajpoots, the latter Vaisyas. These separate castes were permitted by the Brahmans, and most probably were actually constituted by them. This latter supposition seems natural, because of the manifest control which, in the early times, the Brahmans not only exercised over their own caste, but also over all other castes, such as is not needed in these latter days, when caste fills the land, and minute regulations for its due observance are well known to every Hindu.

Thus three castes only existed in primitive Hindu society; and doubtless each of these three was in itself homogeneous,—that is, was not yet divided and subdivided as now into separate branches with no mutual relations and no mutual sympathy. This condition of the Hindus, compared with that which step by step they eventually chose for themselves and adopted, was simple and tolerable. Nevertheless, there was even then at least one other class, though not dignified by the name of a distinct caste, or recognized as such. This consisted of Hindus, bred and born, who, from their menial occupations, and from other causes, were excluded from the three castes, of persons who were the offspring of unions between members of the castes and aborigines, and of aborigines. All these divisions of the remaining people were for a time regarded as outcasts, and were objects of much scorn and loathing on the part of the castes. Special disgust was cherished towards the last named, or the aborigines, who were treated to numerous appellations, especially by the Brahmans, denoting extreme vileness, impurity, and worthlessness.

When it was precisely that the fourth caste, namely the Sudras, was inaugurated, is, I apprehend, unknown; and, moreover, the exact circumstances of its establishment are unknown likewise. Allusions to the Sudras are found, however, both in Upanishads and Sutras. There is good reason for the conjecture that the Brahmans, and perhaps the other castes, finding it inconvenient that such large numbers of their own race, of those who had partly sprung from them and even of the aborigines, should be in the degraded and opprobrious condition of outcasts, determined on the creation of a fourth caste. Then came the pleasing fiction invented to give countenance to this four-fold division of Hindus, that from the mouth of Purusha, or the primeval male, the Brahman was produced; from his arms, the Rajpoot; from his thighs, the Vaisya; and from his feet, the Sudra. The Sudra caste seems to have included all the menial classes, not excepting those aborigines who conformed to the Brahman's sacrificial and ceremonial regulations. The rest were styled Dasyas, whoever they might be, and were held in abomination.

Had the process of caste-making stopped here, the ultimate harm to Hindu society would not have been great. But a dangerous and altogether anomalous principle of national existence had been sown like seed among the primitive Aryans of India. In this prolific soil its growth became rapid and rank. While still keeping to the prescriptive four-fold original generic castes, the castes greatly multiplied, and were said to number thirty-six, but this was only a nominal reckoning, for they increased to hundreds and thousands. It is interesting, however, as a reminiscence of the past, that, even at the present day, although castes were never more numerous, Hindus always speak of them as thirty-six in number, and also as four. The rest of the people followed the practice of their leaders and chiefs in this respect, who found that as they increased numerically, and spread over the country, their feelings towards each other became somewhat like those they cherished towards inferior castes. The Brahman on the banks of the Saraswatee in the Punjab was a being different from the Brahman on the banks of the Ganges or the Sarjoo, and both withdrew their sympathies from the Brahmans of the Narbuddha Valley, of the Godavery, and of the country beyond. Thus, in the course of time, the Brahmans separated from one another, and set a further example to other Hindus on the intricate subject of caste. These latter were always willing learners, and were only too ready to follow in the footsteps of their sacred and highly venerated teachers. The Brahmans becoming split up into numerous branches, according to their geographical position, their observance or non-observance of certain ceremonies and customs, their eating or not eating of certain food, and many other circumstances which, though perhaps in themselves trivial, yet were abundantly sufficient to serve as reasons for separation when the desire to part had once been formed, soon began to exhibit distinct ethnological characteristics. After a few hundred years of disintegration, marked differences showed themselves in the Brahmanical community; and what shall be said of two thousand years and upwards of such disintegration? There are now perhaps not less than a hundred Brahmanical tribes which for ages have had no social relations with one another, and have only intermarried among themselves. Looking upon a Mahrathi Brahman and a Bengali Brahman, the contrast is very striking. They are in appearance as unlike each other as an Englishman is unlike a Red Indian; and yet they are undoubtedly of the same original stock. A difference, more or less manifest, exists between all the tribes which have thus excluded themselves from intercourse with other tribes. To speak, therefore, of the Brahmans as though they were one and the same people, with the same characteristics, the same features, the same habits, and the same temperament, is delusive. For thousands of years they have been a disunited people, with mutual antipathies and non-resemblances, instead of mutual likenesses and mutual concord. The Brahmans themselves, and none others, are responsible for this. Their monstrous arrogance, selfishness, and assumption have proved the bane of their race. In the cultivation of these vicious qualities they are at one, but in all other respects they are the most mutually inharmonious and discordant people on the face of the earth.

The spread of caste and the multiplication of separate, mutually exclusive, and inimical tribes among the lower Hindu grades, also lies at their door. The detestable example they set could not but be slavishly followed by an imitative people without brains of their own and entirely guided by the brains of their social and religious superiors. These Hindu tribes would never have dared to establish an infinity of castes among themselves without the direct sanction and assistance of the Brahmans, enforced by their pernicious practice. Moreover, when the Brahmans perceived that castes were increasing beyond decent limits, until the whole country was threatened with an endless number of caste subdivisions, all for the most part mutually destructive, they might have peremptorily stopped their further multiplication. But they did not. On the contrary it is plain, that they looked on with the utmost satisfaction, pleased at the alienation of tribe from tribe,—pleased that all the castes were animated by the spirit of themselves,—pleased at the prospect of the augmentation of their own authority and majesty with every increment added to the castes,—and pleased above all at the thought that their own order was at the head of the entire system, and exercised command over all its ramifications.

A nation divided against itself is the proper description of the Hindu race. So minute are the divisions of the people that, in most parts of the country, not merely does every profession, trade, and occupation constitute a distinct caste, but over extensive tracts, in Northern India especially, every occupation has given birth to at least seven clans, which are estranged from one another both in respect of marriage and eating together, and, although not so recognized, are to all intents and purposes distinct and separate castes. Even the lowest and most degraded of the people, who are spurned from the temple, and are engaged in the most loathsome employments, have taken their cue from their more respectable neighbours, and have their own castes and subdivisions, together with all the paraphernalia necessary thereto. Indeed, it is a notorious fact in Northern India, at the least, that the most debased castes yield to none in the punctilious strictness with which they observe caste prejudices, and carry out caste regulations. In the city of Benares, not to speak of India at large, there are scores, and probably hundreds, of clans or tribes, which are commonly regarded as out of the pale of Hinduism, being neither Brahmans, Rajpoots, Vaisyas, nor Sudras, and are in reality so many distinct castes, governing themselves with extreme rigidity, and animated with the spirit of pride and exclusiveness, as though they were Brahmans instead of an abhorred race. The epithet applied to them by Hindus of the four original castes, is that of outcasts, a palpable misnomer in this respect, that, although they may not be included in the charmed circle of Hindu caste, they have, nevertheless, long ago constituted themselves into castes, and observe all the rules of their orders with as much pertinacity and sincerity as their betters. Indeed, so much are all the castes, whether high or low, attached to their own fraternities, and so thoroughly are they reconciled to their condition, that, during all the years I have lived in India, I do not remember a single instance of a member of one caste striving to enter another.

The infatuation of pride, self-esteem, and exclusiveness penetrates all the castes, of whatever denomination, through and through. The curse of Brahmanism has fallen on all native society, and blighted it. The spirit of the Brahman, essential to him in the formation and propagation of his distinctive caste, by virtue of which he has isolated himself from all mankind, and the various members of his caste have been led to isolate themselves from one another, and to separate into numerous independent fraternities, each being a distinct unity, has fallen on all other Hindu and non-Hindu castes. This spirit is reproduced in each one, is its *raison d'être*, is its animating principle, is at once the ground of its existence and the cause of its perpetuation. If you carefully observe the working of any caste which you may select, in any rank of native society, you will infallibly find in it the presence of those especial characteristics, which, as previously shown, tended unitedly to the origination, in primitive times, of the Brahmanical caste, and have maintained that caste with its manifold divisions in its condition of isolation. No caste, for this reason, wishes to be other than it is. Though it may be very low in comparison with, and in the estimation of, many other castes, nevertheless it is puffed up with arrogance, and with a strange, and, except for the reasons given, unaccountable conceit of superiority and self-importance. Each caste, down to the lowest, is eaten up with self-satisfaction and self-admiration. It will never defer to another caste in any matter, because it regards itself as an entity, quite as important to its component members, as that of any other caste, of any degree, to the members of which it is composed.

I may state incidentally, that this circumstance,—namely, the presence of these characteristics in all the castes,—is by far the strongest of all the reasons that can be assigned to account for the difficulty of the Hindu race amalgamating with Englishmen, and with all foreigners. Difficulty, forsooth! Such amalgamation is an utter impossibility. If all the castes shun one another with an eagerness amounting to frenzy, we may take it for certain that they will avoid all contact with outside races with not less energy and feeling. If they have determined that all mutual approaches among themselves are impracticable, not to say chimerical, we may rest assured, once for all, that any social approaches of foreigners must be resisted with resentment. This is a necessity arising from the fundamental constitution of caste.

I may further remark, that, as I think I have already substantiated, inasmuch as caste is based on certain vicious qualities of the mind, which have been cultivated in India to an extent entirely unknown in other lands, this circumstance affords, in my belief, the most pregnant of all reasons to account for the great and manifest difference in the intellectual and moral results arising from the spread of education, especially in its higher forms, in this country. A Hindu, with a university degree, indicating that he has acquired extensive knowledge in various branches of human learning, has been, as a rule, drawn but slightly in the direction of true civilization; and his moral sentiments, though confessedly improved somewhat, remain destitute of that robustness, which is one of the grand concomitants of the advanced education which English youths receive. The truth is, the Hindu's mind is enslaved by hereditary pride and exclusiveness. He values English education, but he values his caste more. The former is useful for obtaining a livelihood, but after all is of no vital importance; the latter is of infinite moment, and must be retained at any cost. The possession of vast stores of knowledge, brought from the West, cannot, in his estimation, possibly place him in a higher social position than what he formerly occupied, or raise him into a nobler sphere, or generate in his mind loftier aims and purposes, or compensate, in the smallest degree, for the loss or abandonment of the ancient customs and privileges of caste. Sublime arrogance and moral progress are natural enemies. And thus it comes to pass, that the Hindu, wedded to old prejudices, and inflated with conceit, although adorned with degrees, indicating the knowledge which his intellect has acquired, and in some measure the quickening which it has received, has hitherto made little advancement in the highest forms of civilization. He has failed utterly to comprehend the deep meaning of the Delphian axiom, 'man, know thyself.'

Such is a brief outline of the special conditions of Hindus, under which they have lived for many ages, and by the operation of which they have become a separate people, unlike all other races that have ever appeared on the earth; and have first of all framed, and then, with extraordinary perseverance and patience, perpetuated a peculiar social system, to which, in spite of its unnaturalness and extreme oppressiveness, they have ever passionately clung.

In the second place, having already unfolded what seems to me the essential cause of caste, I am free to admit that one other powerful influence, at the least, has had great weight in producing the result which we see. This is of a geographical character, and is to be found in the country itself, which has been peculiarly favorable to the development of caste. This influence would have had no effect alone; nevertheless, in association with others of a vital and transforming character, it has been of immense use. India, as a country, has been well-suited to be the home of caste in three ways—by its almost perfect isolation, by its climate, and by its physical conformation. We will consider the natural influence on the people of the country of each of these elements separately.

First—the isolation of India.

This land, by its lofty frontier mountains, is almost completely cut off from the rest of the world. True, these mountains have their passes, which at intervals a desolating enemy has traversed, and, bursting on the plains, has fought with, and subdued, the Hindu inhabitants, and, holding them in subjection, has, to some extent, modified their habits and customs. Three great inroads of this nature I will briefly allude to. One was that of the Greeks, led, in the first instance, by Alexander the Great, and subsequently by the Greek kings of Bactria. A second was that of the Indo-Scythians, who destroyed the Bactrian monarchy, and in the first century before, and in the first century after, the Christian era, exercised authority on both sides of the north-western frontier. The third was that of the Mahomedans, who, for eight hundred years and upwards, were lords paramount of India, and during that period were entering the country in a ceaseless, though at times very attenuated, stream. Other incursions of foreigners have also occasionally taken place, as of the Portuguese, Dutch, French, and English. Now, every one of these external influences has produced a certain modifying effect on the caste and habits of Hindus, some much more than others; and yet, as all acquainted with the subject must acknowledge, their aggregate effect on caste has been very slight. Mahomedanism notoriously succumbed to caste, so that Indian Mahomedans, instead of shaking the foundation of the system, which, judging *a priori* from the intolerance and despotism of Mahomedan rulers, was imminent on their taking possession of the country, have themselves become Hinduized, and have been brought into the meshes of caste. Greek art, and science, and politics, were undoubtedly at one time powerful in Northern India. The most violent assailant of the system is English influence in its many-sidedness operating at the present day.

None of these external influences was brought in contact with Hindu caste until it had taken firm hold of the native mind, and had been elaborated into the complicated and cumbrous system which now prevails. Had caste, at the very period of its inception, met with an external opponent, like Mahomedanism, or modern civilization, it would probably have been an abortion. But it had for centuries its own way, and soon grew into a monstrous shape. The opposition it met with at the outset, though fierce, was of men rather than of principles, and, being from within the circle of Hinduism, was short-lived and spasmodic.

In spite of the fact that India has always been a prey to invaders, who have left their mark behind them, it is nevertheless true that, throughout its history, it has been left to itself and its own devices in a very remarkable manner. Few countries have been so isolated. The result has been, that on the whole it has met with little external opposition in carrying out its peculiar social projects. Its subjugation repeatedly by foreign foes has affected its political, but not its domestic life. Without any counteracting authority of sufficient interest and weight, the Hindus have been free to inaugurate and develope whatever mode their acknowledged chiefs invented, as best calculated, in their own judgment, to represent the principles they had formed respecting the ties and relations of Hindu society. They have experienced no friction with other nations. They have not been in the smallest degree amenable to the public opinion of neighbouring countries, which, in some parts of the world, has been a powerful factor in the growth of social customs.

An isolation, almost as complete as that of the Hindus, has fallen to the lot of the Chinese. And with what result? Left to their own imaginings, they have become a people as peculiar and extraordinary in their way as Hindus in theirs. It is manifest from their writings that they have followed their philosophical and religious leaders with as much blindness and infatuation as Hindus have shown in following their Brahmanical teachers. Had Confucius elaborated for them a system of caste, they would unquestionably have adopted it; and would have adhered to it with as much persistency and self-sacrifice as have been exhibited in India. Although they have had a narrow escape from caste, they have, nevertheless, during the long period of their existence, displayed as striking idiosyncracies of national life and character as their neighbours on the plains of Hindustan.

We may regard it as an axiom, that the isolation of a country tends to the generation of national peculiarities, and that the greater the isolation, the stronger and more marked they are. The rapidity with which national peculiarities may develope is illustrated by a country which has risen to greatness in modern times. Scarcely one hundred years have passed since the United States were severed from Britain, and yet the inhabitants, although in the main of British parentage, are in many respects exceedingly unlike their progenitors of the country from which they sprung.

The separation of India from all other countries, and its isolation, have imparted a great impetus to caste; and, although not in themselves affording a sufficient reason for this singular condition of Hindu life, have incontestably rendered it great support and encouragement.

Secondly—the climate of India.

How much the climate of England, combined with its insular position, has contributed to the development of the Anglo-Saxon race, is well known to the philosophic historian. Had England not been separated from the continent, and had its climate been of a milder and more relaxing character, there is every reason to suppose that its inhabitants would have been devoid of the individuality, love of freedom, and common sense for which they are distinguished. Few, I imagine, will doubt that the clear and genial climate of France has fostered the development of the light-heartedness and volatility, which are charmingly exhibited in the genuine Frenchman. And, going further southwards, where the sun exercises greater power, and life is spent in an exquisite realization of nature's gifts, how sensuous, and withal how sparkling, is the enjoyment of the Spaniard, while in spirit and energy he evinces a strange contrast to the lively and yet practical Frenchman?

The hot climate of India has been a powerful modeller of Hindu character. Provoking meditation and poetic sentiment, and at the same time inflaming the imagination to a white heat, it has produced one of the most rhapsodical and unreal beings that ever was created. Thoughts, the most whimsical and fantastic, the most extravagant rhodomontade of which the human mind is capable, and the boldest and most magnificent speculations in ontology and psychology, make up the extensive literature of the Hindus. With minds so singularly constituted by nature, so prone to excess, and endowed with such an intense craving for strange situations and wild fancies, the Hindus have adopted caste with the same mental heat which they have displayed in all other matters. The Brahmanical brain has always been in a state of intense and unrestrained excitement. There are some countries specially adapted to peculiar mental efforts, which would be entirely out of place elsewhere. We are not shocked at monstrous and unnatural forms of thought in a torrid as in a temperate clime. The rhapsodies of the human intellect are not so offensive in India as they would be in England. And caste, though considered by people bred in a temperate region to be opposed to sense, propriety, and humanity, is thought differently of by persons dwelling in the country which has given it birth, who foster and heartily approve of that which all the rest of the world with one voice condemns.

Moreover, while the heat of India inflames the mind as well as the body, it induces, on the other hand, lassitude in both. The 'let alone' principle, as applied to daily practical life, is thoroughly carried out in every grade of native society, and is very apt to creep into the ranks of English residents. There is a fatal tendency induced by the excessive heat, to allow things to remain as they are, from week to week, and from month to month. An effort is required to deviate from the beaten track, which is commonly distressing, if not painful, to make.

Customs, which would not have been tolerated for an instant in a cool climate, have been allowed to grow up, and to exercise gradually a masterly authority, solely because of the general indolence and heedlessness produced by the long and all-pervading summer heat, which enfeebles the mind and prevents it from rousing itself to a contrary action.

Thus caste, which, like rank luxuriant plants of the jungle, could only have been generated under the inflammatory influences of a torrid clime, has been in no small degree perpetuated, until it has become an omnipotent agency in Hindu social life, by the intense lassitude induced by the heat, and by the unwillingness which every body feels to alter that which is already established.

Thirdly.—The physical conformation of India.

Rivers, mountains, forests, and plains, have in the world's history played no unimportant part in the formation of national character. Rugged, bleak mountains produce a love of freedom and independence, as illustrated by the Swiss, or of intrepidity and manliness, as displayed by the Highland Scotch. Forest life fosters a spirit of retirement and exclusiveness; while streams and plains are favourable to meditation and repose.

The Hindu is accustomed to spend half his time on the banks of some sacred stream, from which, having leisurely bathed and performed his devotions, he retires to the cool shade of a neighbouring tree, or to the grove attached to his favourite shrine, where, in silence, or in friendly talk, the hours glide away slowly and lusciously, while he feasts his eyes alternately on the peaceful river and on the gorgeous hues of the trees around him. Thus his existence becomes a romance and a charm. Nothing in his estimation is real. The world consists of phenomena. The grand river before him, the trees which impart their hospitable shade, the lovely flowers, even himself and his friend with whom he delights to converse, are all an illusion, a mere phantom of his own mind. So that he has come to detest what is practical, and to love what is untrue and illusory. This is a faithful picture of the Hindu as he was for many ages. He never was so realistic in his thoughts and ways as he has of late years become under the thoroughly materialistic and unpoetic training of his matter-of-fact English rulers. But I am endeavouring to delineate him as he has been throughout the greater part of his history,—a history in which the human imagination has been let loose, to indulge in the most fantastic freaks and the most contradictory paradoxes, and has been allowed to introduce them into Hindu society, not in sport and jest, but in perfect soberness and solemnity, as though they were necessary axioms for the regulation of the domestic life of the nation, on which all mankind were agreed.

The institution of caste, therefore,—because of its deviation from the forms of human society prevailing in other lands,—because of its intricacy and complexity, its mystery and freemasonry,—because of its intense unrealism, striving to constitute the thousand-fold minute distinctions among men into real and essential differences,—because of its subtle imposition on the intellect, leading it deceitfully to believe that the separation of Hindus into caste is in accordance with the operation of a divine law, by which it is accounted atrociously wicked to attempt to unite clans and tribes which have been, as they imagine, disparted by impassable barriers,—because of these and other reasons which might be stated, is in complete harmony with the Hindu's mind, which has been formed by his peculiar meditative habits, combined with the powerful influence which the physical condition of his country has produced upon him. Moreover, the Hindu acknowledges his obligations to the physical relations under which he lives much more than most people. The noble Ganges, in which he bathes—of which he drinks—by which his fields are nourished—on which he gazes with rapture—and on the banks of which he listlessly dreams,—is to him a divinity, worthy of the homage he devoutly and thankfully renders. If the Brahman, who has taught him what he conceives to be his duty to the river, should teach him other things, though he may not understand the reason of them, he will follow where he is led with unquestioning obsequiousness. He is spellbound, and is wrought upon by a thousand influences unknown to the world beyond. He is not his own master, for his senses have been taken captive by the physical phenomena of the land of his birth, and his intellect has been subdued by the will of a tribe stronger than his own. The seductions of climate—of his national streams—of his dense forests, have robbed him of his mental independence, and have made him an abject slave to the devices of his spiritual and social guides, who have never, like the rest of their race, lost their self-possession; but, calm and unperturbed, have carried out their mysterious plans amid all the strifes and vicissitudes of their country's history.

Summing up the results of these three-fold influences, arising from the physical conformation, the climate, and the isolation of India, on the development of the individual character and the social habits of the Hindus, it is abundantly manifest that these influences have very powerfully affected them. Nor is this at all remarkable. Similar circumstances combined to form the Greek and the Roman characters. Both Greece and Italy were largely isolated, possessed special physical peculiarities, and were favored with a climate adapted to the intellectual training of their inhabitants. Had the Æolian, Ionian, Dorian, and other Hellenic colonists, settled on the banks of the Danube, or in the Caucasus, instead of among the islands and on the mainland of Greece, there is every reason to believe that the Greeks would have had a very different history. In like manner, the Hindus have been highly favored by an extraordinary combination of physical phenomena, allowing the free exercise of the singular talents of a very sagacious dominant race, in the production of what constitutes national character, and in the origination and elaboration of Hindu social usages, among which the institution of caste occupies a prominent place. I shall close this paper by briefly referring to another important matter connected with the establishment of caste, and which may be represented by the following heading :—

TIME OR OPPORTUNITY.

When I speak of time as having played an important part in the production of Hindu caste, all that I mean is, that the time chosen was in the highest degree suitable and favorable, not merely for the origination of caste, but also for its extension among all the tribes of the country.

In the history of mankind, customs have been formed, and events have taken place, agreeable to the circumstances in which nations have been placed. Custom is an exceedingly powerful tyrant, and retains its mastery over a nation long after the reason which gave it birth has passed away. In England, especially in certain countries, towns, and villages, customs of the most grotesque character exist, recalling one to the uncouth and semi-barbarous relations subsisting among men in the Middle Ages ; and are as tyrannical as they were five hundred years ago. Such customs would stand no chance whatever of being started in the present aspect of England, but, having been started, they continue on their course with the childish doggedness of old age. Habits, like weeds, possess a wonderful vitality, and though everything else dies, will continue in unabated vigour.

Were an effort now to be made for the first time to introduce caste into India, it would be received with indignation by all classes, and would create a rebellion in the country. Year by year Hindus are gaining more intelligence and knowledge, and are making rapid progress in the civilization of western nations, so that, did they not find the peculiar institution of caste already in their midst, they are exhibiting, less and less every day, that especially prepared social soil, in which it would be possible for the seeds of caste to germinate and grow. And yet caste having gained possession of the public mind in India, how seriously any blow aimed at it, however unwittingly, is still regarded by Hindus, was recently illustrated in a very decisive manner by the great mutiny and the widespread rebellion of 1857.

The infancy of the Hindu race was not only a well-selected time for the establishment of caste, but was, I contend, the only time when its establishment was possible. The Brahmans had then supreme authority, and immense power; and the Hindus, having recently entered the country, were simple in their habits, and unsophisticated, and had gradually come to look up to their religious leaders with slavish awe and childish confidence. It was necessary for self-defence and for personal security that the Hindus should follow implicitly the teaching of the Brahmans; and, although treated with strictness and severity, they evidently came to the conclusion that this was their best policy. It is manifest from the fragmentary annals of the time scattered about early Sanskrit writings, that the people generally had no voice of their own, but were as children in the hands of their wily instructors, to be moulded according to their will.

Moreover, the Hindu race, compared with what it subsequently became, was a small community. How small it was, we have no accurate means of knowing. Yet, judging from the fact, that it was for a time located within easy reach of the Saraswatee river, now extinct, but formerly flowing in the Punjab, and that it very gradually migrated eastward, coming at length to the Ganges, and occupying the banks of its most westerly streams, we gather that, numerically, it was very inconsiderable as compared with modern times. Few in numbers, inhabiting a circumscribed tract, with strong bonds of mutual sympathy, and still animated by traditions and reminiscences of their common home beyond the Hindu Kush, they were quickly affected by the action taken by their Brahmanical guides, whom they reverenced and consulted, and without whom they undertook no enterprise.

A new people in a new country, the early Hindus were in a highly receptive state, ready to adopt any changes—political, social, or religious—suggested by their leaders. No doubt, caste, even in its rudiments, gave a shock to the primitive non-Brahmanical Hindus, as it seemed a breach of confidence and trust, and threatened their mutual friendship; and for a time some strong resistance was shown. But this resistance could never have been on a very large scale, and probably was almost exclusively confined to the Rajpoots or warriors, who naturally held that they had played an efficient and important part in overcoming the aborigines, and in opening up the country to the entire body of Hindu immigrants. But it is plain that all the Hindu tribes soon perceived the immense sagacity which dwelt in the Brahman's head, and, abdicating their own intellectual functions, were glad to find some one able and willing to think for them. A thinker is a great power, indeed the greatest power on earth; and, if he be also an actor, his actions corresponding in force and grandeur to his thoughts, he is invincible.

This was the Brahman's opportunity—an opportunity which ripened and developed, and which he continued to enjoy for several centuries in early Hindu national life. His will became law to all other Hindus, and has been so throughout their whole history. Nevertheless, his authority was exercised much more emphatically and indisputably in the youth of the race, than was possible in their manhood, and than he could have ventured to display in later ages. I reiterate, that the institution of caste was only feasible in the childhood of the Hindus. The death-blow which caste has aimed at social bonds and relations could only have been submitted to, in the first instance, when the nation was in a condition of mental feebleness and moral helplessness, and would have been met with fierce vindictive opposition had it been commenced at any other period of growth.

DISSERTATION THE SECOND.

THE UNITY OF THE HINDU RACE.

In discussing the conditions of Hindu society it is not sufficient to take note merely of caste distinctions and divisions, which are well nigh innumerable. An analysis of races is incomplete without a corresponding synthesis. We need not only to become acquainted with the dissimilarities in the composition of the multitudinous tribes and castes spread over India, but also with the nature of the agreement subsisting between them. It is much more difficult to illustrate and prove the latter than the former. The fact of the segregation of Hindus into hundreds and thousands of classes, all, for the most part, mutually exclusive, is patent to every body. But to what extent they are bound together, and in what respects they may be said to be related, and to constitute a homogeneous community, is by no means so apparent. In the observations I shall venture to make on this subject, my remarks must be regarded rather as tentative than argumentative, as representing a search after knowledge in this occult matter than as knowledge actually obtained.

The question to be considered is simply this, What resemblances are there among Hindus ? What amount of unity exists between them ? To imagine for an instant that they really consist of innumerable races, corresponding to the minute subdivisions into which they have separated, is preposterous.

Notwithstanding the eager desire now cherished by all the separate castes of India to be severed from one another, yet we know, from the testimony of Manu and other ancient authorities, that, in the period of Manu himself, when caste-rules were very intricate and cumbrous, and when the people generally felt their pressure to be a grievous burden, there was, under certain restrictions, almost free intercourse between the castes, and not only so, but also between the castes and the unclean classes of the outer pale. Intermarriages between Brahmans, Rajpoots, Vaisyas, and Sudras were, in these early times, not merely permitted by the laws, but were every day occurring. The offspring of such cross-marriages did not remain in the castes of their fathers, but formed separate castes, and set up as distinct tribes on their own account. They were, however, not merely countenanced by the law in so doing, but were protected likewise; and their condition became, in the new sphere they occupied, one of honour and comparative respectability. In this way castes rapidly multiplied, and would have continued to increase indefinitely, had not a stop been eventually put to these intermarriages; though when they actually ceased, is uncertain.

By referring to the statements in Manu's Code, it is abundantly manifest that the blood of the Hindus was in those early times greatly intermingled. If the detailed accounts given by Manu be correct, we gather facts of immense importance to our subject; and the answer to the question, whether the low castes were always disconnected from the high, is ready at hand. Brahmans, Kshatriyas, many Sudras, and many more outcasts are allied by the closest ties of consanguinity. Carpenters, fishermen, merchants, leather-sellers, hunters, jailors, executioners, burners of dead bodies, and other persons, now reckoned among the vilest and most degraded outcasts, have Brahman blood flowing in their veins, and their ancestors were united to Brahman parents by lawful marriage. These observations will sound startling to those who are unacquainted with the accounts given by Manu on this topic, which are so elaborate and minute, and withal are so matter of fact, and have so strong an appearance of truthfulness about them, that it is utterly impossible to doubt that they are a faithful representation of the picture of Hindu society in that distant epoch.

The testimony of this ancient work is irrefragable on the very extensive intercommunion between Hindu tribes of all ranks, and also between Hindus and non-Hindus. The example of Brahmans freely marrying women of lower castes, was evidently readily followed by the castes immediately below them. Kshatriyas availed themselves of the privilege of multiplying their wives. Vaisyas also allied themselves with inferior castes. The inferior castes likewise intermarried. And thus the blood of the castes and of the non-castes became considerably interfused.

The Brahmans have ever been over-much given to add to the number of their wives. In these early ages they were notorious as a wife-seeking people; and they can hardly be said to have improved in modern times. I may remark in passing, that, from the custom which the Brahmans of the period of Manu adopted of taking their subordinate wives one after another from women of lower castes, it is very clear that their own proper caste was numerically too small to supply them with what they wanted. After a time, though when is unknown, Brahmanical women had sufficiently increased to supply the Bráhmanical demand, and then marriages with other women were once for all forbidden. These observations are also applicable to both the Kshatriya and Vaisya castes, which from their comparative weakness sought alliances with Sudras and outcasts. Demonstrably, therefore, the upper castes, especially the Brahmans, and next to them, the Kshatriyas, were at first, and for many years, much fewer in numbers than the Sudras and outcasts combined. That the higher castes would never have degraded themselves by such connexions, legally made, had they not been under a necessity to do so from the paucity of their own women, and that they would have infinitely preferred to select wives from their own sacred order, is a position as historically as well as morally certain, as any that can be maintained respecting events of two thousand years ago and upwards, which are not susceptible of positive proof.

Although there can be little or no doubt, therefore, that there has been thus an extensive intermingling of classes in India, whereby most of them have lost much of their individuality, yet we must not rush to the conclusion that Hindus have become confusedly mixed together, and that all traces of their original distinctiveness have been lost. This would be a blunder as great as the opposite one, of regarding every caste as representing a separate race. In Indian social history the astuteness of the Brahman is an important factor, and must never be for an instant lost sight of. He has been far too clever to allow himself to be tainted, or his sacred blood poisoned, by contact with the inferior Hindus. The marriages of his ancestors with lower caste men and women left the Brahmans unpolluted, inasmuch as the offspring of such unions never took rank in the Brahmanical order, but were kept at a distance from it, more or less great. Such was evidently the case too with the Kshatriyas, and most probably likewise with the Vaisyas, though not to the same extent. The consequence was, that new castes were constantly being formed; but the old castes, especially the Brahmanical, remained scarcely touched by the process which was filling the country with mongrel tribes destined to play, each one for itself, an important part in the future annals of India.

We may thus account for the comparative numerical smallness of the Brahmanical, Kshatriya, and even Vaisya tribes in the present day, and the immensely greater number of Sudra and outcast tribes. The original numerical superiority of the latter would not have been sufficient, without this additional reason, to account for the enormous excess of the lower castes of India over the higher, which we now see. It was only the progeny of Brahman parents, of pure blood on both sides, which contributed to the increase of the Brahmanical fraternity, while the children of a Brahman's other wives, a second, third, fourth, or more, as the case might be, and also of a Kshatriya's and probably of a Vaisya's, secondary wives, ranked among the lower castes; and by intermarriages with them rapidly swelled their numbers, already fast multiplying by natural increase among themselves.

It is plain, moreover, that, the lower the descent in the social scale, the more numerous were the intermarriages, owing to the fact that the obstacles to them became less and less, and the greater was the increase in the population. Where the blending of castes was most complete, there naturally their growth was the largest. Again, where a caste limited itself in any way, either in its occupation, manner of life, or place of abode, a restriction was thereby put on the measure of its development. Brahmans and Kshatriyas not only strove to keep their tribes free from the introduction of base elements, but also placed themselves under various limitations of this nature. They were not alike, however, in the methods they adopted, and consequently their internal growth has been different. The Kshatriyas have lived on the whole under more rigid restrictions than the Brahmans, with what result their condition numerically, as compared with the Brahmans, fully shows. The Brahmans have endeavoured to found colonies of their order all over India, and have undoubtedly been the most successful of all Hindu tribes in spreading themselves throughout the country. There is scarcely a district in the land, however small, which has not at the least a few Brahmans. Every town and large village has some representatives. Even remote corners, barren wastes, inaccessible hills, crags, ravines, jungles infested by wild animals, the abode of wild aborigines, resound with the shrill notes of the sacred shell blown by the Brahman ascetic, who has chosen these regions for his habitation. With a clear and over-mastering conviction of the importance and need of his services as a religious teacher and guide, the Brahman has gone forth to the spiritual conquest of the multitudinous tribes of India, speaking many languages, and exhibiting diverse habits, and has triumphed everywhere. They have been spell-bound by his sublime presence, and oracular utterances. The irresistible power and authority of the Brahman are acknowledged among the snows of the Himalayas, on the burning plains below, in the fastnesses and dismal regions of Central India, on the banks of the Ganges, Nerbuddha, Godavery, Krishna, and other rivers, among the Dravidian races of the South, along the picturesque Ghauts, and throughout the changing scenes and diversified tribes beyond, to Cape Comorin. Hence, the Brahmans, in spite of their exclusiveness, stimulated by their spirit of enterprise and research, have wonderfully prospered as a people. It should be added, that, while they have, as a class, professed to abstain from agriculture and other secular pursuits, they have, nevertheless, in some places, devoted themselves in considerable numbers to such modes of obtaining a livelihood, and have thereby not merely increased their wealth and comfort, but also their own population.

On the other hand, the Kshatriyas, who in primitive times were probably more numerous than the Brahmans, pursuing quite a different course, have come to be numerically far behined them. Professedly, like the Brahmans, eschewing manual labour together with the cultivation of the soil, they for ages rigidly followed the profession of arms, and of government, and settled down in certain localities with which they remained content, until conquest or defeat led them either to enlarge their borders, or to quit them for other regions, where they established themselves on precisely the same principles as had previously regulated their lives. They have thus taken three thousand years and upwards to extend their tribes over Upper and Central India, beyond which they are little known, and their influence is little felt. In Bengal Proper and in the countries of the Dekhan they have almost no authority, and are altogether insignificant. The consequence of the policy the Kshatriyas have adopted, in conjunction with their strong adherence to caste rules, though with less strictness than the Brahmans, is that their augmentation comes far behind that of some other great Hindu classes.

The higher castes, though possessing many favouring circumstances denied to the lower, have been nevertheless enormously outstripped by them in the numerical increase which they have severally made. There are some of the inferior tribes which individually outnumber the whole of the Brahman tribes, or the whole of the Kshatriya tribes. Take for example among the Sudras the Kunbi, or agricultural caste, which under various designations is scattered over the greater part of India. Copying the migratory principle of the Brahmans, the Kunbis have gone on planting their villages, until the country, especially those regions which they have cultivated, is full of them. And yet this is only one out of an almost countless number of Sudra castes.

The marriage customs of the Sudras, and of the castes below them, are much less stringent than those of the higher castes. Many permit the re-marriage of widows. Some of them, like the Ahirs and the Nuniyas, compel a man to marry the widow of his deceased brother. Perhaps the most prolific cause of fruitfulness among these castes, which is seen in some more than in others, lies in the diversity of their occupations. If a tribe, as for instance, the Rajpoots, is restricted in its pursuits, so that many of its members are unable to obtain a livelihood for themselves, but lead an indolent life as dependents on their wealthier brethren, its increase is thereby seriously affected. But this is not the case with the castes in question. They have been free to choose various employments, which their families have followed from generation to generation, with such regularity and strictness that many castes are known by their occupations. Thus they have apportioned out among themselves nearly all the modes of gaining a livelihood in which men, whether in civilized or uncivilized countries, are usually engaged, leaving only a very small number to the castes superior to them. From this division of labour, which doubtless has its serious drawbacks as practised in India, arising from the circumstance that a trade or profession when once taken up by a Hindu family is too rigidly followed from generation to generation, leaving at last little scope for enterprise and the exercise of the inventive faculty, the great internal prosperity and extraordinary numerical increase of the Sudras, and castes below them, have nevertheless chiefly resulted.

Some minor castes are especially worthy of notice for their vigorous vitality, and for their consequent growth beyond that of other castes. The Chamârs afford an excellent specimen of a caste of this character. The hereditary occupation of these people is the manipulation of leather, as dealers in hides, tanners, shoemakers, harness-makers, and the like. Their caste has seven divisions, each of which undertakes a separate branch of the general trade, while, in order to give full scope to each, so that one may not intrude on the province of another, they maintain no mutual intercourse in the smallest degree, and permit no intermarriages, or any social or festive union. But the caste has been much too wise to restrict its labours merely to the pursuits of its ancestors. Many Chamârs have become servants, grooms, day-labourers, and coolies; and a very large number has taken to agriculture. In the Upper Provinces, and throughout a large portion of Northern India, extensive tracts are entirely cultivated by this caste. As cultivators they are laborious, persevering, and fairly intelligent. Thousands of villages are in their hands, in most of which they are only tenants; yet in not a few they are in the position of landholders. While an ignorant, despised, outcast race, they bear a good character for industry, and for a readiness to turn their hands to any calling by which they may obtain a livelihood. And what is the general result of this praiseworthy conduct? They have not improved their social position, for that was absolutely impossible under a pernicious and tyrannical caste system, nor have they as a class much risen in wealth; but they have increased numerically in a wonderful manner, and now form a community of several millions of persons. As they are all self-reliant and industrious people, though comparatively poor, they are healthy and contented, multiply rapidly, and are conspicuous for their large families.

Having seen by what means castes in earlier times were multiplied, and that, although they were destined individually to acquire a separate vitality and independence, yet that by far the larger portion of them were originally related to one another, it is necessary to enquire to what extent this relationship still exists. Blended together by intermarriages, it was natural, that they should for a time retain some of their primitive characteristics, both physically and mentally, and that likewise they should in a measure, and some tribes more than others, continue to exhibit them throughout their long history. It is impossible to look at some specimens of both sexes among several of the lower castes, without being struck with their likeness to Brahmans and Rajpoots. Take, for example, the Chamâr caste, to which reference has just been made. I have seen many members of this caste with very handsome features, equal to those of Brahmans—thin lips, a well turned chin, expressive eyes, an elegant mouth, a head compressed, and symmetrical in all its parts. This physical conformation is especially visible in Chamâr children; who occasionally vie in beauty with lovely English children whom one sometimes meets. Generally, however, these charming features are worn down and indurated by severe toil and spare living, long before middle age is attained. Yet even to old age many Chamârs retain their delicacy of form and make, which are distinctly traceable like lines of beauty in a faded flower, in spite of the rough usage they have experienced. The question forces itself upon us, whence have the Chamârs acquired these physical graces? Certainly not from the aboriginal tribes, from which probably they are partly descended. Judging from the purest of these tribes of the present day, which, so far as is known, have kept themselves quite free from contamination with Hindu and other races, as, for instance, the Ghonds and Khonds, the Kols and the Santals, and which are, almost without an exception, intensely ugly, the Chamârs, on their aboriginal side, were no more good-looking than these semi-barbarous people, we are driven to the conclusion, therefore, that the Chamârs have inherited these graces from their other ancestors, the Brahmans, and from, it may be, other Hindu tribes of the better castes. The Chamârs are manifestly a mixed race. Some are tall, and not unlike Rajpoots, others are fair; but the greater mass of the caste consists of persons rather short in stature, of slim make. and although not unfrequently, as already stated, of well cut and handsome form, yet for the most part very brown, or dark in colour. But this duskiness of skin may easily be accounted for, and arises doubtless from the constant exposure of their half-naked bodies to the sun's rays, whereas Brahmans living an easy, luxurious life, avoid the intense influence of the direct ray. Moreover, it must be acknowledged that the Chamârs, like nearly all low caste Hindus, are very dull of intellect, and, even when taught to read and write, develope with exceeding slowness; so that, after years of painful application, they seem utterly unable to acquire more than the mere rudiments of knowledge. Yet their luckless condition in this respect may be sufficiently explained. For many long ages they have been a down-trodden and oppressed race, have been treated by the higher castes almost as savages, have been purposely kept ignorant and debased, have been compelled to labour very hard for the scantiest fare, and have been led to regard themselves in the same light in which they were regarded by other castes, namely, as an unclean, vile, ungodly, and contemptible race, not worthy to enter a temple, or to come near a Brahman, or to perform any religious duty, except vicariously through the priests, or to receive the smallest amount of useful knowledge, or to hold any position, except that of serfs and clods of the ground. What wonder, then, that they should have degenerated to their present miserable condition. Education, however, is beginning to tell even on this mentally abject race; and they are slowly, though perceptibly, gaining intelligence. As they are most industrious and persevering in whatever they undertake, the prospect before them is hopeful.

Let us direct our attention to quite a different class of natives, in order to see among them, though in a very different manner, proofs of their high origin and relationship. These are the Kayasths, or the Writer caste. Respecting the origin of this caste there have always been great disputes among Hindus. They claim to be descended from Brahmans, on the father's side; in which claim they are supported by Manu, who says that they are the offspring of a Brahman father and Sudra mother. The Brahmans themselves refuse to recognize the Kayasths as in any way connected with them. The Padam Purana affirms that they sprang from Brahmâ, while the Jâtimâla states that their first parents were both Sudras. Wilson, in his Glossary, gives it as his opinion, though without authority, that they are descended from a Kshatriya father and Vaisya mother. Thus it is manifest, the whole subject is involved in doubt and uncertainty. While destitute of satisfactory historical evidence as to the true position among the castes which the Kayasths have a right to occupy—for no one, whether Hindu or non-Hindu, is able to say who and what they are—we have evidence at hand, derived from other sources, of a powerful and indisputable character.

The Kayasth has not the striking appearance of the Brahman. His features are intelligent; in some cases, exceedingly so. But he has none of the majesty of the Brahman, none of that mixture of unconscious pride, superiority, and greatness, which so wonderfully characterizes many of his class; yet he exhibits a family likeness, nevertheless. You may not know where to place him, or how to designate him; but on looking at him, and conversing with him, you feel quite sure that you are in the presence of a Hindu of no mean order of intellect. He has not the keenness and shrewdness of the Brahman, but his understanding is as well balanced, and perhaps a little safer to follow. You find him in the Courts of Law in various capacities, some of great responsibility, and you especially admire his gifts as an advocate, in which position he proves himself to be quite equal to the Brahman in argumentative power, and in all the qualities which, in their just combination, constitute the successful pleader. In Northern India the Kayasth has become the greatest competitor of the Brahman for important posts demanding considerable natural acuteness and mental training, whether connected with the government of the country, or with trade, which were formerly considered to be the exclusive right and heritage of the Brahman, for which he alone was specially fitted. And in regard to the future there is every probability that the Kayasth, during the next fifty years, will be a much more prominent figure, and will be a much more useful and efficient personage, in promoting the welfare and progress of his country, than the Brahman. Moreover, he displays an ability as a ruler, when called upon to exercise such functions, which show him to be to the manner born. Under the Kings of Oudh numerous Kayasths occupied posts of high trust, and among the principal Rajahs who rose to distinction, as many as fifteen were of this caste. Thus on the one side they are linked with the Brahmans, and on the other with the Rajpoots. And, in the opinion of the author, it is unquestionable that the Kayasths, who are naturally looked upon with extreme jealousy by the upper castes, have some of the best blood of India coursing through their veins.

The numerous tribes composing the great Vaisya caste, to which most of the merchants, bankers, and traders belong, may be classed together, as they have many features and peculiarities in common. It is difficult to affirm with any degree of precision how far this class represents in the present day the class designated by the same name in ancient times. Its numerous branches now strive to maintain a vigorous adherence to caste rules, so as to preserve undefiled whatever degree of caste purity they have inherited from the past; but this affords no criterion of the changes they may have undergone a long time ago. From the statements of Manu, it is abundantly clear that Vaisyas formed alliances with Brahmans and Kshatriyas above them, and with Sudras and other castes below them. Coming thus midway between the castes, and having apparently no strong will of their own, the Vaisyas were exposed to powerfully destructive influences.

It is questionable, therefore, whether they have been fortunate enough to retain any of their original characteristics, especially when it is remembered what their primitive condition was. According to the statements of early Hindu writings, the Vaisyas, on our first acquaintance with them, were, for the most part, an agricultural people, but were also, to some extent, engaged in trade; their chief occupation, however, was the cultivation of the soil. At that time they were the third and last great division of the Hindus, the Sudra caste having not as yet been constituted. As we look at the principal Banya or Vaisya castes, as we now find them, it requires a strong imagination to believe that they were ever employed in practical agriculture. Fair in complexion, with rather delicate features, and a certain refinement depicted on their countenances, sharp of eye, intelligent of face, and polite of bearing even to excess, the upper classes of the Vaisyas, it is quite certain, must have radically changed since the days that their forefathers delved, and sowed, and reaped. The lower division of the Vaisyas, on the other hand, are much more fitting representatives of their assumed progenitors, as they exhibit in their persons signs of toil and hardship, which are altogether wanting in their wealthier and better educated neighbours. But they may be, and doubtless are, on this very account, in a more direct line of succession from the original Vaisyas than their more fortunate brethren. Yet, however this may be, these latter have higher Hindu relationships than the former. Their better blood and more exalted birth are revealed in their physiognomy, deportment, and manner of life. They exhibit a strong Hindu type, but a type of a superior kind, and thus testify to a fact, which cannot possibly be doubted by any one acquainted with ethnological laws, that they are of one and the same race with Brahmans, Rajpoots, and Kayasths. Moreover, I would not have it to be supposed, from these observations, that the inferior order of Vaisyas are a distinct people from the upper. A little study of both will soon show a close union between them, the difference evidently being that the one class came originally more in contact with the higher castes, while the other class came more in contact with the lower castes. Yet both are emphatically Hindus, and differ no more from each other than do agricultural labourers in England from the trading classes in towns and cities.

Descending to a lower grade in the social scale, we come to the Sudras, a very mixed class, numbering at least a third of the entire population of the country. Judging from the first notices of Hindu castes in the earliest Sanskrit writings referring to the subject, only the three castes of Brahmans, Kshatriyas, and Vaisyas, were originally established. A period of comparatively short duration, yet how short is not precisely known, sufficed for the formation of the Sudra caste, which naturally assumed the fourth place in rank, and soon occupied a position consisting, partly of that formerly filled by the Vaisyas, and partly new altogether. Gradually the Vaisyas retired from agricultural duties, which were taken up chiefly by the Sudras, who were likewise herdsmen, shepherds, breeders of camels, and took charge of all handicraft occupations, were servants to the upper castes, in numerous capacities, and became a necessary class of producers of raw material to the general community. Indeed, in all probability, it was the manifest usefulness of this class in the early ages of Hinduism which soon led the Brahmans to perceive the mistake they had committed in not having given them at the outset the status of a distinct caste, and to remedy it without much delay by bringing them within the sacred pale of Hindu castes as a separate order of the fourth degree. Yet who, and what they originally were, and what is the nature of the relationship subsisting between them and the more favoured castes in modern times, are questions hardly open to dispute. Entering the country as slaves or menial servants to the chief men of the Aryan tribes, they associated, on the one hand, with the families of their masters, with which they made numerous marriage alliances, and, on the other, with the aboriginal races, with which also they intermarried, their numbers rapidly swelling, especially as the children of the upper castes married to castes other than their own, generally settled down as Sudras. What wonder, therefore, if the Sudra castes soon presented a very motley character, and that in such condition they have come down to us. There are consequently very marked distinctions among these castes, such as are not found in the three great castes above them. These latter, although exhibiting certain important differences, nevertheless preserve a strong family likeness and unity, so that it is impossible to doubt the sameness of their origin. But it is far otherwise with the Sudras.

Three broadly marked characteristics, at the least, distinguish the Sudra castes from one another. First, there are Sudras who exhibit unmistakably the true Hindu type. Secondly, there are those who display just as distinctly an aboriginal type. And thirdly, there are others whose countenance, contour of head, and general figure, are a blending of these two extremes, sometimes the one, and sometimes the other, slightly preponderating. Many other intermediate types often present themselves, but these are the chief distinctions, under which all Sudras may be classified in a general manner. The Sudras which come under the first heading are manifestly much more intimately connected by descent and by their personal qualities with higher caste Hindus than the lower grade of Vaisyas, just described. Similarly, the second class show that they are mainly descended from aboriginal races; while the third class doubtless are the fruit of numerous intermarriages between Hindus and other races, causing great confusion in the original types on either side, so as in their mutual blending to obliterate, for the most part, their separate distinctive attributes.

As representatives of the first division of the Sudras here referred to, I would single out two classes, one living in the towns, the other in the open country. These are the Sonârs, or caste of goldsmiths, jewellers, and silversmiths, and the Agricultural castes. The two greatly differ in numbers, the latter being fifty times more extensive than the former; but they will, nevertheless, be fair examples for our purpose. Moreover, it should be borne in mind, that, while a few castes are very large, there are many which are comparatively small, and it is important that all, of whatever extent, should be brought within the scope of the argument.

The Sonârs, like the Kayasths, lay claim to high birth. This, however, is a weakness common to many castes. But it is generally not a mere weakness. The castes which indulge in it have derived their convictions by traditions received from the remote past, handed down from generation to generation, and, although not susceptible of proof, lay firm hold of the imagination and belief of all concerned. The Sonârs of the city of Benares profess to derive their origin from the Kshatriyas. On the other hand, the Sonârs among the Mahrattas regard themselves as partly of Brahmanical origin, and apply the designation to one another of Upa-Brahmanas, or minor Brahmans. Whatever may be their origin, their occupation shows them to be of Sudra rank, in which, however, they must be allowed to stand high. The reasons for this supposition are twofold: first, their own traditions, sustained and sanctioned by other castes; and secondly, their physiognomy and general physical appearance. Many Sonârs have all the politeness and gentility of Vaisyas, whom they resemble in fairness of skin and delicacy of countenance. In short, although having peculiarities of their own, they have the thin lip, the intellectual forehead, the sparkling eye, the handsome fingers, and the complete style of thorough-bred Hindus, and are without doubt as much Hindus as Brahmans themselves.

The Agricultural castes, spread over a large part of India, differ in outward signs very greatly from Sonârs. But we must remember at the outset the difference between the two in occupation and place of residence. The agriculturist spends his time chiefly in the open fields, exposed in the summer to scorching heat, and in the rains to drenching storms; besides which, while a few of their number in most districts are landholders, and live more luxuriously than the rest, yet the masses are employed in the hard and toilsome duties of cultivating the soil. The Sonârs, on the contrary, need never expose themselves to the rigours of the weather, and are usually able to acquire a comfortable livelihood without severe labour. The latter, therefore, would be in a far better position to retain the sharp outlines of their original Hindu type than the former. The primitive form of the Hindu countenance and other physical conditions, are consequently not so easily discerned in them by a cursory observer as in the other class. Such an observer too will be very apt to draw a wrong conclusion from their mental characteristics, especially as they are, in many respects, so unlike those which he can so readily trace in the keen-witted Sonâr.

The Kumbhi, or Kurmi caste, as it is variously styled, is in point of numbers the principal branch of the cultivating castes, and, as everybody acquainted with the subject knows, is a very fair representative of all such castes. The Kurmi has a strong bony hand, natural to a man of his employment. His complexion is of a deep mahogany colour, never black, nor approaching to it. He is sometimes, and in Upper India frequently, tall and powerful; is manly, outspoken, and independent in manner, and is altogether free from the cringing obsequiousness so peculiar to many of the self-contemning outcasts below the Sudras. As a drawback to this, he is rather dull of intellect, which is no matter of surprise, considering the nature of his duties, which in every country exercise a deadening influence on the understanding. These castes exhibit various qualities, not seen in lower castes, and forming striking characteristics of the higher. They are free from the servility and sense of fear, amounting frequently to terror, which are so distressingly visible among the outcast races in their intercourse with the superior castes. But the genuine Kurmi never descends to this, but, on the contrary, manifests the intrepidity and calmness of the Rajpoots, whom in his general spirit he much resembles. He has no cunning, no quickness of perception, no versatility, and is consequently very unlike the Brahman. The Rajpoot is his pattern; and, if he were placed in better circumstances, there is little doubt that he would become very like his model. Again, his physique is that of the Rajpoot, and not at all that of the outcast tribes. It is true he is not so fair, nor so handsome, as the Rajpoot; nevertheless, he is of the same figure and cast of countenance. He has the endurance, composure, and above all, the self-respect, which are some of the prominent and distinguishing attributes of a true Hindu. He may be poor, as he often is, but you never find him sacrificing his dignity to his lot, or exhibiting an abject, miserable demeanour. His social position is comparatively higher than that of the agricultural labourer in England, and consequently he commands greater respect from others; but his respect is due very much to his excellent bearing, which is free from the Brahman's vanity and the Rajpoot's pride.

The next two classes must be looked at together, inasmuch as both may be found in different clans or branches of the same caste. How frequently are you suddenly astonished, in mixing freely with the great Sudra family of Hindus, with the dark skin, thickish lips, and heavy cast of countenance, united with a lowering and wily expression, of some of the persons you meet with, belonging to one of the Sudra castes, and regarded by Hindus as undeniably of their number. The Kahârs, or palankeen bearers, have this peculiarity. While all of them seem to be of a dubious type, some much more so than others, and a few approaching the type which the Kurmi presents; some, on the other hand, are so dark, indeed almost black, and manifest such a decided negro expression of lip and cheek, that we should be inclined to believe they were Africans, were we not assured that they belonged to the Kahâr caste, which occupies a position of no mean respectability among the Sudras. These observations are also, to some extent, applicable to the artizan castes, such as carpenters, blacksmiths, masons, and the like. Many members of these castes are in appearance like the better class Kahârs, though few are broad and stalwart, like some of the Kurmis. Yet there are many likewise, stupid and gloomy, and of a physique resembling that of the outcasts. Respecting these castes, which are very numerous, and contain a large population, I would remark, that, on the one hand, they are clearly allied to genuine Hindus of the superior castes, and, on the other, are as manifestly connected with the aboriginal races. They display a great intermingling and confusion of races. Every caste exhibits this confusion, some of its clans or branches, rather than its individual members, evincing strong Hindu characteristics, and others just as striking opposite qualities. They offer a living and practical testimony to the fact, that, in former times, the upper and lower classes of native society, by which I mean the Hindu and non-Hindu population of India, formed alliances with one another on a prodigious scale, and that the offspring of these alliances were, in many instances, gathered together into separate castes, and denominated Sudras. I say, in many instances, but certainly not in all, for some, like the Chamârs, who had much more of high caste blood in them than many Sudras, were thrust down to a position far below the Sudras, professedly because they touched skins and worked in leather, though more probably because, as Manu shows, they were partly descended from a Brahmini, or female Brahman, whose union with a husband of a caste below Brahmanical was regarded with abomination by the twice-born, and was invariably punished with social ostracism.

Not only is there a great diversity in the physiognomy of the lower grade of Sudras, but also in their intellectual gifts. Some are of quick perception, imaginative, and light-hearted, while others are sluggish and morose, susceptible of malice and fierce anger, relentless, and intensely ignorant. Why these latter should be included among the Sudras at all, is by no means clear. In estimating roughly the proportion which Sudras of an aboriginal type bear to those of a Hindu type, the great majority, perhaps two-thirds of the whole, are in my judgment in the latter category, and one-third in the former. If this estimate be correct, it proves that an immense number of the Sudras chiefly belong to the great Aryan family, though not in an equal degree. And even of the remainder, who have strong leanings to the aboriginal races, not all have this in the same measure; while doubtless most of them, notwithstanding their degenerate appearance, originally received some slight infusion of high caste blood, so as to warrant their being placed in the Sudra ranks.

Many of these Sudra castes retain traditions of their descent from Brahmans, Kshatriyas, and Vaisyas; and some of their separate clans or sub-castes still bear the designations of those branches of the higher castes, from which they profess to have sprung. It will be interesting to furnish a few examples.

The traditions of the Bhâts, or native bards, are threefold: first, that their common ancestors were a Kshatriya father and a Vaisya mother; secondly, that they were a Kshatriya father and a Brahman widow; thirdly, that they were a Brahman father and a Sudra mother.

Among the Kokâs, Barhai, or carpenter caste, are two clans, called severally, Bâman Barhai and Ojha Gaur, both which terms connect them with the Brahmans; while a third clan is styled Janeodhâri, or 'wearers of the sacred cord,' a habit of all the members of the clan, by reason of which they regard themselves as much superior to the rest of the caste, and thus preserve the outward sign of the better social status their progenitors enjoyed.

The Kumhâr, or potter caste, has a branch with the lofty title of Chauhânia Misr, the former appellation being derived from the Chauhân Rajpoots, the latter from the Misr Brahmans, and in all likelihood the twofold title shows faithfully the origin of the clan.

Several of the Agricultural castes have Rajpoot names attached to some of their branches, thus corroborating, in a measure, the supposition already made, that these castes bear considerable resemblance to the Rajpoots, and were partly derived from them. For example, the Koeris have a Kachhwâha clan, and so have the Kâchhis, the Kachhwâhas being a well-known powerful Rajpoot tribe. The Mâlis have a Baghal clan, the Baghal being a strong tribe of Rajpoots in the Rewah territory.

The Phâtak Ahirs, a clan of herdsmen, claim to be descended from a Sisodiya Rajah of Chittore, and the daughter of Digpâl, Rajah of Mahaban, an Ahir, to whom he was married. An account of this Rajah and of his marriage is given by Mr. F. S. Growse, in a memorandum inserted in the Report of the Census of the North-Western Provinces for 1865. The Ahars, a tribe probably connected with the Ahirs, and engaged in the same occupation, have no less than two branches with Rajpoot titles, namely, Bhatti and Nagâwat.

The Nuniya or Luniya caste, formerly engaged, as the name implies, in the manufacture of salt, has two important clans: one, the Bach Gotra Chauhân, who wear the sacred cord, and believe themselves to be the descendants of Chauhân Rajpoots, whose ancestor was Bach, or more properly Vatsa; the other, the Bhuinhâr; and are thus apparently connected with the Brahmanical tribe of this name.

These instances in some of the principal and best known Sudra castes are sufficient to illustrate the carefulness with which they have preserved the memory of alliances formed with the superior castes in former times.

We will now make a further descent in the social scale, and investigate the relations of those numerous tribes which are generally regarded as outcasts,—that is, as quite distinct from the four great Hindu castes, of Brahmans, Rajpoots, Vaisyas, and Sudras,—and yet which are more or less intermingled with them, performing various duties, and engaged in many kinds of occupations, all, in public estimation, of a degrading character, and only to be entered upon by a debased and unclean people. I am not now referring to the pure aborigines, who in the main keep themselves aloof from Hindus and their dependants, and who must be separately considered; but to that multitudinous class, of great diversity of colour, habit, intelligence, and demeanour, which fills up the lowest stratum of society in the towns and villages of India. Many of these low castes are regarded as too impure to live in the immediate presence of the four Hindu castes, but are compelled to live a short distance outside a village, or in entirely separate hamlets. They are scowled upon by the Brahman, spoken roughly to by the Rajpoot, kept at a respectful distance by the sleek well-to-do Vaisya, and heartily despised by the Sudra of all grades.

This repugnance to the outcasts is hereditary. Its origin, from the lapse of time, is forgotten; yet is not difficult to account for. In endeavouring to understand and account for it, we must compare the feelings of Hindus in relation to the pure aboriginal tribes, like the Ghonds, Kols, Santhals, and others, whose constant effort for many ages has been to hold no intercourse whatever with Hindus, but to keep rigidly apart from them; with their feelings in relation to those miserable outcast tribes which are located in their immediate neighbourhood, and minister in many ways to their necessities. The independent tribes are treated by Hindus with some amount of honour and deference. Indeed, they would resent any other kind of overt treatment, for they have their own chiefs and their own system of government, which is largely of a patriarchal character. Hindus may, as they do, cherish an antipathy to them, from a sense of their own superiority as a civilized and intelligent people ; but this is quite a different sentiment from that of abhorrence and detestation.

Yet this is precisely the sentiment, not merely felt in their hearts by Hindus towards the low castes beneath them, but also that which they delight to exhibit in their intercourse with them. They foster this spirit of intense repugnance; they impart it to their children ; they hand it down from generation to generation ; they display it perpetually in their dealings with this unfortunate race, whom they vilify by the use of every epithet of abuse which can possibly pourtray the loathing and disgust with which their minds are filled. Why is this ? What is the sufficient reason to account for this extraordinary mental phenomenon ? How is it that no amount of patient, faithful, and ill-rewarded service performed by a member of these despised tribes, can soften the heart of the Brahman or Rajpoot, and lead him to think and act differently ?

The outcast tribes were originally constituted by the offspring of alliances formed between the higher and lower Hindu castes, and between pure Hindus and aboriginal tribes, in a manner such as to arouse the strong reprobation of Hindus. Marriages of a certain kind only caused the degradation of children proceeding from them to the condition of Sudras, and perhaps even not lower than Vaisyas ; and there does not seem to have been any absolute social dishonour springing out of such unions. But other marriages—for marriages they were, and not concubinages—in which a Sudra husband was joined to a Brahmani or Rajpootani wife, or worse still a Dasya man,—that is, a man of one of the primitive tribes,—was united to such a wife, involved the extreme penalty of complete excommunication from Hindu society, the children born being regarded as the uncleanest of mortals. Such and similar marriage contracts, in days when, as is very plain from the records of Manu, great laxity existed among the earlier Aryan tribes in their intercourse with one another, and also in the intercourse of Hindus with the indigenous races, were evidently very numerous, and new inferior castes were rapidly formed.

It is indisputable that the same spirit of pride, self-esteem, and exclusiveness, which in the beginning led the Brahman to separate himself from all other Aryans, and to establish the system of caste, whereby he might be the better able to carry out his ideas, also induced him to hold in extreme abhorrence all social connexions which tended to degrade and corrupt his own order. In his violent, not to say absurd, efforts to maintain the purity of the Brahmanical priesthood, the strongest feelings of enmity and opposition were awakened in his breast against all those persons who, if admitted into his hallowed circle, would, by the untoward accident of their birth, completely defeat and overthrow all his projects, and cause his caste to be regarded as no better than any other. He therefore from the first sternly set his face against every alliance of this nature, spurned the children of such unions, and by degrading them to the lowest social position by the most stringent regulations that even his brain in its most active and fiery mood could invent, effectually shut out all hope, as he imagined, of their ever ascending to the highest. And this unnatural animosity, which, in his case in primitive times, had reasons, however inhuman and cruel, for its existence, the early Brahmans transmitted to their successors, who, in total ignorance of the reasons, and led at last to believe that these tribes were in reality what they were described to be, namely, inherently vile, filthy, and scandalous, and were, and had always been, separated from them by the most impassable barriers, spared no pains to communicate to their posterity this monstrous and fatal judgment, which has come down to the present age to the perpetual and absolute ruin of the tribes concerned.

Moreover, to add to the iniquity of the proceeding, these wretched and abhorred castes, treated from generation to generation with the utmost ignominy, soon began to despise themselves, and to believe they were as black as they were painted. Give a dog a bad name, and hang him, is an adage never more justly applied than to this unfortunate class, who are not merely exposed to the petty persecutions of all around them, but also to incredible coarseness and harshness in their treatment of one another; so that it sometimes seems that it would have been better had they never existed. It should be remembered, moreover, that some individuals of these tribes are as fair and much more handsome than many Brahmans, exhibiting in their countenances proofs irresistibly strong of their original connexion with the highest castes; and yet these castes, disavowing the relationship, and intent only on their own exalted position, eye them with scorn, speak of them as worms crawling on the earth, apply to them the most opprobrious epithets, and account the air they breathe poisoned, and the street of mud huts in which they live unfit to be trodden by their sacred feet.

Were there not some instinctive consciousness in the higher castes of a remote ancestral blood relationship subsisting between them and the outcast tribes, it would be impossible to account for the intense loathing of the former in sight of the latter. A difference of race, supposing it existed, or of occupation, or of social position, or of civilization, would necessarily cause considerable difference of feeling, but of another type. It would not convey with it a sense of intolerable repulsiveness and disgust. The transmission of this gross moral sentiment from father to son, through a course of time extending over thousands of years, in regard to a numerous body of their fellow-creatures, who surrounded them on every side, and contributed in many ways to their comfort and security, is in itself a most suspicious circumstance, which cannot be explained by the mere supposition of a compulsory distinction between conquerors and conquered races, or of the social contrast subsisting between the habits and occupations of these two opposite classes of the national community. For any one who has never resided in India, and who has had consequently no practical experience of the extreme violence of the feelings of abhorrence and contempt cherished by Brahmans, Rajpoots, and other Hindus, towards the outcasts, who of course are never spoken of as Hindus at all, but have various disparaging appellations applied to them as terms of reproach, by which they are known,—to attempt to understand the relative social condition of Indian tribes and castes, is for him to endeavour to comprehend that which is altogether beyond his penetration. There are no parallels for him to judge by in the social status of the various classes and ranks of England and elsewhere. He may sometimes meet with class bitterness and even rancour in other countries; but that is not the feeling which separates high castes from low castes in India. The feeling of intense abomination and contempt, amounting to utter loathing, with which the latter are regarded by the former, is a feeling, one is proud to say, which could not find an entrance into a high-minded country like England, where men with all their differences are equal, and in the main pay respect and honour to one another.

However detested the inferior tribes may be, it is nevertheless beyond the power of their calumniators to obliterate the marks which nature has stamped on many of their forms. These marks are missing ethnological links, uniting the extremes of native society. In some cases, the features of the low castes are of a very decisive character. For example, wherever you meet with thin lips, a well developed and expressive nose, a symmetrical forehead, a fair countenance, a well knit body, as in some of the Chamârs and many other outcast tribes, there you may be quite sure of the nature of their origin. They are indisputably of high caste descent. But we must be careful lest we fall into a mistake, for in the very same tribes, and even in the same clans, and perhaps in the same families, you will also meet with a development of an opposite character—thickish lips, dark skin approaching to black, a dull eye, high cheek bones, broad face, and gloominess or heaviness of expression. This proves just as strongly that the blood has been greatly mixed. Whole tribes, however, will show a preponderance of the one set of qualities, and again whole tribes of the other set, with here and there strange and contradictory varieties, carrying conviction to the mind, if such were needed, of the intermingling of blood in them all. The greater development, and on the largest scale, of the one kind of qualities or of the other, affords, in my judgment, as convincing a proof as is possible to obtain, apart from actual historical testimony, of the origin in the main of the one class or of the other. Some of these outcast tribes will thus be shown to have had an origin chiefly of a high caste character ; while others will appear to have been derived, for the most part, from low tribes ; and others still will be non-descripts, partaking of the attributes of Hindus and non-Hindus in a very puzzling manner. The Doms, Pásees, and other castes in Northern India of their standing, burners of the dead, eaters of carrion and vermin, rearers of pigs, executioners, sinister, ugly, dark, heavy browed, downcast, and gloomy, have confessedly scarcely a line or trace of noble breed in them. These are the lowest in rank ; but above them somewhat, yet far below those of the first rank, is a heterogeneous mongrel class, with no distinctive peculiarities, individuals of the same tribe being occasionally very different from one another.

This attempt, however, to range the lowest or outcast tribes under three general divisions, must not be too closely insisted on or criticized ; for it is purely imaginary, and has no foundation in fact. The truth is, between Hindu tribes proper and the lowest section of the outcasts, there is room for a great diversity of type, and this great diversity actually exists. Yet, while even the very lowest of the despised tribes exhibit some traces of the resemblance to genuine Hindu, though in some cases they are doubtless exceedingly faint, and can only be recognized by an eye accustomed to the detection of differences in the human form, it is very remarkable that some of these inferior tribes should be much more like Hindus of the best type, than many castes, especially among the Sudras, acknowledged to be within the charmed circle of Hinduism, and universally regarded as true Hindus. I reiterate, therefore, the statement already more than once made, that, in spite of Brahmanical pique and prejudice and pride,—in spite of sentiments amounting almost to malice cherished by the upper class, sentiments which, whatever their origin, do them immense dishonour,—in spite of the scorn, contempt, detestation, and absolute abhorrence in which they are held, such inferior tribes have a better right to be called Hindus than many which are so called; that they show marks and signs of purer Hindu blood than some tribes about whose Hindu purity no question is ever asked; and that, if all the Hindu and non-Hindu tribes, of every grade, freed from caste symbols, sacred threads, and every decoration, ornament, and peculiarity, could be passed before a committee of Brahman experts, to be scrutinized, and an opinion to be formed of them entirely from observation, some of these abject tribes would be assigned a high rank, while some of the Sudra tribes would, undoubtedly, be relegated among the outcasts.

There remains a large class of tribes of which we have as yet taken no notice. These are the numerous tribes in all parts of the country, but in some provinces more than in others, which have striven for ages to keep themselves separate from the Hindu race, and from all other races that at various periods have entered India. In ancient times they held possession of India, but were gradually driven from the plains into the hilly regions, forests, fastnesses, and inaccessible tracts, which they made their homes, and in which, at the present day, they are mostly found. Of less skill and tact, and of far inferior civilization, even the best of them, than their conquerors, it is evident that, finding they were no match for the Aryan invaders, they retired before them, and sought out other lands where they might dwell securely. They were not a timid people, and doubtless strove to defend themselves and their property wherever practicable; but, at the same time, the great mass of them yielded to the invader, and were driven before him. Nevertheless, the early annals of Hinduism show that collisions between Hindus and the aborigines were for a long time of perpetual occurrence, the issue of every struggle being the steady advance of the one, and the steady retreat of the other.

There is one circumstance connected with the primitive races of India, of much importance in the investigation before us. This is, that while the main body of the tribes kept together and fled from the invaders, many persons attached themselves to them, ministering to their wants, and acting the part of menial servants. Notwithstanding the pride displayed by the Hindus, which has always been characteristic of their treatment of subordinate tribes, those members of these tribes, who were separated from their own people, soon became necessary to the Hindus, who in the course of time formed alliances with them, while they on their part lost or abandoned their federal condition, and, severing themselves from their own tribes, left them altogether; and finally, in the progress of ages, forgot their original relationships. Meanwhile, the Hindus drew closer to the aboriginal separatists, and intermarried with them. From the fruit of these intermarriages the present outcast tribes were partly formed, though, as already described, they were partly formed likewise from the offspring of marriages between the Hindu castes themselves, some of the most degraded of the outcast tribes having been thus instituted. But these outcast tribes, whether originated in the one way or in the other, were not, as a rule, elevated above the separating line, and allowed to rank among genuine Hindu castes. The rule was not without a few exceptions however, some of which are noticed in the second section of the Introduction to the second volume of this work, in special relation to the Rajpoot tribes. And even occasionally Brahmanical tribes have been added to from the lower castes ; but the occurrence has been rare.

The aboriginal tribes of India which have kept themselves apart from Hindus are numerous, and some of them are populous. They are generally ranged under two classes, namely—those that originally entered India from the north, and north-east, by the way of Thibet, and are described as exhibiting characteristics of the Chinese race; and those that came through the passes of the Himalayas to the north-west, and are generally regarded as of Aryan origin. This two-fold division leaves out of sight many small tribes confessedly of very remote antiquity, which have little or nothing in common with either the one set or the other. Undoubtedly, not a few great tribes of Central India and of other parts are of a strongly Mongolian type, to which belongs the family of the Gonds and Khonds, people with round heads, distended nostrils, wide mouth, thickish lip, straight black hair, and scanty beard and moustache. The other series is of a very different cast, and is unquestionably another race. One entire collection of tribes of this series bears the name of Kolarian, for the reason, that the great Kol tribe, and others intimately related to it, are its principal members. These Aryan tribes were originally of the same family as the Hindus, but entered India before them in separate independent batches. The Santhals are also of this race, and probably arrived in India about the same time as the Kols. There is ground for supposing that the Khairwars of Singrowlee and Sirgujah to the south, are in reality a branch of the Kols. Further west and south-west we find the Gujars, Jats, and Bheels, all more or less claiming to be somewhat connected with the Rajpoots. In many places, the two former are reckoned as Rajpoots without dispute, but not everywhere; and as to the Bheels, while in some districts they claim to be degenerate Rajpoots, in others they appear to be only aboriginal tribes, almost as wild now as they ever were. All these three races, which have played such an important part in the history of India in former times, may be classed among aboriginal tribes in the same sense that Kols and Gonds are. And yet they are properly foreigners, as these too are, and in the distant past immigrated from the west and north of the Hindu Kush into Aryavastu or ancient India.

Yet what is to be said of some of the strange tribes of southern India? Take the Todas, for example, of a noble appearance, well proportioned, powerful, with aquiline nose, with a somewhat receding forehead, speaking in a voice described by a keen observer of them as strikingly grand, of copper-coloured complexions, their women being fairer than the men, and often tall and handsome. Who are these lords of creation? Whence have come these magnificent people? Unlike Aryan and Thibetan, with a fine and remarkable physique, in what category are we to put them? Their language, says Bishop Caldwell, is Dravidian. Taken in connexion with their antiquated customs and ceremonies, and with the fact that there are some important resemblances between them and the builders of the cairns which are found on the hills they inhabit, we cannot hesitate to regard the Todas as some of the very oldest inhabitants of India.

But the Todas are not the only primitive tribe scattered about the Neilgherry hills. The Kota, Burgher or Badaga, and Trula tribes, different from one another and also from the Todas, are likewise found there. Each has its own traditions, and all were formerly not in the same positions which they now occupy. Moreover, the three former are confessedly not of such remote antiquity as the latter. And yet all were in India prior to the Hindu immigration. About this, I apprehend, there can be no controversy.

Some of the aboriginal tribes are still in the lowest stage of degradation, and live like savages. The Koragars of Canara are a tribe of this nature. In manners, customs, dress, and dialect, they are separated from the rest of mankind. The men are scantily clothed, and the women are not clothed at all, with the exception of a bunch of leafy twigs. Strange to say, with all their ignorance, lying, stealing, and adultery are crimes unknown to them, and no Koragar has ever been known as a criminal in a court of law.

The Vaidan and Naiadi tribes of Travancore are among the most debased specimens of humanity. The former are a dark and timid people, wearing shells round their necks, and leaves round their loins, and avoiding human society; the latter are as degraded, and perhaps more wretched, for they are carefully shunned by every body of every class of natives as the most unclean and abominable of mortals.

Colonel Dalton, in his valuable and interesting work on the Ethnology of

Bengal, has given more or less detailed accounts of numerous tribes on the northern and north-eastern frontier of India, among the Rajmahal hills in the province of Chota Nagpore, and in other tracts, and has furnished illustrations of the tribes he has described. It is very manifest from his statements, as well as from the illustrations, that none of these tribes have any relationship with the Hindu race. Physically, intellectually, socially, they differ from Hindus in a very striking manner. Not only so, but they never care to consort with them, and have for ages kept themselves to themselves.

Thus there are many distinct and separate tribes outside the Hindu circle, scattered about India from the Himalayas, in the north, to the Cape of Comorin, and from the Brahmaputra, on the east, to the Indus and beyond, on the west. Some of them are without doubt related to the outcast tribes, which have allied themselves to the Hindus, and perform numerous menial services in their behalf; but have been so long dissevered from their primitive clans, that all traces of their original connexion with them are altogether lost, and the fact of the connexion itself is partly derived from tradition, but chiefly from conjecture and probability. These independent tribes maintain a separate entity, and hold no intercourse either with Hindus proper or with the outcast races. Indeed, one important feature in their existing distinction from the latter is, that, while these, namely the outcast races, are spoken of, like Hindus proper, as divided into castes, and are designated as castes, and not as tribes, the independent tribes are never spoken of as castes, but always as tribes. In their case, the word caste would be a misnomer and without meaning; and yet it is full of meaning, and felt to be the correct term as applied to the low outcast races, waiting on the Hindus.

It is one of the great and distinguishing peculiarities in regard to native races in India, that, notwithstanding the immense population of Hindus and outcasts, and their vast preponderance over the numerous indigenous and aboriginal tribes, yet that so many of these tribes should have for so long a period been singularly successful in preserving their isolation and distinctive autonomy. At times encroachments have been made upon them both by Hindus and Mahomedans; nevertheless, the fact is patent and indisputable, that they have been every bit as tenacious of their own national or tribal life as the Hindus of theirs. Indeed, it is easy to show that they have been more so, for, although Hindus of all the castes have occasionally robbed them of some of their families, and have gradually attached to themselves a numerous people, so that the descendants of aborigines now in connexion with Hindus are ten times more than have remained loyal to their original tribes, yet the effect thus produced on the Hindus themselves has been of a very levelling character, and nearly all the castes, having to some extent allied themselves with renegade aborigines, have to that extent lost their Hindu purity and genuineness, their blood has been diluted, and, although they may possibly object to the statement, they and such aborigines have in reality become one people.

The Hindus have thus, after all, and notwithstanding the exclusiveness and strictness of caste prejudices, shown much less care in the preservation of their own proper organic and national life than the aboriginal tribes which they have driven before them into inaccessible regions of the country. These tribes have never been corrupted internally, have never lost their autonomy. This cannot be affirmed of most Hindu castes, for, while they have retained their autonomy in all its potency, they have been internally corrupted to a very great extent. We have never heard of Hindus becoming Gonds, or Kols, or Todas; but we know well enough that many Gonds, and Kols, and other aborigines have left their tribes, and have gone over to the Hindus, chiefly to swell the ranks of despised outcasts. And so it has come to pass that the aboriginal tribes, which have kept themselves at the greatest distance from Hindus, and have had least intercourse with them, are among the purest races in India.

Extremes often meet. Here in this country we are presented with a singular instance of the truth of the statement. Among the Hindus the only caste which can possibly lay claim to caste purity is that of the Brahmans. And even they, though they have on the whole kept themselves remarkably free from contamination with other races, have not been completely successful. Still, after making all possible abatements, they must fairly be pronounced to be one of the purest and least corrupted races on the face of the earth. Many of the aboriginal tribes of India, however, while differing in almost all the characteristics which separate a civilized and highly intelligent people from uneducated, degraded, and besotted tribes, may, so far as I am able to perceive, lay claim to an equal amount of blood purity with the leading tribes of Brahmanical caste. They have had no motives for internal changes and developments and for making external alliances, such as the Brahmans, especially in their earlier days, have had; and have been perfectly satisfied with remaining from age to age in the same condition. But the Brahmans were in a very different position. Moved by ambition, pride, self-consciousness, and desire of greatness and glory, it might have been *a priori* imagined that to gain their ends they would have been ready to sacrifice some of their principles. Herein the Brahmans have shone with conspicuous and unapproachable lustre. They have exercised amazing self-restraint, have imposed severe strictures on themselves, have promptly excommunicated all offending members, and have erected formidable barriers against other castes and tribes, which I cannot say have never been crossed, but which have ever been guarded with unflagging attention and extraordinary skill.

Next to the Brahmans in purity of blood, but at a great distance removed, come the Rajpoots. These have intermingled not a little with other castes, as well as with the lower tribes. Nevertheless, they retain a considerable amount of purity, though, it must be confessed, even in modern times, under the stress of female infanticide, they have largely replenished their clans from beautiful girls kidnapped or purchased from the Bhars and other inferior or outcast tribes. We would compare with the Rajpoots at the one extremity of native society, the lowest and most degraded castes at the other extremity. By these latter I refer to the lowest stratum of castes, consisting chiefly of aborigines who have formed marriage connexions only slightly with Hindus, and yet are their servants, and live outside their villages and towns, being held in contempt and abhorrence by the Hindus properly so called. Now these low and miserable people, by the very fact of their degradation and exclusion from Hindu society, have been able to retain, to a large extent, the purity, such as it is, of their race; and certainly may claim to be as genuine representatives of primitive tribes as existing Rajpoots are of primitive Rajpoot castes.

After the Brahmans and Rajpoots is the large mixed class of Vaisyas and Sudras, possessing more or less low caste blood, with whom we must compare the large mixed class of low outcast tribes, excluding the very lowest. These two classes, although of very different social status and rank, are in reality much alike, with Hindu characteristics preponderating, exhibiting here and there signs of aboriginal alliances, especially in certain castes, or clans, or families, and yet manifesting Hindu traits in the main. These united form the great mass of Hindu society, and are the chief source of its prosperity, and of the prosperity of the country at large. Though this enormous class, constituting five-sixths of the native population, is divided into innumerable castes and sub-castes, yet ethnologically it is one race, just as much so as the Anglo-Saxons are now one race, and also the French, and the Italians.

The conclusion at which we have thus gradually arrived is, that, in spite of the extraordinary division of the people of India into multitudinous tribes and castes, which, whatever may have been their condition in primitive ages, are in these latter days, for the most part, socially separated from one another by the most stringent rules that human ingenuity could devise, the Hindu race, nevertheless, consists of one great family. It has its varieties and provincial differences, undoubtedly; it exhibits more high caste blood in some directions than in others ; it shows itself to have been, under certain conditions and circumstances, more strongly affected by intercourse with aboriginal races, than under other conditions and circumstances ; it has plainly experienced more interfusing of tribal relations in its earlier history than in its later ; and it displays marked distinctions in its numerous branches, so that every clan or caste is stamped with its own special characteristics. Yet all this diversity is perfectly consistent with inherent unity. Because an inhabitant of Suffolk has a peculiar twang in his speech, and a peculiar expression of countenance, and because a Yorkshireman differs from him in both, and because, moreover, the denizens of nearly every county in England have, in a similar manner, their idiosyncracies and significant marks, are they then not the same people ? Must we on these grounds separate them from one another, and regard them as so many distinct nationalities and races ? Obviously not. And so, in respect of the vast Hindu family, from the highest Brahman to the lowest outcast, divided and subdivided into hundreds of castes, cherishing mutual animosity and dislike, yet each contributing in his own sphere to the welfare of the other, and being necessary in some degree to his happiness, are we warranted in making invidious distinctions in speaking of the race as a whole? If Hindu blood, more or less, runs through them all, are we to draw a hard and fast line anywhere, and to say, these are Hindus, the rest are not? Because in some parts of England there is more of Danish blood, or more of Saxon blood, or more of Norman blood, or more of Celtic blood, and consequently because in reality there is less Anglo-Saxon blood in certain districts than in others, should we be right in affirming, that therefore all are not Englishmen, and some must be denied that honourable appellation? Would not the slightest doubt cast on the right of any one of these classes to the title of an Englishman, be scouted as preposterous and absurd? Similarly, the term Hindu is rightly applied to, and may be justly claimed by, every member of the Hindu family. Of whatever nature its component parts may originally have been, the family is now one. However much the family may be split up into innumerable branches, through the pride, folly, and inhumanity of its recognized heads, it is nevertheless one in spite of them. They cannot destroy family relationship, although, like proud and cruel parents, they may refuse to acknowledge their poor relations, who have gone astray and disgraced themselves, and may, for the maintenance of their own honour, prefer to treat them with derision and contempt.

In making these observations, I of course exclude from their scope all the aboriginal tribes which have kept themselves apart from Hindus. These are numerous, and have as distinct and special customs and rules of their own as the Hindu castes. It is not about them I am writing, but about the household of the Hindus, who, although at strife with one another, a family strife which to their shame has lasted for several thousand years, and indulging in the most disgusting terms of reproach in their mutual intercourse, are one community, with, for the most part, the same general habits and customs, the same social characteristics, the same sympathies, the same national hopes and aspirations, the same religion, and the same blood.

DISSERTATION THE THIRD.

THE PROSPECTS OF HINDU CASTE.

It has been said with some truth, that caste promotes cleanliness and order, and is, in a certain sense, a bond of union among all classes of the Hindu community. Yet surely these ends might have been attained in a simpler manner, and by a less antagonistic process. The invention of a project so wonderfully elaborate and intricate,—a project for bringing into absolute subjection two hundred millions of the human species by robbing them of their independence, and by imposing on them an intolerable burden of endless and unmeaning ceremonies, for the regulation of themselves personally, of their families, and of their tribes,—a project for ruling them with a rod of iron, and for introducing among them an all-pervading despotism, from which there should be no appeal,—a project founded on unnatural principle, by which family should be pitted against family, and class against class, to the utter destruction of all mutual friendship and sympathy,—a project which should bring lasting honour and glory to one or two great tribes, and lasting dishonour, reproach, and contempt in varying degrees to all the rest,—the invention of a project like this, so prodigious and far reaching, was not needed to accomplish such useful and beneficent aims. That another and very different object was in view from the very first, is abundantly manifest. This object was neither more nor less than to exalt the Brahman, to feed his pride, and to minister to his self-will. It was by no means his purpose to do good to the subordinate castes; and if they have received any incidental benefit from caste, such benefit was foreign to his intention, and is as the small dust of the balance when weighed against its pernicious fruits.

Caste is sworn enemy to human happiness. Laws, customs, social compacts, and the sweet acts of self-denial so frequently practised between man and man, are intended to promote the welfare of mankind, to increase the sum of human joy, to make homes tranquil, and to strengthen all the ties by which one family is bound to another. Caste was instituted for a different purpose. It seeks to sever natural ties, to alienate friends, to harden the heart, to stifle sympathy, to increase pride and self-esteem, to generate misanthropy, to repress the kindly affections, and to destroy mutual confidence and trust, without which society is beset with stings, and becomes a stranger to genuine comfort and peace.

Caste is opposed to intellectual freedom. It stereotypes thought. The rules of barbaric ages, of a nation in its infancy, are still enforced with unswerving rigour, though the nation has arrived at manhood ages since. Learned men, professors of colleges, leaders of public opinion, counsellors, judges, magistrates, editors of papers, and a multitude of other persons of talent and education, are bound, hand and foot, by the most childish and inane customs, from which, if they deviate by a hair's breadth, they are in danger of excommunication from the society in which they move, and of which they are ornaments, and of being utterly abandoned by their closest and dearest relatives, as well as by all professed friends. Moreover, unless they be of the same caste, they can hold no social intercourse of an intimate character with one another. Although they may be on terms of friendship with each other, yet they cannot intermarry, cannot partake of food together, cannot therefore meet at the festive board, and are in fact much more mutually estranged than if they belonged to separate nationalities, for this circumstance would admit of occasional inter-communion, of a nature not permitted by caste.

Caste sets its face sternly against progress. Social improvement, abandonment of old landmarks, advancement in civilization, reform of absurd and antiquated national habits, repression of follies, striking out new paths, searching after wisdom, and walking in her ways,—caste will have none of them. Caste abhors change, and compels the Hindu, under threat of its perpetual ban, to be a laughing stock to the whole world. That the thoughtful and educated men of India should so patiently endure its tyranny—a tyranny the most relentless, and at the same time the most senile and unreasonable, ever conceived by the human mind in its greatest corruptness, is a phenomenon unparalleled in the history of our race. That Englishmen, after having ruled over this vast country for upwards of a century, should, even in the persons of its most refined and accomplished representatives, rarely have been able to approach beyond the official presence of polished natives of rank and education,—should have held genuine social intercourse with only a very few of them,—should seldom have known the most friendly more than in a formal manner, and from a certain measured distance,—should never have felt, even with the most sympathetic, a perfect oneness of spirit, or have received from any one overtures of geniality, corresponding to their own, such as true friends cherish towards one another, and all because of the reign of caste-terror and superstition, under which Hindus of every grade live, is a circumstance which proves the malicious potency and infinitely subtle and fatal fascination of this social syren.

Caste makes no compromises. The most ignorant Hindu is able to compel the obedience of the most intelligent. No shortcomings are suffered for an instant. After observing forty-nine silly punctilios, which have been handed down by a hundred generations, the omission of the fiftieth brings with it condign punishment. A man may break all the laws of the decalogue with impunity, but if he touches grease or tallow, or drinks water from the hands of a man of inferior grade to himself, he exposes himself to the condemnation of his brethren and to its attendant ills.

The ties of caste are stronger than those of religion. A man may be a bad Hindu, so far as the practice of his religious duties goes; but caste rules must be minutely observed or he will have to reap the consequences of his neglect. With many Hindus the highest form of religious observance is the complete fulfilment of the claims of caste; and most of them conceive of sin as a breach of caste discipline rather than of moral law. I have frequently remarked with much astonishment and pain, that a Hindu, in his daily life, places caste on a higher platform than religion, and pays much greater heed to the sanctions of the one than of the other. In fact, caste is his real religion, for the sacred feelings and sense of duty which religion should inspire, are inspired much more commonly by it. So that it is quite true, and I would add distressingly true, that caste is inseparable from religion, and is very often its chief and most conspicuous feature. I have repeatedly known a Hindu, when pressed not to perform some trivial caste duty, as it really was a matter of no consequence, and no one would know of his neglect, and the omission would certainly be to his immediate profit, make the reply, that although none of his friends would know of it, yet that God would, and this thought has restrained him from yielding to the temptation. This illustrates the moral influence of caste, and shows how it occupies in the Hindu's mind the place of religion, and oppresses his conscience with its pseudo moral and sacred obligations.

Caste is intensely selfish. The object of each separate caste is to seek the welfare of its own small and often insignificant community, without the least regard to the interest of all others in its neighbourhood. Every caste thinks only of itself, is an empire in itself, is dependent on, and associated with, no other caste, cares nothing for any other caste, seeks diligently its own prosperity, and is utterly unmoved by the adversity which may befall a hundred other castes in its immediate vicinity. A Hindu does not live for himself, but for his caste. He will look upon men and women in the utmost distress with perfect callousness when he knows that they do not belong to his caste.

This extraordinary and anomalous institution sits as an incubus on the Hindu race. Their social blood has been poisoned, and their social life has been strangled, by the deadly sting and foul embraces of this serpent. It is impossible that there should be any true and widespread public opinion, or any strong united action, among Hindus, until this monstrous evil has been destroyed. Education, Christianity, and a thousand beneficial influences from the west, may be, as they are, affecting the minds of the people powerfully in every direction,—who may be, as they are, manifestly becoming more civilized and enlightened from year to year; but all these good influences with their gracious results are being constantly and resolutely thwarted by the operation of this pernicious and destructive agency.

Not merely in domestic, but also in moral and political matters, and, in short, in all the concerns of the Hindus connected with their progress in every possible way, the great and almost overwhelming obstacle is caste. It fosters jealousies, foments faction, prevents union, and thus represses the natural growth of the nation, and keeps it stunted and unfruitful. I would ask any thoughtful Hindu, whether he believes any practicable measures for the promotion of some general scheme of action whereby the interests of the entire community may be advanced, can be adopted so long as caste wields its present authority. The Hindus are without any mutual bond, are a mere rope of sand, while divided and subdivided in their plans and purposes by the incessantly clashing antagonisms of caste. They cannot trust one another,—they can have no faith in disinterested patriotism,—they cannot combine together on a large scale in any matter of national importance,—they can, in fact, do nothing extensive, either great, or good, or honorable, until they rid themselves of this social enemy and pest.

One important and very hopeful sign, as a presage of the coming reformation, is distinctly visible in the strongly expressed wishes of a large proportion of the educated and intelligent members of Native Society. The desire for a radical change, cherished by many of the leaders of Hindu thought, although their number in the aggregate may be comparatively few, is of incalculable value. Such desire is essential before any movement can take place, and this is the very class of people who can best of all awaken it in others, and can transmit it to the various grades above and below them.

But although the desire for a change is acknowledged by most persons of culture, yet it is necessary to add at once, that it is very differently evinced and acted upon. The desire, excellent as it is, and at the outset most urgently required, is not sufficient. And here national timidity, national hesitation, and national stagnation become formidabie opponents. Many are afraid to talk on the subject, except to Englishmen and to other persons of the same views as themselves, lest they should beget suspicion in the minds of their strict Hindu relatives and friends. They very seldom, therefore, speak on the matter; and although convinced of the folly and evil of caste, are not in the slightest degree inclined to take any step, certainly no initial step, for its eradication. Moreover, they have been brought up to the habit of leaving things as they are, of allowing all subjects, good and bad, to look after themselves. They are accustomed to drift with the tide, and are quite contented with doing so.

Now it is plain that such persons are almost useless in any effort that may be made to counterwork and undermine such a well-fortified and exceedingly powerful institution as caste. They may in their hearts desire success to any skilful measures which may be devised for its overthrow; but it is too evident that they will hold themselves aloof from them, until success is being actually achieved. Such is clearly their intention. And yet these persons, whatever their age, and to whatever class of native society they may belong, must be told in the simplest language it is possible to use, that they are cowards, and cannot morally shirk the responsibility of their passive unconcern. That is the opinion which all who know them must and do form respecting them. Doubtless, men of their feeble calibre will care little for such a judgment on their conduct. Nevertheless, it is necessary they should know, that not to raise a finger for the welfare of their country, and though perceiving the gigantic ills and errors which oppress it, and convinced too, by the quickening influence and enlightening energy of the education which they have received, that it is their supreme duty to lift their voices against them, yet not to do so, but to be satisfied with calmly looking on and watching the current of events, implies a condition of meanness on the one hand, and incapacity on the other, and therefore of total unfitness to be ranked a whit higher in the scale of civilization than their uneducated, superstitious, and caste-loving neighbours.

But our hope, and comfort too, lie in the fact, that all are not so. While in India the educated class is continually increasing, there is good reason to believe that the active opponents of caste are increasing likewise. But progress is made in this respect in a greater ratio in some parts of the country than in others. Bengalees occupy the van in this movement. To their honour, be it said, they have long been the leaders of public opinion in India. It is they who first formed it; it is they who chiefly sustain it. In them we perceive an amount of active patriotism and genuine earnestness not met with in any other Indian nationality except perhaps the Parsees. Sometimes their enthusiasm becomes excessive, and they are apt to indulge in statements respecting their rulers, and their relation to them, by no means honourable to their judgment, or to their sense of gratitude for the great liberty they enjoy under the British Government. But their inquisitiveness and outspokenness are infinitely preferable to a condition of lifelessness and dullness. And the buoyancy and zeal arising from the quickening influences of education on acute and intelligent minds, producing occasionally strange errors of opinion and singular hallucinations, if not to be admired, are nevertheless to be excused, for it is quite certain that time and fuller knowledge will correct them.

Many, perhaps I should say most, educated Bengalees have the courage of their convictions. Their thoughts wander rapidly over the broad fields of politics, religion, philosophy, and social economy, which subjects they discuss with keenness and ability, searching eagerly into the latest results of European investigation and criticism. With the same haste they have been ready to adopt and to practise the discoveries they have made. They have thrown overboard the theories and dogmas of their ancestors, and have bravely entered on new paths. To the amazement of rigid Hindus they have sternly refused to conform to old superstitions, because education and reflection have revealed to them their illusiveness and absurdity. They may have acted too suddenly before, it may be, they had sufficiently tested and weighed their new ideas. But, be that as it may, an intellectual and religious revolution has been effected during the last fifty years in the educated ranks of Bengalee society, the most striking feature of which has been the determination and resolution which Bengalees have shown in carrying out their new convictions.

And what shall be said of their treatment of caste? Confessedly this is the strongest foe they have had to encounter, and is one which has put their principles and courage to the test. The other enemies were chiefly theoretical and speculative, this was thoroughly practical; those assailed the mind, especially the imaginative faculty; these had a living reality, almost like that of material objects. Some who grappled with the first set of adversaries, quailed before this, or compromised themselves by a partial surrender, or entered on a course of duplicity, resenting caste assumptions in secret, while publicly professing their complete submission to its claims. Yet, notwithstanding the hesitations of these persons, there remains a noble band of earnest and valiant men, who have broken away entirely from the bondage of caste, and have gallantly bidden defiance to its utmost resentment. Their number is still small, but they are individually possessed of great energy,—are fearless,—are of high education and superior ability,—are consciously representative men,—are resolutely bent on carrying out their new found principles—and are already too important and influential a community to be frowned upon and spurned, or treated with contumely. Rigid Hindus feel that it is a serious business to break a lance with them, and prefer to leave them alone. The trimmers, however, who take both sides, come in for hard knocks and many bruises ; and, persecuted and in constant terror of excommunication, suppress their sentiments, and conform, though with a bad grace, to all the punctilious demands which members of their offended castes are prompt to impose on them.

Some of the caste-emancipated Bengalees have a character for adopting European usages. In our judgment, it is far better for natives of India to adhere to their own customs than to adopt those of foreigners. Nevertheless, they are surely at liberty to do as they please. If any class have strength of intellect and will sufficient to abandon caste at any and all risk, we may rest assured it will have enough of the same qualities for its future guidance. A spirit of eclecticism having been produced among the members of that class they will not be satisfied with the mere renunciation of foolish customs and exploded opinions, but will speedily form other habits in accordance with their new ideas. In carrying out their purpose we must not be surprised that their minds take a wide range, and that they adopt views derived from observation on a multitude of heterogeneous objects. In this manner, Bengalees, who have released themselves from caste, in seeking to establish for themselves new forms of social life, are not to be blamed, that I see, for taking as their models the most civilized, intellectual, and advanced people with whom they are acquainted. Nor is it a matter of astonishment, though it is of regret, that they should be prone to copy their bad qualities and habits, as well as their good.

Did we not possess the example of these progressive Bengalees, we might have been inclined to pay some attention to the manifest opinion of Hindus of the old school, that while they might abandon their religion they would never surrender their caste. But an important commencement has been made, and that by the most enlightened and best educated portion of the native community. And it is satisfactory to know, that the work of reformation is proceeding steadily among the ranks of students in all the numerous colleges and schools of Bengal. Many of them may not be in a position to follow out their principles to their practical conclusion; but the seeds of a great social change are already sown in their minds, which are destined in after years to spring up and bring forth abundant fruit.

Moreover, this readiness of the Bengalee to follow his convictions in a practical manner, has caused his mind to react upon itself very singularly. Purposes, whether for good or for evil, if accomplished, frequently give birth to others. And the human understanding no sooner finds itself successful in its projects, than it instinctively conceives others; and so the original stimulus being continually increased produces an ever-augmenting series of results. Thus it has been with the Bengalee. The very effort to deliver himself from his social captivity has had a healthy effect upon his mind. The effort itself was the product of previous thought, which had been awakened by education acting on an inquisitive and busy intellect. Excited by western ideas derived from reading and study, he has endeavoured to put in practice the new conceptions he has formed on many matters, and thereby a fresh excitement has been imparted to him. Or his condition may perhaps be represented as one of *intellectual* excitement, which, having once been generated, and having been nourished by its achievements, has gone on continually increasing. Unquestionably, at the present time, the educated classes of Bengal, especially those persons who having imbibed the true spirit of knowledge have been anxious faithfully to follow its leadings, are in a state of extraordinary mental excitement and restlessness. Englishmen looking on are very apt to suppose that much of this mental state of the Bengalee arises from, and indicates, presumptuousness and conceit. Hence he is commonly spoken against and misjudged, his faults are exaggerated, his motives are distorted, and the very efforts he is making to improve himself are held up to ridicule. Now all this is most unfair and reprehensible. Considering the entire revolution which he is undergoing, intellectually and socially, it would be a miracle if the Bengalee did not make many mistakes, and did not often place himself in a ludicrous position in the opinion of hyper-critical and fault-finding Englishmen. The whole circle of European learning has been suddenly opened out to him,—he has been called upon to alter or abandon his former notions on many important topics in the wide range of human knowledge which he has studied, in the new aspects in which they have been presented to him with all the intensity of his most active mind,—he has found himself transformed into another being, utterly discontented with the stagnation of most of his fellow-countrymen; and is it at all remarkable that many of his ideas should be crude, and that, for the most part, he should fail to master his situation, and that his situation should master him? All his shortcomings are remediable. Knowledge, like strong food, is slow of digestion; but give it time, and the process will be accomplished. The Bengalee has a glorious future before him—a future in which, if I mistake not, he will shine conspicuously as the leader of public opinion and of intellectual and social progress among all the varied nationalities of the Indian Empire. When he attains to the full stature of himself,—when his mind has become thoroughly matured,—when he perceives the true bearings of the knowledge he has acquired, and in his person and life exhibits that advanced civilization, which he only now hears about, and reads about, but which has not yet, except to a very meagre extent, passed into his being,—when he has thus been refined in the crucible of wisdom, and has become a genuine lover of virtue, and a sturdy champion of the truth, then he will occupy that exalted position in India, as a counsellor and guide to its teeming inhabitants, which his talents already indicate to be that which he ought to fill.

I have dwelt upon the character of the Bengalee in order to show, that being at the head of the party of progress in India he has set an example of independent thought which it would be to the interest and honour of the other nationalities to follow. In Benares and other cities are many men of intelligence and education, who are capable of being leaders of their fellow-countrymen in the abandonment of superstitions and the adoption of new ideas and habits, conformable to the education they have received, and the enlightenment their minds have experienced. Like the Bengalees, of whom I have been speaking, they have knowledge, but strange to say, unlike them, they have little or no conviction, no strength of character, no resolution, no clear perception, and no consciousness that increased knowledge implies increased responsibility. With all their weight of learning, the possession of which enables them to carry off University degrees and honors, they are perfectly content to mingle among the most superstitious and ignorant Hindus, to do as they do, to obey their foolish dictum as law, and to have no other aim in life than to conform to the most rigid usages of their ancestors. I would say to all such persons, that education is thrown away upon them, and that they continue to perform with apparent heartiness the most senseless and preposterous customs of the most degraded of their fellow-countrymen,—customs which were originated in the infancy and imbecility of their race; they deserve, so long as they continue such abject cowards, to be ranked among that dishonoured class. Let them not misunderstand me however, for I speak as their sincere friend, not as their enemy. Personally, as I know from long experience, many of them are estimable persons, worthy of all respect and admiration. But so far as their influence extends, as far as they undertake any practical measures for elevating either themselves or their fellow-countrymen in the scale of civilization, and for delivering them from the debasing prejudices and customs of former generations, am I not correct in designating them as mere ciphers, as ornamental, and yet useless, members of the great Hindu society in which they move, and of which they form so important a part?

The question has often been put in England, as well as in India, what has been the real result on the Hindu mind of all the influences which, during the last hundred years, have been playing upon it, derived from English education, English rule and laws, the material improvements introduced into the country, liberty, and above all, Christianity? Have they, to any great extent, remodelled the Hindu? Have they taken the place of the bad influences which wrought his ruin in the past? Has he yielded himself to them, to be recast in their mould? Or has he remained supremely indifferent, his mind and soul hard as adamant in resistance to them? Or has he partly submitted to them, and partly held himself back, determined not in reality, but only nominally, and in words merely, to alter his habits and ways? Great expectations have been formed by Christians, philanthropists, and advanced thinkers of every school. Some have hoped for the rapid conversion of the Hindus to Christianity; others who cared little for this result, have looked forward to the spread of civilization among them and to their increased general enlightenment; while others still have eagerly anticipated that education would work wonders, and that all who were well educated would be filled with wisdom, and would display in their lives the fruit of sound knowledge. These well-wishers, to whatever class they belonged, have been, for the most part, grievously disappointed. While a considerable number of Hindus have embraced Christianity, and the ratio of conversions is becoming greater every year, yet they have been chiefly drawn from the lower castes, the outcasts, and the aboriginal tribes, and only a small, though a very influential proportion, from the educated classes. But the Christian results are superior in kind and in extent to all others. Vast and fundamental changes are, no doubt, visible throughout all classes of the Hindu community, and a spirit of inquiry on every conceivable subject has been awakened in all directions. The people are painfully conscious that the reasons for observing the superstitions and the semi-barbarous customs of the past, are being, one by one, exploded. They are in a state of dissatisfaction with themselves. They feel that their knowledge is better and truer than that of their predecessors, and acknowledge that they are subject to its demands and claims. Yet what is their actual condition? The truth is, practically they are only in the initial stage of great national changes of any kind. By training and habit they love their surroundings, no matter how anomalous and absurd they may appear to foreigners, who, they know, having been taught differently, have no sympathy with them. And as for the educated classes, who ought to be promoters of progress to their fellow-countrymen, and guides to them on the road they should traverse, they are of all classes the most disappointing. They have acquired an enormous amount of knowledge, and there are thousands and tens of thousands of Hindus who may justly be regarded as well-educated men. Yet how little have they assimilated the knowledge they have stored up in their minds! There it lies in heaps, as corn in a granary; but it continues, for the most part, in its original crudeness. It should be received into both mind and heart in such a manner as to change and become a part of their very nature, just as food entering the stomach nourishes the entire body, and becomes indissolubly associated with the living organism, sustaining and strengthening every one of its numerous functions. The brain of the Hindu is wonderfully receptive, and only slightly assimilative. He has little idea of putting in practice the learning which has excited his intellect so powerfully. He is learned without being instructed; he knows much without being wise; he understands the meaning of what he reads without feeling its force—without realizing its living and transforming influence. He is thus a strange paradox, and exhibits the phenomenon of one who has been taught, but who has failed to be instructed in the highest sense. Hence his civilization is on a lower level than that of many less educated men in England and on the Continent of Europe, who have not a whit more knowledge in their heads, yet who strive to turn to practical use that which they possess.

The reason of this laggardness on the part of educated Hindus, with of course some bright exceptions chiefly found in Bengal, to whom reference has already been made, is chiefly two-fold—old habits and timidity. It must be extremely hard for persons brought up from infancy to customs and ways of a repressive character, altogether opposed to the manners of other countries, while surrounded by relatives and friends who insist on strict conformity to them, to adopt a totally different course. And the difficulty is increased tenfold by the natural hesitation to appear singular, by the dread of offending those whom they esteem and venerate, and by the apprehension of being made to suffer socially for the maintenance of new principles. It strikes me very strongly, that Englishmen do not rightly understand or sufficiently appreciate the position of the educated Hindu in regard to these matters. We are too apt to imagine, that it is an easy thing for a man to abandon the time-worn paths so familiar to him, and roughly insist on his braving all the consequences of an honest and thorough avowal of his change of principles. The Hindu is encompassed by the most tremendous barriers. Moreover, he has no will of his own, is not an individual in the French and English sense,—is not his own master in any sense at all. He is a slave to custom, caste, antiquity, and a thousand strange ceremonies established in the primitive simplicity and ignorance of his race.

With everything, however, that can be said in favour of educated Hindus, it nevertheless remains true that, for the most part, they lack honesty of purpose in the pursuit of knowledge, and are devoid of that conscientiousness, that willingness to make use of what they study, without which learning becomes vanity and delusion They shrink from the responsibilities of knowledge, and strive to regard it as of no intrinsic value, but as means of obtaining good situations and of promoting their worldly aggrandizement. It is no wonder, therefore, that with such false aims a very large number of educated natives in this country are imbued with a cursed spirit of perfunctoriness, and have little heart for anything really noble and good.

Pride of caste, the prime evil which has existed from the very formation of Hindu society, is at the bottom of all the mischief of which I am now speaking. Education tends to destroy the unnatural social distinctions which caste fosters! and consequently many educated persons, knowing this tendency, fight against it, just because it is so sweet to a man absorbed in his own selfishness to feel that he is superior by caste-position to a multitude of acquaintances around him, belonging to twenty different castes. Indeed, most men of the Brahmanical order, and of other high castes, adopt their peculiar caste-title, and use them as honorific surnames, by which they prefer to be designated.

On the whole of this subject I would venture to make the following observations :—*Firstly*, so long as educated Hindus are fascinated by caste notions and customs, their minds will remain stunted and stiff, and will reap very little of the most precious fruit that education yields. Caste paralyses the intellect, stifles the soul's generous inspirations, trains the inner eye to gaze on self and nothing else, and perverts the noble end of human knowledge. This is fully acknowledged by advanced Bengalees, who angrily spurn from them with a kind of loathing the noxious thing, which has narrowed their understandings, and, like a worm, has eaten away their heart's sympathies and patriotism. Educated Hindus, and all other Hindus who are anxious for their own and their country's progress, will have to make their choice in this matter, either to retain caste and with it all the prejudices, pride, barrenness, and mental impotence, through which India has been blighted during the dark ages of the past, or to hurl it from them, and, cultivating brotherly love towards all men, to regard Hindus of every grade as forming one family, or to aim at the elevation and enlightenment of high and low, rich and poor, to cherish earnest thoughts for the improvement of the debased and miserable outcasts, so long neglected and despised as an integral portion of the Hindu family, and, thus to feel the glow of hope for their country's freedom, and for a complete deliverance from all the social evils which now oppress it, burning in their breasts.

Secondly, already a struggle between the castes has commenced, and is plainly manifest to lookers on. Knowledge, at all events, is no respecter of persons, and if imparted to all who seek it, the question comes, who will win? In former times knowledge, meaning Sanskrit literature, was restricted to the Brahmanical caste; yet that was not the fault of knowledge, but of the Brahmans. And now that in this later age knowledge is wider, and at the same time perfectly free, it offers its blessings to whomsoever will accept them. The Brahman, therefore, or any other caste, has no special privileges. All are equal runners in the race; and victory will be to them, not whose lineage is derived from the gods, not who by birth are nobles, princes, and warriors, not whose wealth gives them undue influence and authority, but who run the best. The start began some fifty years ago when the Rev. Dr. Duff laid the foundations of a correct system of education in the establishment of the Free Church Institution in Calcutta. But a fresh and very powerful impetus was imparted to the runners in the year 1854, when the famous Despatch on education reached this country, and was speedily followed by the creation of the three Universities of Calcutta, Madras, and Bombay, the establishment of important colleges in the three Presidencies, and the offer of liberal pecuniary assistance to non-Government colleges and schools. Since then the race has become keen, and a great many castes have entered into competition. What the final results will be, is not at present clear. Yet it is very palpable even now, that the Brahmans will not have it all their own way, as they once had, when they kept the entire community of Hindus ignorant except themselves. To single out only one caste, the Kayasths, or writer caste,—although other castes might receive very honorable mention likewise,—in intelligence, earnestness, perseverance, love of knowledge, and ardour in its pursuit, the Kayasths stand at least on an equality with the Brahmans. Indeed, in some places, they have surpassed the latter, and the results which they have achieved, owing not to their superior intellect, but to the greater persistency and heartiness with which they have entered on their studies.

Thirdly, one of the most hopeful and encouraging signs of the times in India, is the indisputable fact that the principal castes are awakening to life. Hitherto the Brahmans alone have been distinguished for intelligence. But now, under the multitudinous exciting influences affecting the people generally, unknown before the British occupation of the country, they are being powerfully moved, and the latent intelligence of a hundred castes is beginning to pierce through the thick mists of dullness which had settled upon them, and to shine forth conspicuously. This welling-up, this intellectual revival, this spirit of inquiry visible on all sides, is the chief characteristic of the Hindus of our time. It is a most healthy sign. I cannot imagine one more so. I can pass over a great many follies committed through partial knowledge, and can forgive numerous indiscretions, the result of zeal unwisely directed, because I know that they are themselves indications of a vital energy, which was before non-existent, and that they will in the course of time vanish away, and be succeeded by just and well-matured thoughts generated by accurate knowledge. The desire for this knowledge, now becoming so universal among all grades of Hindus, will not—indeed cannot—remain merely such. It must of necessity enter on another stage. The information acquired on many topics, although, through the strong obstinacy and opposition of the Hindu mind in its undeveloped state, badly digested, or hardly digested at all, is nevertheless not impotent, nor received in vain. It is slowly yet surely changing the Hindu, is revolutionizing all his thoughts on every subject of human interest. In his eagerness to know, he commits egregious and ludicrous mistakes. He is handling every subject, sacred and profane; and a spirit of criticism has been evoked which, in the opinion of strict Hindus of the old school, he is exhibiting in a very dangerous manner. Yet this, in truth, is the first step to perfect freedom of the understanding—a step which not a few Hindus of very different castes have already taken.

The question of all questions, most important at this time, is—what will be the result of this general mental awakening in India? Let the Brahman interest himself in the answer to be given, for it will be very momentous in its relation to him. Heretofore he has won easily in every intellectual race; but he must now look to his spurs, for in future he will have many competitors and rivals. And he may regard it as certain, that none of his dogmas and theories, which, in previous ages his predecessors imposed on Hindus of all grades for their guidance, will go unchallenged. They must submit themselves to the closest scrutiny, of which the mind of India is capable. That mind has become sceptical, and dares to doubt. It has entered on the initial and most necessary stage of reformation, that of doubting. To on-lookers it seems in a condition of chaotic confusion. But it is not so. It has simply released itself from its old moorings, and knows not the direction in which it is drifting. It wishes to believe, but knows not what. It has become secretly conscious of having been long under the bondage of illusion and deception, and while not yet sufficiently strong to effect its complete emancipation, is filled with suspicion both of its former teachers and its new ones. The Hindu is gradually gaining courage, but his courage is still far behind his convictions, and hence he hesitates. This is the chief and prominent reason why many Hindus do not embrace Christianity, although convinced of its truth—do not altogether abandon superstition, although conscious of its hollowness—do not give up caste, although satisfied of its inhumanity and disastrous results—and do not step out from the crowd to begin life anew. Every educated Hindu I meet is at heart a reformer—a reformer in the widest sense; but he is afraid to act, and so tremulous is he, that, in most cases, he will only secretly avow his sentiments, and that too in an undertone of anxiety. Yet this is a natural state of feeling. If his condition were that of a bravado, and of instant readiness to carry out his new ideas to their extremest consequences, it would show that his convictions were wanting in depth, and might become fickle. But the very secrecy and timidity with which he cherishes them prove their genuineness. While still weak, their strength is cumulative—is growing from year to year, and from day to day. We see now the great body of educated Hindus in their feebleness; but what will they be in their strength?

Aye, what will they be in their strength? When they have gained complete mastery over themselves,—when they have thoroughly thought out the great problems which are now filling their minds, with interest and concern,—when they are delivered from the slavery of fear, and can avow their sentiments with manly intrepidity, determining to uphold them, and to carry them out, in spite of consequences,—when they have attained both mental and moral robustness, and are ashamed of nothing, except vice and error,—when they search after knowledge for its own sake,—when their judgments are formed without bias and prejudice, and their wills are moved to do that which, under the influence of the highest motives and of the purest candour seems to them best to be done,—when they have thus risen to manhood, then we may look for the universal triumph of truth throughout the land, the general abandonment of superstitious ceremonies and rituals, the exchange of idolatry and all fetish worship for a spiritual religion, the worship of one God in Christ, the transformation of society, the abolition of caste, the drawing together of all Hindus of every denomination, and blending into one common brotherhood. They will then be fit for political rule on the broadest scale. Their minds, quickened and energized by a new inspiration, will not merely be powerfully receptive, but will be equally strong in invention; and Hindus will take their legitimate rank among the first thinkers, most careful and painstaking explorers, most critical philosophers, and most acute and brilliant investigators in every department of human knowledge, the world has ever seen. One already catches glimpses occasionally of this latent power, glimpses which glitter through the cloud of obscurity investing the Hindu mind. Sparkling thoughts are sometimes emitted from that mind,—thoughts transcendant in their glow and beauty, proving incontestably the native energy within, and affording a sufficient sign and presage of its effulgent glory when the cloud shall have passed away, and it shall shine forth in its own proper and original strength.

Fourthly, in anticipation of this consummation, which will be hastened or delayed according as Hindus prepare themselves for it, let them first of all believe in their destiny, and next determine to remove out of their path whatever interferes with its fulfilment. They have not had an inglorious career; but its brightness has long since faded away. Let them be fully convinced that hope is not lost, and that in their own persons they possess the elements of greatness, which need only a fitting opportunity, and the surmounting of opposing influences, to be developed to their fullest extent. Let them resolve to avail themselves of all the branches of knowledge placed within their reach, and to submit themselves unreservedly and fearlessly to its plastic and transforming energy. To be puffed up by pride, or to imagine that they have no great alterations to make, or that it is possible to acquire all the varied knowledge of the West, and yet to continue as they are, will be fatal to progress. Knowledge is useless if it be not an active principle in the breast of him who has it. With many Hindus knowledge is mere lumber, encumbering their understandings, and causing them distress instead of exquisite joy and satisfaction. Whatever is sound and true in the knowledge Hindus may acquire, let them have the moral courage honestly to put in practice. They must brace themselves up to the thought that changes will come, and that to effect them is one of the great objects of genuine knowledge. Let them reflect, that the Western world has forsaken its ancient barbarism, and has become what it is seen to be at the present day by the omnipotence of that knowledge—the divine and the human so intimately blended as to form one—which has been shed upon it. If they receive and digest the same knowledge they will display similar results, differing it may be so as to be conformable to their altered requirements and circumstances. Yet just as the nations of the West, under the supreme influence of this many-sided knowledge, abandoned their degrading customs—their foolish superstitions—their coarse and vulgar habits—and their inhuman and filthy practices—so must Hindus be ready to surrender every custom, superstition, habit, and practice at variance with the elevated moral tone and spirit of the divine and human wisdom which has come to them from the West, and which they all welcome and pronounce to be very good.

Fifthly, as caste is a social distinction dependant on the assumption of an essential and natural difference among men,—a difference by virtue of which one class is accounted pure and another vile, one blessed another cursed, one from head to foot inherently and necessarily good, in every imaginable sense, without blemish or stain of any sort, and another utterly abominable, and incorrigibly bad,—should such a vain assumption continue to be maintained in the face of the intellectual and moral growth of Hindus of all grades, it will infallibly produce fierce strife and animosity among them. Can it be supposed for an instant, that young men of inferior and degraded castes, who by their acquisitions and talents leave all competitors behind them, and under the authority of a liberal and impartial Government, vault into commanding positions of trust and honour, will be content to live subject to a social ban, despised and loathed by a proud class of their fellow-countrymen—to the brightest and best of whom in capacity, education, virtue, and energy they have shown themselves to be fully equal? Already such men—of such abilities—and of such grades—are coming to the front. The democratic system of education pursued throughout the country, but with more thoroughness and impartiality in Mission than in Government colleges and schools, is training thousands of youths of Sudra castes, and of numerous castes inferior to them; and is at the same time producing in their minds a sense of injustice and wrong. The heavy gloom of conscious inferiority is passing from their faces, which are becoming bright and cheerful like those of youths of the higher castes; and they are fast losing the hang-dog expression, the shadow of social slavery which the lower castes almost invariably bear on their countenances. It is idle to affirm that, as the castes have for many ages maintained a loyal confidence in one another, so that those in a subordinate position have never murmured at those in a higher, and all have been in a measure contented and satisfied, this loyalty of subjection will be displayed by the inferior castes even when they are as well educated, and exhibit as much ability, as some of the superior. They who reason in this way forget that of knowledge is power. They forget that one of the many results of knowledge is to inspire the mind with a sense of personal dignity and self-importance. Nothing is more certain than the lower castes, when raised intellectually, and when fully awake to the fact of their political equality with the upper castes, will rebel against the cruel caste laws by which they are forcibly kept in a mean and depressed condition. If the Brahmans, and the upper castes generally, determine at any cost to continue their reserve, and make no approaches towards the lower castes, notwithstanding their great improvement in intelligence and knowledge,—if they insist on preserving fully and without abatement those social distinctions which were enforced in the dark ages, when nearly all Hindus except the Brahmans were sunk in ignorance and barbarism, it requires no prophet to foretell that a social rebellion,—a caste convulsion—is at hand. It is demonstrable, that just as the tyranny of a monarch must fall before the growing liberty of a people, so must caste fall before the increasing enlightenment and progressive civilization of the Hindus.

Sixthly, if these statements be true, admitting of no dispute, as I believe them to be, how important it is that the higher castes should thoroughly understand this great social question, and in a spirit of magnanimity make the first approaches towards the lower castes. In Bengal the remarriage of widows has been sanctioned by a very respectable class of the community, showing that if there be common agreement, a most stringent custom, coming down from ancient times, may be abolished. Moreover, some of the most advanced and highminded Bengalees have consented to intermarriages among the castes, that is, virtually to their suppression. In Upper India, where caste is very strong, and its regulations are rigidly carried out, obstacles to intercommunion among the castes may be more powerful than in Bengal. Yet it is necessary even there to take note of the growing influence of what may be termed the Middle

Class of native society, consisting of the Vadyas, the Kayasths, and the higher grades of Sudras. These are incontestably the most energetic—most pushing—and most successful of all the castes in that part of India. Intelligent, intensely active, and of immense force of character, some of their members having been educated to the highest pitch of learning which the colleges there are capable of imparting, should they choose to make demands of the castes above them, and those demands should be resisted, they have sufficient strength to drive those castes to extremities, and not only so, but by a close combination among themselves, to subject them to abject humiliation. At present they evidently have no such feeling or desire, because perhaps they have no real consciousness of the enormous power they possess. But let them suddenly arrive at that consciousness—let them suddenly awake to the thought that they are as well educated, as able, as intelligent as the Brahmans—are much more successful in their secular schemes—and exert a much deeper and a far better influence over Hindu Society at large; and they can, if they be so inclined, destroy Brahmanism, root and branch—can utterly annihilate it.

Seventhly, if the superior castes are wise as well as politic, they will lose no time in holding out the right hand of fellowship to the lower. Such a step would, by its magnanimity, secure to them much of the respect and honour which they at present enjoy. The Brahman would not lose his position of eminence as the time-honoured leader and instructor of the Hindu race. He would be *primus inter pares*, would still be first among his fellow-countrymen, though no longer of a different order. All Hindus would be proud of him, as the noblest and most finished specimen of their nation's intellect; and he would continue to be looked up to as the most subtle thinker and most astute counsellor the country possessed. But let him bear well in mind, that his fate in the future depends upon himself and the movements he intends to make. The first overtures must come from him, for the inferior castes will naturally feel their powerlessness to make any overtures at all. Let him beware of that passive unconcern—that recklessness of indolence—that supercilious indifference to the sentiments of others—which in bygone ages have proved so frequently fatal to the Hindu race. The fear is, that he will totally disregard these warnings, or will consider them as inopportune, or will say, "there is plenty of time yet," or will determine blindly to pursue his own way, and face the consequences. He may even, as doubtless many of his class will, deride these statements and these exhortations to reformation, as the maudlings of a foreigner, unable to appreciate the social beauty and fitness of Indian caste.

Be it so. He will at least give the writer credit for being a friend, and not an enemy. For more than a quarter of a century has he associated with Hindus of all castes, and striven to become acquainted with their habits, thoughts, sorrows, burdens, hopes, and fears. Much in their character he admires—some of their customs he highly approves—many of their sentiments he believes would do honour to the most civilized countries in the world. He has always spoken in their praise so far as truth would admit. He seeks nothing from them, neither wealth, nor rank, nor even honour. He has no motive but their welfare. Having studied the nature and the workings of caste much more perhaps than they have themselves, he has come to the conclusion, that it is the most baneful, hard-hearted, and cruel social system that could possibly be invented for damning the human race. Furthermore, by patient reflection he has come to the conviction, that if the superior castes do not presently invent some scheme for its eventual suppression, the inferior caste, when sufficiently educated, and thoroughly awakened, will rise up in furious and unappeasable indignation, and peaceably, though none the less surely, brand them with an indelible stigma of shame.

Eighthly, what is the attitude which non-Hindus, dwelling in India and interested in its prosperity, should take in regard to this question of caste ? Let them avoid the profound and pernicious mistake committed by the Mahomedan population. Many of these are converts from Hinduism to the faith of Islam, who have been permitted to retain numerous caste usages, and in doing so have indoctrinated with their sentiments the Mahomedans whose ancestors in former times entered the country ; the consequence being, that Mussulmans in India, with exceedingly few exceptions, have become semi-Hindus, practising caste in a modified manner, while, what is much worse, many of them, especially among the lower ranks, conform to some extent to the idolatrous customs of the heathen. It is remarkable how easily and imperceptibly strangers in India fall into the ways and habits of its Hindu inhabitants, by reason of their immense multitude and the all-pervasiveness of their peculiar institutions. And thus it comes to pass that Englishmen and other foreigners, although on their first arrival in the country setting their faces strongly against superstition, caste, and other evil influences, yet, gradually becoming familiar with them, cease to oppose them strenuously, and, after a time, even begin to speak of them approvingly. In no other way can I account for the favour often shown to caste by Government officials ; Brahmans, Rajputs, and other members of the superior castes being constantly preferred to members of lower castes. In regard to not a few situations of importance under the Government, the question is at once asked of candidates, 'To what caste do you belong?' Official notices commonly state the castes of Government servants; and thus those of low caste, although holding, it may be, as good positions as those of higher castes, are held up to obloquy and contempt. I believe this is altogether unintentional on the part of the Government. Nevertheless, it is beyond dispute, that caste is invigorated and honoured by the public attention which is thus paid to it. Moreover, Hindus of good caste naturally feel that they stand in favour with the Government by virtue of their caste, and in proportion to its rank, to the disadvantage of Hindus of lower castes, who, on the other hand, are painfully conscious of the comparative dishonour with which they are regarded and treated on account of caste inferiority. So inveterate is the habit, in some Government departments, of stating in official documents the castes of Hindu employees, that even when a Hindu becomes a Christian he is still compelled to state his caste, which in his case is the Christian *caste*. This recognition of caste by the British Government in India is a custom which it most likely inherited when it took possession of the country, and which it has unwittingly observed to the present time, for it would be unjust, as well as absurd, to imagine that the Government, which has so determinately severed itself from all connexion with Hindu idolatry, would knowingly lend its influence to the propping up of Hindu caste. Still it has done so. Henceforward, however, its connexion with it should cease. It should not recognize the institution in any way whatever. Its official documents, its monthly forms, pay-bills, and other papers containing descriptions of its servants, should make no allusion to it. Specially, should the question never be asked of a candidate for a post under Government, what is your caste? The candidate's suitability for a post should be decided by his qualifications, altogether apart from the subject of caste. In short, the Government should carefully abstain by fitting regulations from sanctioning such an obnoxious and terrible social evil.

Ninthly, the managers of Indian railways, and of the Indian telegraph, European merchants, bankers, planters, and others have also been occasionally guilty of fostering caste in the selection of their clerks and servants. Some have paid little regard to the matter, but not all; and there are those who on no consideration would allow one of the outcast tribes to hold any situation in their gift. Caste prejudice thus creeps into the minds of Europeans, who nevertheless profess to be inimical to the system. This no doubt has arisen from the fact, that until recently the persons best qualified for situations in merchants' offices, on the railways, or in other similar posts, were drawn from the better castes. And many heads of offices are strangely unaware that of late years education has made immense progress among the people generally, so that multitudes of men of the lower castes are as well fitted for the posts formerly exclusively occupied by members of respectable castes as these members themselves. European gentlemen holding important positions unconnected with the Government, in which they have native clerks under them, cannot be too forcibly and emphatically counselled on the subject. Probably they little think that by their conduct they may be powerfully sustaining or repressing a great national adversary. By thoughtlessness—by an undue preference for high caste men—by cherishing a distaste for change—they may be lending the weight of their authority towards an institution which, theoretically, they denounce. They should know that on them rests a heavy responsibility. They may do much, if they will, to bring caste into disrepute, as much indeed as the Government itself with all its English officials. If they will have nothing to do with it in any shape or form, but will in future select their men totally irrespective of caste, and will continually frown on it whenever and wherever they have the opportunity, they may administer to it a severe, if not irreparable, blow

Tenthly, hitherto little or nothing has been said of the direct and indirect influences of Christianity in eradicating this great social evil from the homes of India. All Christian people, and all Christian Missions, in this land are not equally affected with a sense of its perniciousness. Some, as for example, Roman Catholics, regard it favourably, and permit it among their converts. Even a few Protestants are not enthusiastic for its destruction and give it their partial sanction. Both these instances of support rendered to caste have, I believe, the same reason, namely, the hard difficulty of obliterating it. Hence a kind of compromise has been effected. Moreover, it is undoubted that many Protestant Missions in Southern India, in their earlier history, adopted this system and allowed it among their native Christians. They have, however, to their honour, long since repudiated all connexion with it, although having once sanctioned the evil, it was no easy task to get rid of it. But it was effected, however, very bravely and resolutely. Still in many parts of the country, notwithstanding the utmost vigilance of Missionaries, it occasionally crops up, and destroys the peace of a community for a time. Wherever it appears in a Mission it produces immense mischief. Pride, discord, selfwill, selfishness, separate interests, disrespect, anger, and heart-burning are some of the vices which it infallibly engenders. The serpent is apt to lurk in the most unlikely places, and its poison sometimes corrupts the minds of earnest God-fearing men. Speaking generally, Protestant Missions in India are nowadays very slightly affected by caste, inasmuch as in the Missions of nearly all the Societies a sleepless watchfulness prevails, so that its slightest manifestation is detected and forthwith suppressed. Not only are forty-nine out of every fifty Protestant Missionaries determinately opposed to it, but the same proportion of Protestant native Christians are so likewise. So that, with a small number of abatements only, the consentient voice of the Protestant community attached to the Missions of India is directly and strongly antagonistic to the institution. Indeed, it is not stating too much to affirm, that this community is its direct and most pertinacious foe. It is this community which perceives more powerfully than any other the viciousness of its nature, and the social disorder and misery it entails; and is most anxious for its overthrow.

Impelled by the peace-loving principles of the Gospel—by the earnest desire to promote in every way the happiness of mankind—by a love of order and harmony—by a hatred of dissension and strife—and by that larger hearted benevolence and kindness which characterised the Great Teacher in all His dealings with men—Christian ministers, Christian laymen, Christians of every race and colour in this land, by their counsel and conversation, and by their influence, should steadily oppose this monstrous and most corrupt system of social life; and in their intercourse with Hindus, especially those of education, should ceaselessly strive to counterwork and thwart the intricate and subtle power by which it charms and subdues them. They may accomplish great results by pursuing such a course. It should be remembered that Hindus are a very imitative people; and it is because they are so that they have followed in the footsteps of their predecessors so long and so ignorantly. Nevertheless, when once they begin to move in another direction, it is likely they will do so in crowds, especially if they have wise and popular leaders. The initiatory step in a thorough social reform is manifestly the most difficult to take, and the difficulty is a hundredfold greater in a country like India, where the people are wedded to old customs, which they still cling to, and relinquish most reluctantly even when convinced of their criminality and folly. This first step has already been taken, as before intimated, by some of the foremost thinkers and actors in Bengalee society, and a great change for the better has commenced.

INDEX.